KNOWING

HEPBURN

KNOWING HEPBURN

and Other Curious Experiences

James Prideaux

ff

Faber and Faber
Boston · London

First published in the United States in 1996 by
Faber and Faber, Inc., 53 Shore Road, Winchester, MA 01890

First paperback edition published in 1998.

Library of Congress Cataloging-in-Publication Data

Prideaux, James.
   Knowing hepburn and other curious experiences / James Prideaux.
   p cm.
   ISBN 0–571–19941–0 (paperback)
   1. Hepburn, Katharine, 1909– . 2. Motion picture actors and
actresses—United States—Biography. I. Title
PN2287.H45P75   1996
791.43′028′092—dc20   96-15730
[B]   CIP

Cover design by Hania Khuri
Printed in the United States of America

CONTENTS

IN MEMORY OF "HILLY"
HOWARD HILDENBRAND

PART ONE

1968

"And where do you find yourself?"

These were the first words Katharine Hepburn ever spoke to me. I hadn't a clue as to what she meant. There was a pause that was, indeed, pregnant.

"And where do you find yourself?" she asked again.

We were standing in the living room of a suite at the Hotel Bel-Air, having just been introduced by Irene Selznick. The pause lengthened.

"Huh?" I managed to say at last.

Miss Hepburn gave a slight shrug as if to indicate that, being retarded, I needn't answer.

Finally, hopelessly, I said, "In New York I live at the corner of Eighth Avenue and Twenty-seventh Street in the Penn Coop South."

"No, no," said Miss Hepburn, "I mean where do you find yourself *here*? In Los Angeles."

Ah!

I embarked on a somewhat lengthy description of the Sunset Tower West, my sunny room, the cheery kitchenette, the handsome swimming pool, the underground garage.

She sighed.

"I think we'd better have a drink," she said.

And what was I doing, poor and obscure as I was, being served drinks by Katharine Hepburn and Irene Selznick that September evening in 1968?

Well, it all started one Sunday afternoon in July when Clinton Wilder telephoned me from his house on Long Island. I loved Clinton. He was rich and eccentric and, when it came to the theatre, a total professional as a producer. I knew him because I'd worked as a flunky in the office he shared with Edward Albee and Richard Barr on West

Forty-sixth Street in Manhattan. I was an aspiring playwright, yes, but I had to make ends meet.

It was Clinton who taught me, among other things, to always go in early and check that the theatre was cool if I was doing a comedy.

"Jimmy," he said on the phone that July afternoon, "what are you doing for the month of August?"

I confessed that I was doing nothing for the month of August.

"Well, would you be free to go to the coast?" he asked me. "Irene Selznick is out here at Quogue and she needs a writer to work on a project. It would mean going to Los Angeles for a month."

He got a little mysterious. He mumbled something about the person I would be working with being on the coast. I took that to mean Mrs. Selznick already had a writer on the project and he probably wasn't working out.

I said yes, yes, yes! I was free, I could go, I would love to. I didn't tell him that the only plan I had for August was to worry about where the September rent was coming from.

He was delighted and said he would tell Irene. She would be calling me later in the day, when she got back into New York.

"By the way," he added, "you come very highly recommended for this job." He then said he had a cold and had to hang up. I didn't get a chance to ask him who had recommended me so highly.

It was a sweltering July in Manhattan and the windows were open that evening when Mrs. Selznick called—I hadn't dared go out—and the traffic noises drifted up from Eighth Avenue. Not easy to hear on the telephone even with shouting, and Mrs. Selznick, at least on the telephone, was a whisperer.

I did make out from her furtive little whispers that she wished me to come to her suite at the Pierre the following day at noon. She started to give me the address of the Pierre, but I gaily told her that, of course, I knew where the Pierre Hotel was.

"Some people don't," she whispered and then, having uttered something that might have been good-bye, she hung up.

At exactly noon the next day, I rang the bell at Mrs. Selznick's suite. And rang. And rang. Finally, I went down to the lobby and inquired if Mrs. Selznick had left any message for Mr. Prideaux? She hadn't. Was this the way the rich treated the poor? I carefully worded a note to Mrs. Selznick, not mentioning the rich and the poor, simply stating the facts: "Dear Mrs. Selznick. Missed you. Do give me a call. Best, James Prideaux."

I walked a bit in Central Park and then decided that, like Clinton, I was coming down with a cold. I would go home and go to bed, pulling the covers up to my nasal passages.

As I entered my apartment, the telephone was ringing. It was Mrs. Selznick, all apologies. She had been in her bedroom at the far end of the suite, she had not heard the bell; she had thought me utterly unreliable; she had talked with her "friend on the coast" and said we can't work with him because he doesn't even keep appointments. But then she had queried the hotel staff and discovered my note. Come right back, she insisted.

I got rather grand. I said I thought I was coming down with a cold. I touched upon my postnasal drip. Going out again could be extremely dangerous.

But, she said, I must read the two books this movie would be based on right away! Oh, said I, do send them down by messenger, then, and I'll read them in bed. She said she supposed she could get a messenger through the hotel. And I was to call her the minute I'd read them—the minute. It didn't matter what hour it was. She was actually talking quite loudly.

I remember wondering if I'd ever hear from her again, if the books would arrive, if we were playing games.

An hour later a very old messenger boy, easily a grandfather, puffingly handed me the books.

Written by the British author, Margery Sharp, *Martha in Paris* and *Martha, Eric and George* are one book really and delicious. I curled up in bed and cooed over them. There were problems, I could see, when it came to dramatizing them—the leading character, Martha, seemed quite unlikable and totally without charm—but the books also had what I considered my kind of humor and they did make a valid statement about the creative artist. This project was right up my boulevard!

And so I telephoned Mrs. Selznick at midnight and told her I was very interested. She whispered excitedly that I was to come to her apartment the next day at noon. She'd be listening for the bell.

The door was opened by a motherly maid in a starched uniform. Mrs. Selznick appeared almost instantly, her hand extended. We looked each other over. She was short, thin, her dark hair in bangs over her forehead. She looked like Anita Loos if Anita Loos had been ground in a pencil sharpener. The eyes were level and intense.

She wore a quite girlish flowered red summer frock with a full skirt. My impression that day was that she was younger than I had expected. I pegged her at fifty.

What she pegged me at, I don't know, but I was well into middle age, pudgy, and feeling fairly shabby.

She led me down the hall and into a den, a charming book-lined room with family photographs in silver frames, and prominently displayed, a replica in miniature of the famous streetcar named Desire, presented to her on the first anniversary of her production of the Tennessee Williams play.

She made very little small talk. She sat on a sofa and I sank into an armchair which, to my surprise, reclined when I leaned back, causing my legs to pop up in front of me. Unfortunately, I was attempting to light a cigarette at the time. (This was back in the days when we all smoked.) I struggled to maintain my balance. The impression I gave was of a gravely uncoordinated person with a possible history of seizures. I clutched the match, but dropped the cigarette.

Mrs. Selznick pretended not to notice, although I saw a fleeting frown sweep across her brow. What had she gotten into?

After this unfortunate display, she got right down to business. She wanted to know exactly what I thought of the books. She wanted to go over them, point by point. She quite clearly wanted my opinions and ideas and suggestions.

I had sworn to myself coming up on the subway that, since I wasn't on salary, I would not permit her to pick my brain. Don't give it away, I had cautioned myself over the din of the subway train. At this point, Mrs. Selznick proceeded to pick my brain and I flowed like a fountain. I gave her opinions and ideas and suggestions. Mind you, at this juncture I hadn't an inkling of what the deal was. I only thought that there was a writer out there on the coast who was in trouble.

Mrs. Selznick learned a great deal about me and my grasp of the books before I learned a thing about her and the deal.

We were interrupted by the telephone. It was "Doris." Mrs. Selznick chatted warmly with "Doris," ending the conversation with "love to Jules!" When she'd hung up, she told me that Jules Stein and Universal were very interested in this project. I was duly impressed.

She then explained that she was scared. She had never produced a film before and she was terrified that it would grow into a monster. She wanted a small, relatively inexpensive production, one she felt she could control. I nodded sagely, saying that the material was perfectly suited to exactly that kind of production.

But I kept wondering why I was there. New York—not to mention Hollywood—was crammed with writers who were far better known than I and with screen credits, which I didn't have. I had had one play on Broadway, briefly, and was trying to get a second one, a historical drama called *The Last of Mrs. Lincoln,* on the boards, but I was, by her standards, strictly nobody.

I'd decided that I liked Irene. There was something appealing about her, something lonely. I had to keep reminding myself that she was the daughter of Louis B. Mayer. Watch out! The only conclusion I could come to, as we talked and I looked into her eyes and she looked into mine, was that I was there because she thought she could get me for practically nothing.

"Listen," she said suddenly, possibly sensing my growing suspicion, "are you free at all this evening?" I said I was. "Then have dinner with me." I said I would.

As I was leaving, my spirits revived. Going down in the elevator, I hummed happily to myself. After all, the fabled Irene Selznick wanted me to go to Hollywood with her.

Why discuss money?

When I arrived that evening the double doors to her suite seemed like old friends.

She let me in herself. In the few hours since we had parted, I'd contrived not only to remember her as rich, intelligent, and articulate, but young and cute as well. This evening, despite the flaming red lounging pajamas or perhaps because of them, she looked a good ten years older.

I had foolishly imagined, too, that this would be a social event, a first exciting taste of her world with Marlon Brando or Noël Coward dropping by. Instead, we were alone and she led me with hardly a word back to the den.

She offered me a drink and poured herself an Aquavit. She reclined on the sofa again and I gingerly lowered myself into that chair.

"Have you been thinking about the picture?" she asked. "What have you come up with?"

I hadn't been thinking about the picture and I didn't want to think about the picture. I'd had enough of that for one day. Nevertheless, she began talking about the picture and we started to bat some more ideas back and forth. Irene was, to say the least, single-minded. For the next few hours we were to talk of nothing but the picture.

She did break off long enough to order dinner sent up. From a desk drawer she produced the hotel menu, which was mostly in French, and surprisingly she kept asking me what everything was. Unsurprisingly, I kept saying I didn't know. I began to feel rather glad Noël Coward hadn't dropped by.

Dinner arrived with astonishing rapidity. A white-jacketed waiter set up a table in the center of the living room and Mrs. Selznick and I sat opposite one another as she talked about the picture and I ate. As she droned on, I gradually became aware that the soft, continual voice and the food were making me drowsy. She, on the other hand, seemed fresh as a daisy.

"I've got a wonderful ice cream to top this off with," she said. As she was dishing up the ice cream, she suddenly seemed terribly serious. "Maybe it's too early to be talking like this," she said. I shrugged. With the drowsiness, I was beginning to feel depressed again. Were we ever going to talk about money?

When we'd finished off the ice cream, she silently rose and walked out of the room. After sitting alone for several minutes, I realized that she had gone back to the den and possibly meant me to follow.

I did.

She had flopped down on the sofa again and was lying on her back. Her eyes were shut. At this point she really began to talk turkey.

"You know who's going to direct this picture?" she said.

"Who?" I looked dutifully blank.

"Katharine Hepburn is going to direct this picture," she said. She opened her eyes, enjoying my reaction.

"Katharine Hepburn? But . . ."

"How do you think I heard about you?"

"Well, I thought that Clinton Wilder had suggested . . ."

She sat up. "I checked you out with Clinton, but it was Kate who recommended you."

I sat down and my legs flew up.

"Why?" I asked.

"Kate says you're a wonderful writer."

Well, I knew that, but I wasn't aware that anyone else knew it, least of all Katharine Hepburn.

And then I remembered. A producer named Charles Adams (not the cartoonist) had *The Last of Mrs. Lincoln* under option. For two years he had paid me $200 a month, a windfall that at least paid the rent over the rough times. Indeed, friends said, "Prideaux, don't get it produced—your income could end overnight!"

Charles Adams was daunted by nothing. He informed me that the perfect person to play Mary Todd Lincoln was Katharine Hepburn. I felt in my heart that Katharine Hepburn would have devoured Abe in one bite, but the possibility of having Katharine Hepburn in any play of mine overrode my reservations.

Charles Adams could get anyone's private telephone number (he used Roz Starr or Celebrity Service or somebody) and one day he had called me excitedly to say that he had given my script to Katharine Hepburn—given it to her, handed it to her. He explained that he had telephoned Miss Hepburn at her house on Forty-ninth Street, talked with her, and then he and his wife, Peg, had personally taken her the script.

(What a happy mix-up! Later I was to learn that Phyllis Wilbourn, Kate's companion-secretary, had picked up the phone in the kitchen just as the crosstown bus was going by. Kate and—irony!—Irene Selznick were in the next room, chatting. Phyllis called out to ask if Kate would talk to Mr. Charles Adams about a script. Kate shouted back no. But Irene stopped her. She said if this was Charles Addams, the cartoonist, then she knew him because they had vacationed in the Caribbean once in neighboring houses and he was an astute man and if he had a play for Kate, then Kate should read it. Kate shouted back to Phyllis to find out if it was Charles Addams, the cartoonist. Phyllis put the question to Charles just as the bus, having discharged and picked up passengers, roared past the kitchen window. She couldn't hear. Charles says he said no. Phyllis claims he said yes. At any rate, Kate came to the phone and agreed that Charles could drop the script off that afternoon.)

Peg and Charles had dressed in their best and presented themselves at Miss Hepburn's door. She had come to the door herself and been perfectly pleasant, although—he couldn't quite disguise his disappointment—she hadn't invited them in. She wore blue denim shorts with a ragged edge, a loose white shirt, and sandals. She accepted the script, saying that she would get back to him in a matter of days.

Charles was aglow. I could tell he felt that this was what show business was all about: meeting people like Katharine Hepburn. I thought so, too, and I couldn't help feeling a little peevish. It was my play, but he was meeting Katharine Hepburn!

I'd never get to meet Katharine Hepburn, in all probability.

The very next morning, Miss Hepburn telephoned Charles at the crack of dawn and he excitedly reported to me that she would very much like to play Mary Todd Lincoln. However, she was flying to the coast the next day to confer with Alan Jay Lerner about a new musical based on the life of Coco Chanel. There were, unfortunately, book problems; she wasn't at all satisfied with the script. It was iffy. She would get back to Charles within the week with a definite decision.

Within a week, a letter came. KATHARINE HOUGHTON HEPBURN was printed in small letters across the top of the blue note paper. We read and reread it: "Dear Mr. Adams—The play is remarkable—and I am not available. It is hopeless. Many thanks for letting me read it—and all sorts of good luck. Katharine Hepburn."

We were desolate, but not really surprised.

And now it was paying off.

Mrs. Selznick went on to say that Kate had called her long distance from California and read much of *The Last of Mrs. Lincoln* to her.

"See how he creates scenes within scenes," she quoted Kate as saying. "Listen how he uses humor in the serious scenes." They had concluded that I was the man for this job.

I was overwhelmed.

"She's a great lady and a great actress," I heard myself saying, rather theatrically. Mrs. Selznick agreed.

"She's also a great friend," she added. "She's my closest and dearest friend. She knew I was hunting for a director and she read the books and one night she came by and said, 'Well, I've found a director for you— *me!*'"

She picked up a small statuette from the table and handed it to me. "Have you noticed this?"

It was exquisite, but I hadn't a clue as to why she had chosen this moment to point it out. It appeared to be a young lad, barefoot, rather in the manner of Huckleberry Finn. I didn't know what to say.

"It's perfect of her, isn't it?"

Only then did I realize that it was Katharine Hepburn. I said it was perfect and handed it back to her. She was again all business.

"I've never produced a picture before and Kate's never directed one. We've been friends for years, but we've never worked together and we don't know how it will work out. Kate might not go through with it."

I asked her if she would continue with the project if Miss Hepburn didn't go through with it.

"No," she said, "and that's why I don't want lawyers and agents and contracts."

I was instantly on guard.

"Let's talk money," she said.

We parried. We hedged. Neither of us would commit ourselves. I said that because we didn't know how long the project would take or whether I would end up writing just a treatment or go on to a screen-play—"At that point," she interrupted, "we'll have contracts"—I should be on a weekly salary. Plus expenses. She agreed to that. In reference to the expenses, she concluded that I couldn't live on less than $150 a week, which would cover an apartment and a rented car. (Those were the days!)

"I must have a swimming pool," I declared, as if all my life I'd had swimming pools. She quite understood. And the apartment, she in-sisted, must have a full kitchen. Every writer should have a full kitchen.

At $250 a week plus expenses, we shook hands.

Surprising as it may seem, I was ecstatic. With Charles's option mon-ey, this came to what I considered untold wealth.

As she walked me to the door, Mrs. Selznick informed me that she'd be flying to Los Angeles at the end of the week and would be staying at the Hotel Bel-Air. Kate was living not far away on St. Ives, at the top of Doheny Drive. They'd find me a place close by. Her secretary, Peggy Dalton, would see to my ticket and I would fly out probably the follow-ing Tuesday or Wednesday. I would be notified when to come.

Heady though I felt, I did have the presence of mind to suggest that since I would be reading and rereading the books and making notes and, in fact, actually working, that I go on salary immediately. She seemed to agree. Peggy Dalton would send me a check.

We hugged. When next we met, it would be in California!

"Don't forget to pack your swimming trunks," she said. And then she slammed the door after me.

The check didn't come. And didn't come.

Weeks passed.

I telephoned Mrs. Selznick's New York office. Mrs. Selznick had gone to California. Peggy Dalton was home, ill.

When I finally contacted Peggy Dalton, she gave me the oldest line in the world: the check was in the mail. No, there was no word from Mrs. Selznick as to when I was to fly west.

I went through the books line by line, word by word, a drudgelike process but absolutely necessary if I was to understand what I was doing. I felt fully confident—and heartened. It was all there, it was simply a matter of organizing the material properly and putting it into cinematic terms. I liked the material better and better, although I recognized the enormous problem that was posed by having a heroine who was utterly without regard for the human race. How to make her palatable to audiences?

I was prepared to fly to the coast at a moment's notice.

And I continued to wait.

Had it all been a dream?

My friends were in a state of excitement. "We're so proud of Jim," someone said at a party one evening. "You know, he's going to Hollywood to work with Katharine Hepburn."

But was I?

One morning a check, a week's salary, actually arrived in the mail. I rushed off to Mrs. Selznick's bank to cash it. The lady officer to whom I presented it said blithely, "Oh, they're overdrawn. They've been overdrawn for a long time." I went limp in the knees. After all this, a rubber check!

However, the lady officer excused herself, went into a hushed huddle with another officer, came back and finally okayed the check as I stood trembling. I cashed it and shot out of the bank before she could change her mind.

More time passed.

Still no word.

And then Peggy Dalton called to say that Mrs. Selznick herself would be telephoning me in a day or two. Yes, I would be leaving in a week.

Actually, I was glad to have that week because the next morning I started doing a full outline, with a rundown of scenes.

Mrs. Selznick called me from the Hotel Bel-Air. Tennessee Williams had finally vacated and she was in her favorite suite. I was to fly out on Monday; Peggy Dalton would get the ticket to me, but would I be upset if she hadn't found a place for me to stay yet? I suggested she call my old pal, Jim Tartan, in West Hollywood and see if he couldn't suggest something. She said she would.

"You do have notes, don't you?" she asked. I said I had, but I didn't mention that I also hoped to have an outline by the time I arrived. That was meant as a surprise.

She invited me to dine with her at the hotel on Monday night after I got in. Not with "us"—with her. No mention of Hepburn. Was she already out of the project?

Jim Tartan met me at the Los Angeles Airport.

I thought the apartment he'd found me at the Sunset Tower West (at $75 a week) was fine, although I was a little concerned that Mrs. Selznick hadn't bothered to find one. There was also a white Chevy convertible for me ($110 a month, plus four cents a mile)—not new, not grand, but a white convertible certainly seemed appropriate. And the breeze was balmy and the palm trees were swaying and the sun was shining and I knew I was going to have a grand time.

I called Mrs. Selznick and she welcomed me to Los Angeles and, giving me directions, said she'd expect me for dinner at the hotel at 7:30. No mention of anyone else. Just the two of us, apparently. Miss Hepburn was clearly out of the picture.

One's first view of the Hotel Bel-Air must be one of the pleasantest moments life has to offer. I was enchanted. Walking through its gardens was a little like strolling through Oz. I might add that I wasn't in the least nervous. I thought I was the right man for this project and I knew I could do it. I figured they were lucky to have me. And I proposed to enjoy it.

I checked at the desk and was directed to suite 264, a little walk away and then up a flight of red-carpeted stairs. The desk had telephoned ahead and Mrs. Selznick was waiting at the top in the doorway to her apartment.

We embraced. Over her shoulder, seated on a sofa in the living room, I saw Katharine Hepburn.

She got up immediately and came forward to meet me, her hand extended.

"And where do you find yourself?"

My first impression was that she was somewhat nervous. She was also shorter than I expected. The magnificent face had pinkish splotches, as if badly sunburned and peeling. No makeup. The arms and hands were a bit pudgy and deeply freckled. The reddish gray hair was loosely swept up on top of her head. She wore a beige slack suit with a high

Nehru collar and sandals on her naked feet. She appeared only slightly older than I had expected. And she looked a little tired. But the voice was electrifying.

We sat around a coffee table. Miss Hepburn was drinking from a bottle of red wine, I had a scotch, and Irene—as she became that evening—was again at the Aquavit. We settled in comfortably and, after that initial awkwardness, had no difficulty in finding conversation. Miss Hepburn really was interested in where I was staying. It was my first glimpse of her astonishing empathy.

(Later that week, as we were working at her house, I suddenly felt a draft, but said nothing; Kate immediately disappeared and returned with a sweater, which she flung at me. "Aren't you feeling a draft?" she said.)

After offering them to us, Miss Hepburn nibbled nuts incessantly until Irene said amiably, "Kate, that's enough—put the lid on the jar." Miss Hepburn—she didn't become Kate that night, but soon afterward when "Miss Hepburn" seemed too formal and I was practically at the "Hey, you" stage—then turned her attention to the water chestnuts, curling her nose and cooing over them as if they were the most delightful thing in the world. She said she would peel them and serve us, whereupon she started carving them into three pieces.

"They look dirty, but they're not," she informed us.

I said I'd had a bit of a day (I was still fearful of flying in those days) and Kate said hers had been very rough. She was working with her niece, Katharine Houghton, who was going to do *Sabrina Fair* in Ivoryton, Connecticut.

"I read the script and I didn't know what to say to her," Kate sighed. "I had to read it twice before I could make anything out of it. I don't see how Maggie Sullavan did it."

Kathy was to appear at the same theatre in which Kate had made her first stage appearance, a theatre near Hartford, "thereby assuring a large audience of relatives." But while Kate had worked practically for nothing, Kathy was making a bundle of money.

"How much?" asked Irene, always interested in money.

"Fifteen hundred a week," said Kate, "but she's done a picture. I was glad to be on a stage. I played a forty-five-year-old sophisticate so I went into New York to Bergdorf's and bought tremendous hats . . . that Dad paid for."

We talked about the utter confidence of youth. "When I first started on the stage, I thought I was perfectly wonderful," said Kate. "It's only later when you begin to learn something that you're terrified. It never occurred to me to doubt myself. When I first worked with John Barrymore, I watched him a bit and thought, 'Why, he's a *ham*! I can handle this perfectly easily!'"

I listened enthralled as Kate reminisced about her early years.

"When I went to New York, I even had a car. I always had a car. I had everything. And I'd do the most ridiculous things to attract attention. I had a green coat and instead of sewing on a button or a snap to fasten it at the throat, I pinned it together with a huge safety pin — *huge*! Now, why did I do that? It was obviously to draw attention to myself."

I tried to imagine a time when Katharine Hepburn had difficulty in drawing attention to herself. I failed.

Irene said it was time to order dinner sent up.

I explained that the plane trip had put me off food and I wasn't hungry.

"Oh, but have a steak," Kate insisted. "Have a small one, if you like, but you should have a steak." So I ended up ordering a small steak and a salad.

"How about soup first?" said motherly Kate. "A nice brisk consommé. Only a cup, if you want." So we ordered consommé. It wasn't easy, I observed, to say no to Kate.

As we waited for room service, I told Kate that everyone in New York was very much looking forward to the opening of her latest picture, *The Lion in Winter.*

"Well, it's a magnificent script," she said. "I believe the script is everything. If you don't have a good script nothing can save you. And the boys who play my sons are marvelous. Every one of them could be stars. One of them understudied Larry Olivier, you know. And Peter O'Toole is brilliant."

I asked how soon we'd see *The Madwoman of Chaillot*, also in the can, and she replied that it couldn't be released until after the musical had opened on Broadway.

"*Dear World*," she sniffed. "Isn't that a terrible title?"

"Terrible," agreed Irene.

And what about her own musical? The one about Coco Chanel?

"Well, the script isn't right. We've abandoned it for the time being."

The waiter appeared with dinner. He was very conscious of Katharine Hepburn's being in the room, which caused Kate to grow silent.

Conversation was stilted while he was with us. Once he was gone, we were easy again.

"Now you sit there," Kate told me, "and we'll serve you."

I thought what a wonderful profession I was in! Here was I, broke and unknown, being served dinner in the Hotel Bel-Air by Katharine Hepburn and Irene Selznick.

"I'd hate to be a waiter," Kate remarked, ladling out the consommé. "Serving all those fat people."

"You'd be very good at it," said Irene.

"Of *course* I'd be good at it," said Kate, "but I'd *hate* it."

Kate sat down at the table, while Irene was still standing over the meat course on the metal cart. I waited politely for Irene before eating, but Kate dug right in. She didn't bother using a spoon for her consommé; she lifted it and drank right from the cup.

As we ate, Mary Pickford's name came up.

"Somebody brought her to watch me filming once," Kate remembered, "and I thought she was just some silly society woman—hadn't the faintest notion who she was—and she said could I come to dinner and I said I couldn't possibly because I was always in bed by seven. I was very condescending. And everybody came rushing up afterward saying did I know who that was? So of *course* I went to dinner and I sat at Douglas's right and thought myself a great success. And was never invited again. Years later she and I happened to be on the same plane going to France and I went up to her and introduced myself and she said of course I know who you are and I said may I sit down and then I said, tell me the story of your life. And she *did.* It was fascinating. She has total recall. *I* can't remember a thing."

"I saw Sam Goldwyn last night," said Irene. "You wouldn't believe how sharp he is—at eighty-seven. Frances's mother is in this terribly expensive nursing home . . ."

"I know the one," said Kate, "and it's a thousand dollars a week."

"And Frances said she went out to visit her and who should come racing down the hall at her in a wheelchair but Louella Parsons! And she shouted at Frances, 'Don't forget, I gave Sam lots of scoops!' "

"Frightening," said Kate, "frightening. I talked to the director of that place once and you know what he said to me?" She did a brilliant imitation of a pompous official. "We're proud to say we have several residents over one hundred!"

I said the problem of what to do with the aged was very sad, but I didn't know what the answer was.

"Big houses used to be," said Kate. "There was plenty of room and you could keep a crazy relative around somewhere. And they all did."

I was to learn that evening—later fully confirmed—that nothing pleases older stars so much as reminiscing.

"When I was first new out here," said Kate, "I kept a drawerful of money at home—literally a drawerful. And finally I thought I might as well spend it so I rented a very fancy foreign car and my friend, Laura, and I went touring up the coast with a very handsome chauffeur who turned out to be a midget when he got out of the car. Anyway, we had a lovely trip and were so elegant I decided to keep the car when we got back, renting it by the week and I thought impressing the hell out of everybody. Well, it turned out every extra in town had rented that car at one time or another. It was the most recognized piece of rented property in Hollywood!"

We moved back to the coffee table for coffee. Kate stretched out on the sofa, Irene sat in a chair, and I sat cross-legged on the floor.

The subject of hippies—then very prominent—came up. Kate had seen two dirty, barefooted girls sitting on the curb on Sunset Boulevard that afternoon and was indignant about it. (In those days, we had never heard of the homeless.) I said—having made a pact with myself on the plane always to say what I thought—that I liked the hippies and felt I understood them. Kate was eager to hear my views and, for the first time, the name of Spencer Tracy was mentioned. I was soon to discover that her conversation was frequently peppered with references to "Spencer." Spencer thought this or Spencer thought that. Obviously, he was not a taboo subject.

As a matter of fact, in the weeks to come I was surprised by her candor about her personal life. I had expected her to be very private and quite reticent. Not at all.

I was amazed, too, that we laughed so much that night. To this day I am astonished that nobody has ever said how *funny* Katharine Hepburn can be.

It was nearly midnight and we hadn't stopped talking. Nor had Irene, showing great restraint, brought up the subject of the project, the thing nearest and dearest to her heart. Now, as I rose to leave, I went to a manila envelope I had casually dropped on a side table (and

Irene had eyed hungrily) and presented them each with a copy of the twenty-two scenes I had outlined.

Kate said she would read hers the following morning, but I knew Irene would be at them the moment I was out the door.

It was arranged that we would meet to work every afternoon at two at "the house on the hill," a small house Kate rented high up on Tower Road, but didn't live in.

"But come up there at noon tomorrow," Kate said, "and have lunch first." Irene would call me in the morning and give me directions.

I asked Kate if I could see her to her car, but she said no because she was parked in a special lot in the back of the hotel. She took me to the window and pointed it out so I could use it next time, "because it's so much easier." Meaning one could sneak in the back way.

She shook my hand very cordially, touched me on the shoulder, and told me what a pleasure it was to meet me and how nice it was of me to come to California for them.

I murmured something about the pleasure, indeed, being mine.

Driving home, I felt that in Katharine Hepburn I had made a new friend, although I suspected it wasn't as simple as that. I knew she was cautious. I deduced from the evening's conversation that she treated her life and career with the greatest respect and carefully protected them. I was certain that, while she might extend a warm and friendly hand to anyone with whom she came into contact, she did not lightly admit strangers into her home and hearth. One earned that right, and it took time.

I also realized that working with Miss Hepburn would include something I hadn't counted on. It was going to be fun.

Irene telephoned me early the next morning.

"Kate called to say how much she likes you," she whispered. "She says you're intelligent and charming and thoughtful." I was delighted, of course, but the way Irene told it to me gave me pause. It was clear that if Kate hadn't thought I was intelligent and charming and thoughtful I'd have been on the next plane out. For the first time, I felt ephemeral.

Irene gave me directions. I was to drive west on Sunset Boulevard and, just past the Beverly Hills Hotel, make a right on Benedict Canyon Road, and she would meet me at the corner of Tower Road at five minutes to twelve. I would follow her up to the house. Otherwise, I'd never find it.

As it turned out, Irene couldn't find it either. And I know because I was with her in her car, my rented convertible having stalled and died as I waited for her at the corner of Benedict Canyon Road and Tower.

Irene came by a couple of minutes later and I could see she was less than enchanted to find me standing by a stalled car. She was annoyed by problems of that sort.

"Just leave it," she said brusquely. "Get in." I got in and she started up the hill on steep, winding Tower Road. And got lost. She didn't know where she was, which didn't help her disposition. She'd obviously made a wrong turn, a thing Irene Selznick just didn't do. Since I could be of no help, I sat silently as she went back down again and started over. She tried a different turn and at last we came to the house.

I could hear Kate's voice ringing over the countryside even before we saw the house. Boy, did that voice carry!

It was a dusty, countrylike road, and we parked parallel to a concrete wall behind which, thanks to shrubbery and trees, the house was barely visible. There was a little iron gate—never locked, to my knowledge—and then steps leading up to the side of the house, which was on two levels. On the second level was a balcony and there Kate was frequently to appear, as one entered, leaning on the railing and looking down at you as you approached. She was always wreathed in smiles, madly energetic, and likely to greet you with, "I played the best tennis of my life this morning!"

She greeted us now as we continued up the steps to a back patio. There was a round, metal table there under an umbrella and it was set for four. Had the trees been thinned, the view would have been spectacular.

A small, birdlike woman fussed about cooking hamburgers, but Kate made no move to introduce her so I assumed she was the cook.

I explained about the car and Kate was all sympathy.

"Well then, I'll go down after work and push you to the nearest garage," she said.

Irene seemed not to be listening.

The small, birdlike woman was putting food on the table.

"Kate," said Irene, "I don't believe Jim has met Phyllis."

"Oh," said Kate, "I thought *everybody'd* met Phyllis."

And she introduced me to Phyllis Wilbourn, who'd been her secretary-companion for years.

If this tiny British spinster had lived to write her memoirs, half the greats of the world would shudder. Originally a companion to Constance Collier, Phyllis had met most of the theatrical notables of that day including Kate, who studied Shakespeare with Miss Collier. When Constance Collier died, leaving Phyllis whatever estate she had, it was to Kate that Phyllis came. One cannot now imagine the one without the other.

I was occasionally shocked by Kate's treatment of Phyllis. She could be very brusque, but there can be no doubt of her love for her. And as for Phyllis's devotion to Kate, it could move mountains.

(Some years later, Kate called and invited me up for dinner. When I arrived, I was stunned to find we were alone. Phyllis was in New York on a week's holiday and staying in her own apartment in Manhattan. I couldn't imagine Phyllis taking a vacation any more than I could imagine her having an apartment of her own somewhere. The whole evening seemed quite abnormal.)

As we sat down to lunch, Kate made the definitive statement about her secretary-companion:

"Phyllis," she said, "lives solely for others." Lucky for Kate!

We had a splendid, quite simple meal. One of the nice things about knowing stars is that you eat well, and always the best. Phyllis, I was to learn, arose early and motored far across town to find the freshest vegetables.

Indeed, it was Kate who instilled in me a wariness of restaurants, which remains to this day. "I won't pay those prices," says the frugal New Englander, "and I won't let anybody *else* pay them." Also, she says she can't eat while people are staring at her.

The telephone rang and Phyllis hurried into the house to answer it. She called out to Kate, "It's John Ford. Will you talk to him?"

"I've been talking to John Ford for forty years," said Kate, rising. "I'm not going to stop now."

I watched her as she bounded into the house. Last night she had seemed much older and almost sedentary. Today she appeared youthful and athletic, a really marvelous specimen of a woman. She was wearing shorts and her freckled legs were, I noticed, still very good. She was, I suppose, about sixty at the time, with Phyllis possibly five years older, but old age seemed a long way off.

After lunch, I was shown the house.

"I love this house," said Kate. It was tucked into a corner of the former John Barrymore estate—I never saw the rest of the estate; it was higher up and totally hidden—and it was called The Aviary.

"His birdcage," said Kate. "Look at that!"

She pointed to a stained-glass door in which the young figures of John Barrymore and Dolores Costello glittered in the sunlight. I was often to glance at it in the weeks to come.

The house was long and narrow, and due to faulty wiring the lights worked on only one side of it. The second floor was composed of a large studio room, in which we stood, sparsely furnished, but what furniture there was was deep and comfortable. Small rugs of animal hide were scattered about. Mobiles of mounted photographs, taken by Kate's nephew, hung from the ceiling and swayed gently. On this floor, there was also a small bedroom and a bathroom. I later discovered there were stairs that led down to a living room with a fireplace, a dining room and the kitchen.

The studio room was big and airy and had a faintly Mexican quality, very southern California, I felt. It was a great shock some years later to leaf through a magazine and see this room as redecorated in screaming modern by the current tenant, Candice Bergen. ("The landlady threw me out," Kate reported.)

Other than the mobiles, there were only two photographs in that house. One was of Katharine Houghton, which sat on the commode in the bathroom, and the other was of George Bernard Shaw, which was on a living room table. In her own California house, the one that Spencer had rented from George Cukor, Kate had no photographs at all.

And then there was Lobo, the German shepherd Kate had bought for Spencer and whom they both adored. After Spencer's death, Kate claimed, Lobo was never the same, and when I first met him he seemed old and fairly inactive, although he was always ready to accompany Kate on her early morning hikes around the reservoir. Lobo really looked like a wolf, but he was the sweetest and gentlest of creatures. I grew to love him. And Kate would sometimes break off work to exclaim, "Look at Lobo! Look how beautiful he is!" All the furniture in her house had slipcovers so that Lobo could hop onto any chair or sofa he fancied. I think to Kate he was an enduring link to Tracy.

We settled down to work. Kate stretched out on the sofa, feet up, as she was always to do. Irene sat perched in a straight chair. I sat on the floor, cross-legged.

They had mentioned at lunch how much they liked the outline I'd done.

"I don't see why we have to meet at all," Kate said. "You've done it all. You don't need us."

They then proceeded, in the most charming and professional way, to consult their notes and change everything I had written.

We spent two hours going over every scene, all of us making suggestions. We threw things out, kept things in; we voted. It was perfectly relaxed and quite invigorating. If one of us insisted on something, we had to explain why and try to prove the mileage we'd get out of it.

Kate was to make suggestions, throughout the coming weeks, that I found brilliant. She had a marvelous sense of what was funny or witty or moving in cinematic terms. I sometimes disagreed with her—I thought she sometimes went too far—but generally her instincts were sound.

The trouble was that she was a frustrated writer. Never work with a star who thinks she's a writer—unless she is. Kate wanted to be a writer. She was inordinately proud of a little article she had written for a small Virginia quarterly.

I told her one day how much I liked *Bringing Up Baby* and she said, "Oh, that's the film that Cary and I wrote every morning before the director arrived." I was shocked that she could be so cavalier about such a thing. I'm sure she and Grant made suggestions and ad-libbed, but Dudley Nichols and Hagar Wilde wrote the screenplay, and Howard Hawks directed it. Howard Hawks never directed a script written by Katharine Hepburn and Cary Grant.

Kate admitted that she was, especially in her early days, equally arrogant regarding directors. She summoned the young George Stevens, then virtually unknown, to her home when she was told that he would direct *Alice Adams*, interviewed the nervous young man, and concluded that she would obviously have to direct the film herself.

She admitted, too, that she revised her thinking after the first few days of shooting.

Anyway, as time went on, I would write scenes and Kate would write scenes and she would love hers and I would love mine. We batted them back and forth and ended up compromising.

Very early on, I made an important discovery. I saw our heroine, Martha, as a great lump of a girl with virtually no charm. Kate saw her as a young Katharine Hepburn, oozing with charm. Once I realized how our views differed, I at least knew where we stood.

I should make clear that it was purposely never made clear to me exactly what I was hired for. We talked about a treatment, but at the end of the first afternoon's work it was decided that we would meet daily for discussion and then I would spend the next morning writing the scenes, dialogue and all, and present them that afternoon to the ladies.

I was, in short, writing a screenplay. My assumption was that my work would be so dazzling, I would naturally be kept on to write the final script. Without ever saying it in so many words, both Kate and Irene nurtured this assumption of mine. They were deliberately vague. They never said I would and they never said I wouldn't.

I suspect that even then it was in the back of their minds to move on to William Rose when the time came. Kate especially was inclined then, as now, to think big. She would want an established writer to do her screenplay. I was merely breaking the ground.

After work that first day, we drove down the hill to my stalled car in Kate's handsome black sedan. She handled the curves like a veteran. She told me there was nothing to worry about, that she was marvelous at fixing automobiles.

She said Spencer was in a hospital in New York once and he confessed to her that when he came out what he wanted was a snappy little sports car.

"But then he said, 'It wouldn't do, would it—with the white hair and everything?' And I said, 'Shoot, if it's what you want, get it.' So he ordered it and it was delivered to the hospital the day he got out and we went down together and there it was at the curb. All the nurses were leaning out of the windows, watching us. So he got behind the wheel and I got in beside him and he tried to start the motor and it wouldn't start. And it *wouldn't* start. So I jumped out, opened the hood, took a bobby pin out of my hair, and in two minutes flat I had it fixed. All the nurses started applauding. I took a bow. And we drove off in a blaze of glory." She laughed. "It was my finest hour."

I said I hoped she had a bobby pin handy.

"Always," she said.

But when we got to the car, it started instantly. I was a little disappointed; I had hoped to catch her bobby pin act. I kept the motor running and we stood beside the car talking as other cars slowed down to watch us.

"We're two strong-minded women," she said, suddenly. "Don't let us walk all over you." I said I wouldn't.

But, in the end, I suppose I did.

Life was very pleasant. I looked forward to our sessions in the afternoons and I thoroughly enjoyed my solitary mornings, busily writing away. We all adored the books and were united in a common effort to make it the best possible picture. For the time being, we were like a little family, just as actors on the road with a play become a temporary family, although, once home, they may never meet again.

I began to care about Kate and Irene. I knew they gossiped about me the minute I disappeared down the hill, but I knew that they liked me, too, and respected me. And it was really such fun working together.

In time Kate was to confess to me that she was riddled with doubts about her ability as a director.

"I wake up in the morning thinking what am I doing?" she moaned.

I can remember the two of us sitting on the back steps one evening as twilight came on, alone, and her telling me how frightened she was. Could she do it?

It really didn't surprise me that Kate Hepburn was frightened. She was, like all intelligent people, frightened. I told her what I felt to be true, that she would not only be a good director, she could be a great director.

"Bless you," she said, taking my hand.

I am even now sorry that Kate never got the chance to direct. (I was there the day the telephone rang, Kate answered, chatted, and came back into the room saying, "That was Alan. He's fixed *Coco*.") She had embarked on this particular project not only because of her affection for Irene and love of the material, but because she was possibly unsure of her future as an actress. Directing might be the only course open to her. I wish, for that short time, that it had been.

Kate was lovable, huggable, touchable. And she was herself a toucher. She reached out for physical contact. But she was extraordinary in that she was not, to use the vernacular, a "ball-breaker." She knew how to be forceful and strong and decisive without ever making the man she was with feel less a man. She was always a woman with a man, never attempting to usurp his role or to demean or belittle or emasculate. I think she must have learned a great deal from her relationship with Mr. Tracy.

Irene was quite different. Irene didn't know many of the things that

Kate knew by instinct, was born knowing. Irene was more calculating and, because calculation takes time, she couldn't be as spontaneous and open as Kate. And she was suspicious, which Kate really wasn't. (Kate was protective of herself, but not suspicious.) And yet Irene, the Jewish mother, had oodles of love to give, whether she knew how to give it or not. I suspect she could be possessive and obsessive and, as I say, single-minded. And I would watch her like a hawk in a business deal. But underneath it all, there was a good person and a warm person and, I should think, a loyal friend. And always, always a certain aura of being alone that was touching.

But, Lord, was Kate exhausting! Her personality was so strong, so overwhelming, I'd often drive down the hill at the end of the afternoon with a crashing headache. And I began to talk like her. I couldn't help it. I'd go to the store for cigarettes and lapse into Hepburnese in spite of myself . . . the phrasing, the inflections, the voice. Clerks began to look at me askance.

Susan Dudley-Allen came to visit me.

"Bring your friend up for lunch tomorrow," Kate said.

"Really?" said I. Where was the Katharine Hepburn who protected herself so carefully from strangers?

"Really," said she.

So Susan came to lunch, Susan so lovely with her honey-colored hair, exquisite British features, and quick English wit. I had thought she'd be pretty impressed when I told her Katharine Hepburn had asked her to lunch, but she was perfectly casual about it. Too casual, I thought.

"After all," I pointed out, "it isn't everybody who gets invited to Katharine Hepburn's for lunch."

"All right, all right," she said. "Let's go. I'm hungry." We went to lunch.

Susan was a terrific success. I felt quite left out. The three girls huddled around the lunch table gossiping like magpies. It turned out that Susan knew many of the people in England whom Kate and Phyllis knew, and they had a grand time catching up on everything. Irene got her two cents' worth in. I managed to occupy myself with the food and nod pointlessly now and then, totally cut off.

At the end of it, Kate said to me, "Susan must come to lunch again tomorrow."

I was quite put out. "Susan can't keep coming to lunch," I said.

"I don't see why not," Kate replied.

So Susan came to lunch again the next day and we relived the lunch of the day before. When it was over, though, Kate and Irene took the afternoon off while Phyllis escorted Susan and me over to the MGM lot in Culver City, a deserted lot then except for James Garner filming one movie and Peggy Fleming taping an ice show.

Kate rarely took an afternoon off. The only days when there was definitely no work were those when one of her family, a niece or nephew, was in town. Then all else stopped. She might even go to Disneyland, crowds and all, so great was her devotion to her family.

I told her one day that I was planning to see *Cabaret* at the Ahmanson Theatre the following week.

"Make it the Wednesday matinee," she said, "and I'll go with you. I like matinees."

So I telephoned my friend, David Rounds, who was in the cast and said, "Look, I'm bringing Katharine Hepburn to the Wednesday matinee. Can you arrange proper tickets?"

David almost fainted. He could do anything, he said, for Miss Hepburn. And he arranged house seats for that performance. But would I kindly bring Miss Hepburn backstage? The cast would be thrilled. I told him I could promise nothing where Miss Hepburn was concerned, but I'd try.

On Wednesday morning, however, Kate telephoned me.

"With my back this way, I can't possibly go to the theatre," she said.

"Your back?"

"I've wrenched my back."

"Oh," I said, "I'm sorry." I was also slightly annoyed. It sounded sort of phony. I thought of the special seats arranged for Miss Hepburn.

"Well," I said, "I'll have to find somebody else."

"If you don't," she said, "maybe Phyllis would like to go."

"Why don't you ask her and call me back?" I said.

She hung up. Ten seconds hadn't passed before she called back.

"Phyllis would love to go," she said. "And why don't you come back here for dinner afterward?" That was her peace offering.

So I took Phyllis and we had a grand time, although the cast looked daggers at us when we went backstage to thank David, even as Phyllis kept telling everybody how sorry Miss Hepburn was not to be there.

On the way home, we picked up ice cream for dinner—boysenberry, that great favorite of Kate and Spencer's.

It was my first invitation to the house Kate lived in on the coast, Spencer's house, the little house at the corner of St. Ives and Doheny. It was surprisingly close to the Sunset Strip and at a fairly busy corner, but so camouflaged by fence and shrubbery, L.A. style, it wasn't even visible from the street. Since Spencer's death, Kate had rented it from their good friend, George Cukor.

A smaller house, tucked away somewhere nearby, housed Margaret and her husband, a Swedish couple Kate employed as domestics and keepers of Lobo when she was away.

Phyllis clicked the electric gate open and we drove into the carport. Then we entered the house through the kitchen door.

Kate showed no indication of a back injury, nor mentioned it, as she showed me around the house.

It was quite small, all on one floor and built California style in the shape of a U around a patio. The living room was large with wood-paneled walls and a wood-burning fireplace. It had a kind of elegance, but in the most comfortable sense.

"I designed it," said Kate proudly. "Doesn't it look like a man's room?" It looked to me like more than that. It looked like Spencer Tracy's room.

The rest of the house consisted only of a couple of bedrooms and a fairly large kitchen. The perfect house for a man living alone.

We established, that evening, a routine that we were to follow over the years whenever I was invited to dinner there. Kate sank into a high-backed black leather chair ("Spencer's chair") with her feet up on a stool, facing the room. On the floor in front of the chair was a small throw-rug with a star design in it.

"There you are, Spence," she had said when she bought it for him. "Put your feet on the stars."

Phyllis sat on the sofa to her right.

I pulled up a chair and sat facing Kate with the coffee table between Phyllis and me. This became such a pattern it would have seemed outrageous of me, in time, to have plopped down on the sofa in Phyllis's usual place, and the very idea of me sitting in Kate's (and Spencer's) chair was unthinkable. We knew our places and we went to them. Lobo might occasionally leap into Phyllis's spot or even mine, but even Lobo dared not eye that black leather chair.

We had a drink or two. That is, I had two; they had one.

There was always an ashtray on the table and Kate had an annoying habit of counting the number of butts at the end of an evening or, when we were working, the day. I was still a smoker. Kate, on the other hand, had recently given them up and flew at me with the zeal of the convert.

She said her father had taught her that smoking, like drinking, was a pleasure and should never be indulged in as one worked. For years she consequently never smoked on the set, but then she'd come home and consume an entire pack before bedtime.

"Fifteen!" she would cry triumphantly, counting my butts, "Fifteen!"

I formed the habit of emptying my ashtrays during the day when she wasn't looking, which wasn't often.

Whereas with Irene, at whatever hour and under whatever circumstances, one always talked about the project, Kate and I rarely discussed it once the day was over. We talked about everything else, which included religion and politics.

"Miss Hepburn and I believe in the goodness of man," Phyllis would say, lapsing into "Miss Hepburn" when she felt the occasion warranted it. (But when she was annoyed with her and her patience was at an end, it would be, "Now, *Kate!*") On the subject of politics, Kate and I were at opposite poles at that time. She was so basically apolitical that one couldn't have much of an argument with her. She said that Eisenhower called her "a pinko," but that didn't dampen her affection for him. She thought that Nixon was terribly "misunderstood," which drove me mad. I expected a woman as smart as she was to know better than that.

After the drinks, I would set up three TV dinner trays and we'd eat in the same chairs, carrying on our conversation as Phyllis brought in a splendid soup, lamb, and luscious vegetables, wine (for me), and the inevitable ice cream.

I wouldn't stay long after dinner. Kate felt that one had said all one had to say during dinner and to stay much after that was to stay too long. Coffee and cookies and out you go. She would invariably walk me to my car at the curb.

"You'll catch cold," I would say, looking at her stockingless feet in the sandals.

"Shoot, I won't catch cold," she would reply, as if no germ would dare.

(Almost two decades later, I was to use these very lines in one of the movies I wrote for her, *Mrs. Delafield Wants to Marry*.)

At the car, we would stand talking a little longer in the dark. I would look at her face in the dim light—that most miraculous of all faces—and feel such affection for this famous lady, who stood there so small and yet so wonderful in the night.

Kate hated any kind of distracting noise.

She and Irene and I were working one afternoon in the downstairs living room when Phyllis started rattling papers upstairs, a sound I wasn't even aware of until Kate shouted, "Stop that, Phyllis!"

A few minutes later I heard a truck stop outside on the road, then start, then stop again. I expected Kate to explode, but instead, all concern, she said, "I think they're lost."

She leaped up from her customary prone position on the sofa and I followed her as she went out of the house, down the steps, and into the road.

An elderly black man sat in the cab of a large van.

"Are you lost?" Kate asked him.

I saw him blink, obviously startled that Katharine Hepburn was standing there in the middle of the road asking him if he was lost.

"Yes, ma'am," he managed to say.

"Where do you want to go?"

He read the address off a small slip of paper. It was the last thing he was to say. Kate took over.

"It may be up there," she said, pointing up a side road that wound around the side of her house. "That'd be a difficult turn for you to make. You stay here. We'll go up and look. Come on, Jim."

So I found myself trotting along behind her as she went at a brisk clip up the hot, dusty road. I felt like a child trying to keep up with his mother. When we came to a house, I was winded. Kate wasn't.

"Nope," she said, looking at the mailbox. "This isn't it."

We went down again.

"It's not up there," Kate told the driver, who nodded, but he made no move and said nothing. He had fallen into the role of being taken care of by Kate.

She swung around now as a car came up the hill. To my amazement, she rushed into the middle of the road and waved it down. I could see the driver's disbelieving eyes as he put on the brakes.

Kate stuck her head into the car.

"Do you happen to have a map of Beverly Hills?" she asked. I thought the man might die of heart failure, but he looked like some sort of salesman and he played it cool.

"Certainly, Miss Hepburn," he said, "in the trunk." He whistled casually as he got out of the car, opened the trunk, brought out the map, and handed it to Kate with trembling fingers. She spread it out on the hood of the car while I looked over her shoulder. On the map, Beverly Hills looked like a pailful of worms.

"I can't read this," Kate said to me, "can you?" I said I couldn't either.

"Thank you very much," she said, folding up the map and handing it back to the man with an air of dismissal. But he wasn't about to leave; the show was too good. He stood there, waiting to see what would happen next.

What happened next was that a second car came up the road and Kate once again rushed out and went into her waving act.

The car stopped, of course, and the driver, who looked as if he lived in the neighborhood (and by that I mean he looked rich), poked his head out of the window. His expression, under his expensive haircut, was one of absolute incredulity.

"Do you live around here?" asked Kate briskly, sizing up the situation. He admitted that he did.

"Well, then, do you know where this address is?" I saw that she now had the little slip of paper, although when and how she had gotten it from the driver I couldn't recall.

"I think that's around the other side of the hill, Miss Hepburn," the man answered.

"Are you going in that direction?"

I saw him hesitate. I could see that he wasn't, but his plans could suddenly have changed. He replied in the affirmative.

Kate sprang into action.

"Good!" she said, getting into his car and slamming the door. "Let's go and see."

To the truck driver, she called out, "You stay here!" To me, she said nothing. I watched as the car disappeared around the curve of the hill.

"Well . . ." I said, shrugging, to the salesman and the truck driver, both of whom were motionless. The salesman remained standing there. If Miss Hepburn was coming back, the show might go on.

I went into the house, unable to believe what I had just seen. Kate the Careful had gone off in a car with a strange man!

"Where's Kate?" Irene asked me, looking up from the script.

"She went off in a car with a stranger," I said, blithely. Irene's eyebrows flew up. For some reason, I suddenly felt guilty. "Should I have stopped her?" I said.

"How?" said Irene.

I settled back down to work, but I was uneasy. There were, after all, such things as kidnappers. Would she be abducted? On the other hand, heaven help the fool who kidnapped Kate!

In half an hour we heard Kate return, her voice booming over the countryside, and the sound of the truck finally driving off.

She came bursting into the house, breathless and cheerful.

"Well, we found it!" she said triumphantly, flinging herself down on the sofa and taking up her script. "Now, where were we?"

Where were we?

We were approaching the end of the first draft and becoming more and more uneasy about the ending. The simple fact was there really wasn't any ending. We all set our minds to this problem and how to conquer it when the time came.

"What happens if we can't get this right?" Irene said to Kate in front of me one day, referring to the script.

"Well then," came her casual reply, "we just say good-bye to Jim and move on."

It was an honest reaction and certainly professional, but it hurt a bit. I had to keep reminding myself that I was expendable; the script came first and my dear friends would drop me in a minute if they thought I wasn't the best thing for the movie. As they should.

At the same time, ending or not, I felt I had a firm grip on what could be a delightful film. I thought I knew exactly what the script should be, whereas I began to suspect that Irene and Kate were going in circles. One day they would go off in one direction, the next day in another. I considered myself the stabilizing force. I doubt if they really cared much for that, although nothing was said. At least, not to me.

Kate impressed Irene and me one day with a speech she had written the night before in which Le Maître, the great artist, counseled his budding art student, Martha. Kate read it to us: "I don't think I can teach you anything—don't mistake me—I know that you have to develop along your own lines—but here I can push you and guide you and show you the competition of great genius—the giants—which must be your competition—what do you want to do—be the big frog in the small pool—how can you keep yourself in line—your best work is a habit—that's why you go to school—to produce your best work."

When she'd finished, Irene and I sat silently. We both knew this speech wasn't Le Maître's—it was Katharine Hepburn's. Kate talking to herself. She had known, those long years ago when she was a struggling actress, that no matter how odd or mannered she might seem, she must develop along her own lines. And she knew, too, the only competition that could be her competition was that of the giants. And she had learned over the many years in small studios and large, great theatres and country playhouses, that one's best work is a habit.

I've always loved that line: your best work is a habit. I've quoted it often and, indeed, with Kate's permission, used it in another of the movies I wrote for her, *Laura Lansing Slept Here.*

I was touched by the speech and told her so. I was wearing Bermuda shorts, however, and I was distracted by a curious itching on my legs. Looking down, I discovered three fleas munching on my calf.

"My God!" I cried, "There are fleas on me!"

Kate was instantly alert. "There can't be fleas on you," she said curtly.

"Well, there are!" I said, jumping up. "And there are probably fleas on Lobo and fleas on Irene and for all I know there are fleas on *you*!"

Kate was off the sofa in a flash and investigating my legs.

"I don't see any fleas."

"I saw one, Kate," said loyal Irene.

"Where? I don't see any."

"*There*!" I pointed. "They're in the *rug*!" It was a thick shag rug and it was alive with little sand fleas.

"Oh," said Kate. "Well, I'll have it cleaned."

We rolled the rug up and continued working. Irene later told me that after I'd left that day, Kate said, "My God, he certainly made a fuss about the fleas, didn't he!"

And the fleas became a kind of running gag with us.

Six months later, on the night of the Academy Awards, I was back in New York and, like the rest of the world, glued to my television set. Kate won her third Oscar that night for *The Lion in Winter*, although it was a tie and she had to share it with Barbra Streisand.

I sent a telegram off to her: DEAR KATE. THERE MAY BE FLEAS ON ME BUT THERE AIN'T NO FLEAS ON YOU. LOVE AND CONGRATULATIONS. JIM.

She sent back a note.

"Well, Jim," she wrote, "you might say there ain't no fleas on *one-half* of me!"

Kate contended that she could give up acting at any time and be perfectly content. She had done it, she said, during those five years when she was nursing Spencer. (I never quite figured out when those five years were.) But, she claimed, nobody wanted her anyway in those days.

"*Now* I'm St. Katharine!" she would trill. "I can do no wrong!"

On the night Spencer Tracy died—and she told me that she had been sleeping in the maid's room, heard him get up and go into the kitchen, heard him running water into the kettle, probably to make a cup of tea, heard the kettle crash to the floor and then a kind of thud, knew he'd fallen but didn't know he was dead until she rushed in and found him on the floor—on that night, Kate's life changed forever. She was transformed (and this she did not tell me) from a devoted companion into an out-of-work actress.

How she must have loved him. They had the most wonderful fights.

"One of the things I adored about Mr. Tracy," she said, "is that we could go at it hammer and tong on the telephone and one of us would hang up on the other and then the other would call back in five minutes and say what time is dinner and the other would say eight o'clock and we'd go on."

Kate sometimes went too far, at least with me. I remember an afternoon when I was rejecting a scene she had written because, I said, I didn't like people poking fun at other people's physical infirmities as one of her characters was doing to Martha.

"That's because you're fat," said Kate.

A shocked hush fell over the room. Irene managed to laugh lamely, as if it were a joke, but I stared at Kate in utter disbelief. She laughed, too. I didn't. In the first place, I wasn't fat (chubby maybe, a little overweight maybe) and, second, even if I was, it shouldn't have been said. She said it to hurt, and it did. Nor was she sorry.

But that was unusual, her "thing" about fat people. Normally, she was all concern and sympathy.

I telephoned her one morning to say I had read in the newspaper that Henry Hull was ill in the hospital. I knew Henry Hull had given Kate her first job in the theatre.

"Isn't life frightening!" she said, a favorite phrase of hers, and I'm sure flowers went right off to Henry Hull. She was equally distressed when Spencer's brother ("Poor old Carroll!") died.

I remember a Sunday evening when I came by her house for dinner and Kate told me to make myself a drink, she was busy, her dentist had died. He was Olivia de Havilland's dentist, too, and she'd heard that Olivia was staying at the Beverly Hills Hotel and she had to telephone her.

I listened as she put through the call.

"Hello, this is Katharine Hepburn speaking. I'm trying to reach Miss Olivia de Havilland. Is she staying at the hotel? Operator, I *know* Katharine Hepburn isn't staying at the hotel. *I* am Katharine Hepburn. No, operator, I am *not* telephoning Katharine Hepburn. I am telephoning Olivia de Havilland. Operator, this is *not* Olivia de Havilland calling Katharine Hepburn. This is Katharine Hepburn calling Olivia de Havilland. Operator, stop calling me Miss de Havilland! I am Miss Hepburn and—!"

But we were both laughing so hard she couldn't go on and had to hang up.

What finally happened with our project, *Martha in Paris?*

To this day I don't know and I'll probably never know.

We finished that first draft, but none of us was satisfied with the ending. Five weeks had passed—a week longer than anticipated—and Irene had to get back to New York. But I was put on a plane first and Irene called me before I left to make sure I would telephone "La Hep," as she always called her, and say good-bye.

I had, of course, planned to do that.

I felt as if I was in limbo. Thrown out. A flop.

Kate was perfectly cheery on the telephone, thanked me for my work, said that we would meet soon again in New York. But she did add that they didn't know what to do with the project. They had agreed, however, that I would work another week in New York and get rewrites to Irene at the Pierre.

When I got in, Irene called me and we had a long, rambling conversation that was mostly about her reaction when she and David had previewed *Gone with the Wind* in Orange County. She had started to scream with nerves when the credits came on the screen and he had to throw his coat over her. She did the same thing at the Los Angeles premiere and again in Atlanta. Hardly a word about the project. Whatever plans they had for it, I knew that I wasn't included.

I sent the rewrites to the Pierre, having worked that extra week, but nothing was said about remuneration and no check ever arrived to cover it.

Nor did I ever see Irene again.

In November, however, I received a note from Kate, who was passing through town, written in her usual unpunctuated style:

"Dear Jim—It's 6:30 A.M.—and I hardly think that I should call you—I tried yesterday about 2–3—no reply—So—we go to London today to work with Margery Sharp—Our 'thing' came out pretty thin and somehow or other one has to get Martha herself in more depth—We'll be back in a month—or three weeks—and I look forward to seeing you when not in such a rush—affectionately, Kate."

Rumors flew.

Mrs. Selznick and Miss Hepburn went to London to confer with Margery Sharp and have Miss Sharp herself write the dialogue for their new movie. But Miss Sharp as a writer of dialogue didn't work out. They then went to the Isle of Jersey to work with William Rose. What came of that, I never heard.

It was, as it turned out, beside the point.

1969

I had left Manhattan and moved to the country to a charming seven-teenth-century stone house that overlooked the beautiful Clove Valley just outside of High Falls, New York. It was a jewel box: totally renovated and completely modern, but with all the rusticity intact. There was a fireplace almost large enough to walk into, great beamed ceilings and stone walls a foot thick. This gem cost me $150 a month, although I was shocked to discover that the electric heating in the winter came to more than that.

Here, surely, I would write the Great American Play. (We were still trying to get *The Last of Mrs. Lincoln* on.) In the evenings, I sat gazing at that beautiful valley, beautiful but not very stimulating. The pinnacle of excitement was a Friday night amateur hour called Joe Runner's Cabaret, housed in the cellar of an abandoned house down the road. The main attraction was a singing goose. The singing goose was famous in those parts because no matter what you did to it—and Joe did every-thing to it—it never sang. Many was the Friday night we waited breath-lessly as the singing goose was gently prodded in every orifice in an ef-fort to get a song out of it. It never even squawked.

You see the level of sophistication.

My spirits fell.

I'd tried, with the support of Richard Barr and Alan Schneider, to get a grant from the Rockefeller Foundation, but the Rockefellers were having no part of me.

I submitted *The Last of Mrs. Lincoln* to the O'Neill Theatre Center in Waterford, Connecticut, and got rejected. (Charles Adams still had the option and was trying to interest Roger Stevens in it, but nothing seemed to work for Charles.)

The money situation was, as always, crucial. I'd bought an old secondhand car and could get around, but beyond that there wasn't much I could afford to do.

It was now that the remarkable Mary Margaret McBride came into my life. She had retired to a sensational house high above the Shokan Reservoir, only a few miles from me, and from that house she did three hour-long broadcasts each week for the local Kingston, New York, radio station. Each broadcast required a guest to be interviewed and you can imagine, being tucked away in those mountains, what a time Mary Margaret had digging up guests. She was sometimes reduced to Girl Scouts.

I was a windfall, being chatty and Show Biz and very much on her humor beam. I was also available at a moment's notice, should her guest get lost driving up from New York City, as they sometimes did. Or simply didn't show, as they sometimes didn't.

I grew to love her and I think she loved me. She wasn't at all what her public image was: the folksy, down-home granny with the Missouri twang in her voice. She was a very sophisticated woman, a former journalist who had stumbled into radio and literally transformed it. I'm inclined to credit Mary Margaret with the talk show as we know it today. (I don't refer to the current crop of talk-show gutter stuff; rather, I mean the likes of Johnny Carson and Jay Leno.) For good or ill, she started it.

So far as I know, I was the only guest she ever paid to be on her show. She used to slip me, sub rosa, fifteen dollars every time I'd broadcast, knowing my financial situation. She was very well off and lived quite splendidly in that magnificent house, a sign outside of which stated PLEASE RESPECT THE PRIVACY I'VE COME SO FAR TO FIND.

I worried about her. She was grossly overweight and had difficulty moving about. In the summertime she loved sitting out in a screened-in gazebo on the lawn, watching the hummingbirds. Insects were the great enemy, and she reeked of citronella from spring until autumn. Scratching insect bites was a torment, especially in areas she had difficulty reaching, which was practically everywhere.

Broadcasting was what kept her interested in living. She fell one day and lay for hours in the wet grass, unable to get up. Finally she was discovered and taken in an ambulance to the hospital in Kingston. I'm told that, as the ambulance passed her sponsors' establishments, she kept trying to look out to see if she could get ideas for her commercials.

I once did a broadcast with her from her hospital bed, where she was confined in a kind of traction. She was in obvious pain and would grimace silently as I talked, but you'd never know it from the cheeriness in her voice. This was a great performer and, I might add, one of the great salespeople of all time. In that whiny little voice, she would rattle on and could sell anything. You absolutely believed whatever she said.

My life was very much linked with Mary Margaret's and I was proud of our friendship. And then one day she died, simply died. Her ashes were buried under her favorite tree on the lawn. And that was that.

I cried and cried.

My friend Barry Plaxen was a nudist. He belonged to a "colony" in New Jersey where every weekend he went, threw off his clothing, and cavorted, happily unencumbered.

It was at this Circle H Ranch that Barry and his fellow nudist, Ken McGuire, saw a production of a 1928 play by Tom Cushing called *Grin and Bare It*. Barry and Ken thought it was a howl. Furthermore, Barry felt that if Ken, who'd done a bit of writing, would update it, this play could be put on the boards in New York.

Oddly enough, Barry had no interest in doing it off-off-Broadway and even off-Broadway, where it belonged. No, he would only be satisfied if it became Broadway's First Nudist Comedy.

There was only one problem that he could see. The play was really just a long one-acter. He needed a curtain-raiser to make it a full evening. And why shouldn't it be one of his favorite plays? Why shouldn't it be my little play, *Postcards?*

I hesitated, but not for long. I didn't wish to engage in sleaze, of course, but no matter how you sliced it, you could hardly call *Grin and Bare It* sleaze. What you could call it was a not-very-good play, perhaps, but not sleaze. It was a gimmick, naturally—all those actors running around the stage starko—but it was perfectly wholesome and healthy, especially if you viewed the nude body as acceptable. That it didn't belong in the Belasco Theatre, one of Broadway's most venerated houses, could hardly be disputed. But there it was.

(And I should like to state—since other productions claim the honor—that it was this production that finally exorcised the ghost of David Belasco, which was reputed to roam the balcony. He never came back after *Grin and Bare It*. Couldn't take it.)

I was convinced my fortune was made. This would run forever. No matter what the critics said, surely audiences would flock to see beautiful naked bodies in a light comedy. Laugh and get your jollies at the same time.

I agreed that *Postcards* could be the curtain-raiser. At least I would have a play on Broadway. What playwright could resist, especially when there was all that money to be made? I could worry about my art later. On the way to the bank.

Barry was circumspect. He really did believe in nudism and tried to avoid sensationalism at the same time he hoped it would sell tickets. I wasn't permitted into any of the casting sessions for *Grin and Bare It* or, for that matter, the rehearsals. Along with the public, I saw the nude cast only at the first preview.

I was booked, however, to spend a day with Barry and Ken at the Circle H Ranch and I was scared to death. Could I do it? I was brought up in a Hoosier household where nudity was unthinkable. We lived like nuns in a cloister.

Consequently, I was trembling as we drove into the ranch. But it was a beautifully warm and sunny day and, after the initial few minutes, the naked families as they swam in the pool or lounged on the grass seemed completely natural. Sexless, too, I might add. It's clothes that make us sexy; I swear, if everybody went around naked, there wouldn't be any sex maniacs.

I shucked off my duds and joined them. It would have been embarrassing not to.

When night fell, though, and everyone headed to a fluorescent-lit cafeteria for dinner, the white bodies under the grim lights looked too awful, at least to me. I put my knickers on. I felt out of place and got some disapproving looks, but nudity and fluorescent lighting don't go together.

Both plays were directed—and very well—by Ronny Graham, who had first caught my attention years before in *New Faces of 1952*. The *Times* reported that Mr. Graham seemed slightly embarrassed by his situation (meaning the nudist play). He estimated that this was his eighth comeback and, to his friends, it was something of a comedown.

"When I told Hermione Gingold I was going to direct it," he said, "she threw a roll at me."

That was nothing compared to William Le Massena, who had to confess to his dear friends, the Lunts, that he was about to appear nude on the stage of the Belasco Theatre. They were horrified.

The reviews were so devastating that I couldn't bear to save any of them, with the single exception of George Oppenheimer's in a Long Island newspaper. All the reviews but his buried *Postcards* along with

Grin and Bare It. Mr. Oppenheimer was obviously a gentleman of rare intellect and breeding.

"Let me add," he wrote, "that the evening had one merit—a fully clothed, fresh and charmingly written curtain-raiser entitled *Postcards* by James Prideaux. Mr. Prideaux's touching and entertaining play is well worth seeing. My only complaint is that it should have come second, as an antidote to the grotesque and cheaply unsensational *Grin.*"

Barry kept the plays running for five weeks, but at a loss, and I was never to see any royalties.

The important thing, as Kate would have said, was to "just keep a-goin'."

So I did, but my career became a thing of rags and patches, indeed.

I was in Manhattan and went down to the Theatre de Lys one night to catch the first preview of a revival of *House of Flowers* that Joe Hardy was directing. It wasn't good. The Harold Arlen score was glorious, of course, but Truman Capote's book was weak and the show was miserably miscast. Joe stopped me as I was leaving the theatre and asked if he could call me later.

When he did, he told me that he'd been talking to the producer, Saint-Subber, and they were prepared to offer me a flat fee ($500, I think it was) if I'd rewrite the book. Truman Capote was in Palm Springs and didn't want to do it and didn't care who did. I quaked a bit at the thought of rewriting Capote—who did I think I was?—but I was calmed by the thought that I was a dramatist and Truman was a novelist and never the twain should meet.

In the end, *House of Flowers*, with some recasting and my rewrites, still wasn't very good. I suppose it needed a real star like Pearl Bailey to pull it off, and the closest we came to that was the angular and arresting Josephine Premice, but she wasn't even the lead.

There were some terrific people connected with it. Joe Raposo handled the musical direction and arrangements, Talley Beatty did the choreography, and Tharon Musser the lighting—but there was no saving it. It was a real thrill to be able to say that I had worked with the great Harold Arlen, a charming and humble man, but beyond that there was nothing. And I took no credit.

I began to get used to taking no credit.

Michael Kasdan had seen a play in London that knocked him out, called *What the Butler Saw,* by Joe Orton. To my mind, Orton was the greatest satirical dramatist since Wilde. Michael picked up the rights, and he and Charles Woodward proposed to produce it off-Broadway. Michael wasn't entirely happy about the ending, however, and he felt, too, that the play should be somewhat Americanized. Since Joe Orton had been murdered by his roommate, there was no question of his attending to this. I was obviously the man to do it.

Joseph Hardy—one was inclined to use one's friends in the world of the New York theatre—was again to direct, and so we sat down together and did what we thought was necessary. It wasn't much. My major contribution, as I remember, was to change "gollywogs" to "tar babies." And we softened the ending, which in London had the characters climbing a ladder in red flame.

What the Butler Saw opened at the McAlpin Rooftop Theatre, which was atop the McAlpin Hotel on Thirty-fourth Street. It was a substantial hit and ran, I think, for a year or more.

The cast was superb: Laurence Luckinbill (who would one day be so wonderful in my *Lyndon*), Diana Davila, Jan Farrand, Charles Murphy, Tom Rosqui, and Joe's former drama teacher, the pixieish Lucian Scott. I never tired of watching it—what a brilliant writer Orton was—and I'd pop in whenever I was in town.

A royalty for me was vaguely spoken of, but I don't think I ever saw it, and, of course, I took no credit.

The papers were full of it.

Katharine Hepburn, of all people, would star in Alan Jay Lerner's new musical, *Coco*.

I could not imagine it.

In the first place, if there was a single gaping void in Kate's world, it was that of music. I won't go so far as to say she hated it, but she came close. Music appeared to be little more than noise to her.

Second, the mere thought of her actually singing was enough to make me shudder.

Third, as she often said, "I get up when it's light and go to bed when it's dark." I knew that she had done plenty of theatre and would do more, but it was difficult to think of Kate acting, let alone singing, at 10:30 P.M.

I was, as she would say, fascinated.

Reports filtered in that she had taken singing lessons on the sly before daring to perform before Mr. Lerner and, when she felt she was ready, she had invited an unbiased audience of one to hear her.

The unbiased audience of one was Phyllis.

"That was just lovely, Kate," I can hear Phyllis saying. After all, Chanel hadn't heard her sing, and probably didn't care any more than Alan Jay Lerner did. Katharine Hepburn was an enormous star and would pack houses. And, of course, there was always the example of Rex Harrison. He couldn't sing, either, but did it sink *My Fair Lady*? Certainly not! One talked a song. Miss Hepburn would, in reality, talk her songs.

I couldn't wait.

And I hadn't learned (and perhaps never will) that just because one works with somebody on a given project doesn't mean you're friends forever. I sent her encouraging little notes. Great stars need great encouragement. And, to her credit, Kate kept the correspondence going.

She must have been in rehearsal when she wrote: "Jim—Think away—that's what I need—lovely country thoughts—Too long and I'm exhausted but it's fascinating—Affection—Kate."

On opening night I sent her a telegram, remembering a day in California when she had admired some sandals I was wearing and asked where I got them. "Ohrbach's," I told her. "And what is that?" she said, "A shop?"

"Well now you know what Ohrbach's is," I included in the wire to her since I knew she had a song about Ohrbach's, not to mention Bloomingdale's and a few other shops she'd never heard of before.

The reviews weren't good, and back came a note in her bold hand with a dig at the critics in defense of Mr. Lerner.

"Jim—you're sweet. The audiences continue to go absolutely mad—They cheer they clap throughout—I think that they're [she meant the critics] so used to the pigsty that wit and glamour and nonsense throw them—and who wrote my part—they are asses. My love and thanks, Kate."

1970

I was dying to see *Coco*, but before that my car overturned on an icy road and I spent some time in bed.

At last, in February 1970, I arranged through friends of friends of the producer to see *Coco*. I wrote to Kate explaining that I hadn't seen her play due to the damn accident and hoping we could meet after the performance for a cup of tea or something.

She wrote back immediately: "Jim—what a sweet note—You make me proud—How terrifying I'm glad you're OK—After theatre OK—no tea, Affection, Kate." I made her proud because I had mentioned what courage it took to do a musical. And there was a postscript: "I finish at 11:15 and get back here 11:45 then I have 45 minutes—Oh fate where is thy—"

I telephoned Kate to say I was definitely coming, and Phyllis answered. She couldn't imagine how I had managed to get a ticket, never had such business been done before in the New York theatre, everybody loved Miss Hepburn, everybody loved the play. I told her how pleased I was and that I would drop backstage after the show. She said she'd meet me at the stage door.

And so I saw *Coco*. I wasn't appalled, but I certainly didn't love it. I thought it was second-rate, interesting only in that it brought Katharine Hepburn to the musical stage. When Kate was doing her big musical soliloquy like Joan of Arc at the stake, I was embarrassed that all it was about was a little red dress. I was even more embarrassed when she walked downstage, looked at the audience, and said, "Shit!"

(Years later she was to criticize a play of mine because one of the characters called something "a piece of shit." When *she* did it, it was wit; when I did it, it was scatology—but then, Kate's never minded a touch of the double standard.)

I couldn't find any wit, although I thought the show did have a kind of visual glamour. And plenty of nonsense. Also, I was saddened to think that Kate would eulogize a woman who had lived cozily at the Ritz in Paris with a German general during the occupation.

Afterward, Phyllis greeted me at the stage door. As we walked to Kate's dressing room, I asked her how Kate had managed to turn her life upside down to accommodate the late hours of the theatre?

Phyllis pulled herself up to her full height, which was short.

"Miss Hepburn," she said, "can do anything."

Kate came out of her dressing room wearing her famous German cap. We hugged and I kissed her on the cheek.

"You've got a mustache!" she exclaimed, disapprovingly.

At that moment, a stagehand passed and Kate whirled on him.

"*Don't you ever do that to me again!*" she said in a tone that would have flattened Ivan the Terrible. The stagehand slunk off, probably to turn in his union card.

I told Kate how moved I was by the magic of her performance. I meant it. She couldn't sing, she couldn't dance, she probably didn't even like musicals, but it had been a challenge and she'd met it and the magic was there.

Luckily, I didn't have to get into the show itself because Phyllis suddenly turned and said, excitedly, "Here comes Bea Lillie!"

And here she came in her little pillbox hat, moving along as if on wheels.

"Well, Bea, what did you think of it?" asked Kate, rashly.

"Oh," said Bea, rolling her eyes in mock ecstasy, obviously less than enchanted, "it was *wonderful!*" Hurt, Kate turned away from her.

I went back to the country.

1 9 7 1

When CBS came to my old friend Joe Hardy and asked if he knew any-body who could write *The Secret Storm*, that venerable old soap, he didn't hesitate.

"Yes, of course," he said, "if you can get him. James Prideaux."

If! I was living at Eagle's Nest now, a ramshackle frame house with great flair on top of a mountain outside Old Hurley, New York, and I didn't have a prospect in the world. But Joe's making me sound hard to get made me irresistible to them. Bethel Leslie (yes, the actress) and Gerry Day had been taken on as head writers and they telephoned to ask if I'd write one episode a week. (These were half-hour shows.) I said yes. They called back to ask if I could possibly write *two* episodes a week. I said yes. They called back to ask if I could possibly write *three* episodes a week. I said yes.

Never having written a soap, I saw no reason why I couldn't.

The little local bank in Old Hurley was stunned by the change in my fortunes. Normally, my bank balance was somewhere around thirty bucks. Suddenly, I was appearing every Thursday with (for me) huge deposits. They were as thrilled as I was.

And it was so easy. I only worked five hours a day—starting at 9:00 A.M. and ending at 2:00 P.M.—for three days a week. It took just those five hours to turn out an episode. And I did it right in the comfort of my own home, looking out from my second-floor study over that wooded mountaintop. Perfect working conditions.

I watched the show daily, partly as a penance for my sins because they rarely if ever said the lines as I wrote them. They just sort of paraphrased them. Some of them had been on the show so long they alone knew how the character would talk. And frequently they'd have to be consulted as to their character's past. Nobody else could remember. "I *can't* marry Bill," Amy might tell us, "because he's my long lost brother!"

Sometimes we'd set up a situation that we'd have to shoot right down again. Two of the characters, for instance, were very much in love and got married. He'd look at her and say, "I love you, Val, and I'll never let you out of my sight." A week later a directive came down saying that the actress who played Val had a vacation coming up. So we had her husband say to her suddenly, "You look a bit pale, dear. Why don't you go to Switzerland for three weeks?"

Stuff like that.

This was all just fun for those of us who created it, but I learned fairly quickly that the viewers took it very seriously. I couldn't be glib about it.

A neighbor stopped in for tea one day—a housewife who was a great fan of the soaps—and I, to make conversation, gaily laughed and said, "Guess what's going to happen to the Gaylords next month?" (Or whatever their names were.) "They're going to be in an airplane crash and *die!*" (They had to because the actress who played Mrs. Gaylord was fed up and quitting.)

The housewife leaped out of her chair and started screaming. She couldn't stop. By the time I got her into her car and saw her down the hill, she was limp as a rag and sobbing hopelessly. I was very careful after that.

I'm a little shocked now, twenty years later, by what they get away with on the soaps. Hopping in and out of beds. In my day we had to think twice before we could even let them kiss, although I was forever slipping in phony pages: SCENE TWO OPENS WITH VAL'S HUSBAND, BRUCE, SUDDENLY EMBRACING ERIK AND PLANTING A BIG, SLOPPY KISS ON HIS RECEPTIVE MOUTH.

Just to make sure Bethel and Jerry were awake.

I couldn't quite get *Martha in Paris* out of my head. I knew that the Selznick-Hepburn forces had lost all interest and dropped all rights. What about doing it as a play?

I asked my new manager, Michael Kasdan, to approach Miss Sharp's New York agent and see if I could take an option on the stage rights. I could and I did, sitting down to write a play version between my work on *The Secret Storm* and the never-ending battle to get *The Last of Mrs. Lincoln* into production. I felt I finally had a solution to the problem of *Martha*'s ending.

When I finished it to my satisfaction, I wrote Kate to ask if she would like to see it and give me her thoughts. Naturally, I included Irene in that as well. Back came an immediate reply.

"Dear Jim—Oh yes—I must read it—What fun—Irene is at the Connaught in London—I finish August 1st—Affection, Kate Hep."

I sent the script off and her response came just as quickly: "Dear Jim—Tried to get you—no ans—no ans—So—You've done a fine job—I like the end very much—Still feel some scenes sticky—and showy and frankly know the material so well it's hard for me to really judge it—I see it as a movie not a play—Do hope you have good luck setting it up—Thanks for letting me see it and congratulations—Kate."

However, I was informed by Miss Sharp's agent that Miss Sharp had changed her mind. She was now planning to write a stage version herself. Could she please return our option money and have her rights back? My initial reaction was a resounding and vehement no, but Michael was kinder than I and agreed to that.

To my knowledge, Miss Sharp has never written a stage version of *Martha in Paris*, which is probably just as well. We should all of us have known not to tackle a heroine who was utterly without regard for the human race.

1972

Would you believe that, after one hundred years of nothing, there would suddenly be *three* plays about Mary Todd Lincoln opening in New York in the same season?

I was lucky. By the time *we* opened, *The Lincoln Mask*, starring Fred Gwynne and Eva Marie Saint as Abe and Mary, had already come and gone after eight performances.

Look Away, a two-character piece starring Geraldine Page as Mary Todd and Maya Angelou as Lizzie Keckley, opened off-Broadway shortly after our opening, but it lasted only through one performance.

Barbara Walters, that great historian, announced that if last year had been the year of Mary, Queen of Scots, this year was the year of Mary Todd Lincoln.

I was afraid this was a bit too much of Mary Todd Lincoln. George Schaefer, the director, and I mulled over our chances. *The Last of Mrs. Lincoln* had packed the Opera House at the Kennedy Center for three weeks. Washington had loved it. Even President Nixon had booked his box (from which I had watched rehearsals), but he was busy that night so Mrs. Nixon came with one daughter and, as her birthday treat, Mamie Eisenhower. Afterward, surrounded by the Secret Service, they rushed backstage to congratulate Julie Harris.

George was always very high on the play and even confessed one evening, over a couple of drinks, that he expected me to win the Pulitzer Prize. That's the kind of optimism that one should go into a production with. I didn't have it. I merely hoped I'd come out of it having made a little money.

We had taken Washington by storm and yet, as the New York opening approached, I was uneasy. I was aware that in Washington the Kennedy Center had made playgoing safe—one drove right into a garage under the building—and fashionable, and that audiences would come no matter how mixed the reviews. But the New York advance was sluggish and, indeed, piddling. And New Yorkers looked to their critics to be told what was good. It wasn't going to be easy. I began to prepare myself for a blasting of the play.

I was startled by how much I cared. I got sick to my stomach when I thought that I might have a flop. I told myself that the critics didn't matter, but who was I kidding? (I'm reminded of a story about that lovely playwright, Beth Henley, who got devastating reviews on a New York opening and was found by a friend sitting on the curb, sobbing, outside the restaurant where the reviews were being read. "Now, Beth," said the friend, "remember when we came to New York to do this play, you said you didn't *care* what the critics would say?" Through her tears, Beth looked up and said, "I lied.")

At the preview on the night before we opened at the ANTA Theatre in New York (now the Virginia), Julie Harris gave a towering performance. I was greatly encouraged, too, that the theatre was nearly full in spite of dreadful weather.

After the curtain came down, our star could be seen in the empty theatre creeping around on all fours in the first two rows. It seemed a friend of hers, overwrought and tearful, had popped out one of her contact lenses during the second act, and Julie, feeling somewhat responsible, was determined to find it. That was our Julie. Unfortunately, she only came up with a couple of tacks, a rubber band, and some sheer filth, all of which she dutifully carried backstage and deposited in a trash can.

Julie dreaded opening nights. She was always nervous and felt her performance was down. On that opening night, she started a little slowly, but she built beautifully and was superb. It was, I thought, the best performance of the play I'd seen. The cast seemed utterly relaxed (try that on opening night), which was a tribute to George Schaefer and his very canny preparation: just the right number of preview performances so as to get the feel of the theatre and a line rehearsal in the afternoon before the opening.

I heaved a sigh of relief. Well, it was over. I would let the theatre empty out and then go backstage to congratulate the cast.

I could hardly get to them, however. The dressing rooms were located on the second floor and the stairs were jammed with people. I waited and let them pretty much clear out.

When I finally got to Julie's dressing room, I was surprised to find the door shut and even more surprised to hear cries coming out of it. I burst right in. George and Millie Schaefer were there, as was Julie's pal, Charles Nelson Reilly. Julie was sobbing almost hysterically. When she saw me, she cried even harder.

"I ruined your beautiful play!" she cried. "I wanted to be so good, but I was terrible and I let you down!"

What could we do but keep telling her how wonderful she'd been? Charles Nelson Reilly was, as usual, delightfully funny as he tried to get her out of it. And Julie hadn't entirely lost her sense of humor.

Through her tears, she told us how her mother, who was in the audience, had gone up to the critic Walter Kerr and asked him for an autograph! How humiliating could life get? Once again, we all told her how magnificent she had been and thanked her profusely and kissed her and hugged her. And left.

The reviews weren't raves, but they were perfectly acceptable to me. Clive Barnes in the *Times*—the paper that mattered most, of course— called the play "a respectable example of its genre, as good, for example, as the once-lauded *Victoria Regina.*"

Julie was universally praised.

Brendan Gill's review in the *New Yorker* was good and because of it I overlooked something that has rankled ever since.

He wrote, "Mr. Prideaux has no ear for nineteenth-century speech. Surely Robert Todd Lincoln would not have been described in a newspaper article of the day as a 'tycoon,' a word popularized by *Time.*"

Now, if there is anything I pride myself upon, it's my ear for the speech of whatever century. I work hard at that and am careful. The article Mr. Gill referred to was an actual article of that day, word for word. Indeed, Abraham Lincoln himself was frequently called "The Great Tycoon" in the press. What Mr. Gill didn't know was that the word *tycoon* was from the Japanese *taikun* and was very much in use in the nineteenth century. I'd done my homework.

It was not a serious injustice, perhaps, but it was incorrect and irritating. I wish I had written to the *New Yorker* and protested. This sort of thing can damage one's reputation and career. However, the rest of the review was good and, right or wrong, I let it pass.

Never criticize the critics, even if they don't know what they're talking about.

Christopher Isherwood and Don Bachardy came to town. I had met them through Franklin Moore a couple of years before, and had even done some interviews with Chris in Los Angeles, which I mailed back east to Mary Margaret McBride to use on her broadcasts.

Knowing Christopher Isherwood was a thrill. He was sixty-eight when we first met and astonishingly youthful, the famous lock of blond hair falling boyishly over his forehead. When he smiled that dazzling smile, I easily (because I offered no resistance) found myself transported back to prewar Berlin and the askew years of the thirties. Sally Bowles, who-ever she really was, admitting the nervous young author into her sleazy room. Or to Bloomsbury, an evening party, perhaps, with Virginia and Leonard Woolf. T. S. Eliot is there. And E. M. Forster. Auden. Or to the south of France and the exquisite estate of Somerset Maugham. Later, to Hollywood in the heady years of the forties. Charlie Chaplin. Paulette Goddard. William Randolph Hearst and Marion Davies. Garbo. Chris-topher had known them all.

"This young man holds the future of the English novel in his hand," Somerset Maugham had told Virginia Woolf, or so Virginia reported to Christopher. And while it may not have turned out exactly that way, he was certainly a most remarkable writer of a very high order.

Julie Harris and I went to a run-through of his play, *A Meeting by the River*, at a small, makeshift theatre in the Edison Hotel. It wasn't en-tirely successful. Chris had given me the manuscript earlier and, very flatteringly, asked for my comments. I saw then that, while being a great novelist, he wasn't really a dramatist.

I took Chris and Don to lunch at Ruby Foo's before a Saturday mati-nee of *The Last of Mrs. Lincoln*. Christopher had fallen on the steps of the Plaza Hotel—the Plaza steps were less than the length of a man's foot and were particularly perilous—and so he was walking heavily with a stick. Consequently, he seemed older to me, although nothing—until the impending cancer—could eradicate the boyishness of his face.

I took them backstage after the performance and left them with Julie, bubbling over with congratulations. Julie had originated Sally Bowles in the play, *I Am a Camera*, based on Chris's *Berlin Stories*. Old friends. I slipped out.

But I must report that one of the most dazzling evenings of my life was spent at the Isherwood-Bachardy ménage in Santa Monica. There were only three guests: George Cukor, Roddy McDowall, and myself.

But the talk, the wondrous talk, was peppered with glorious stories of the old Hollywood, related by people who knew, who had been there.

I knew enough to just shut up and listen.

The Last of Mrs. Lincoln was in its second week on Broadway when I arrived at the theatre one night after the show to find the cast in a state of bedazzlement. Katharine Hepburn had suddenly appeared at the performance and come backstage to congratulate our miracle, Julie Harris.

Julie was as excited as the rest. She adored Katharine Hepburn. "And she said you're to be sure and call her tomorrow at home," Julie exclaimed, as stricken as any movie fan. I said that I would, of course. My stock rose even higher among the cast.

I was surprised the next day, though, at how uneasy I felt about telephoning her. It had been some time since I had had any contact with Kate, despite the occasional note. Feeling at ease with someone so enormously famous required continual contact. I suddenly felt nervous and shy.

Nonetheless, I called her that afternoon at her house on Forty-ninth Street. Kate answered the phone herself.

"Hi!" she said, "Listen, I'm just dashing out. Call me in one hour. I'll be back then. *One hour!*"

I called her back in an hour, but she hadn't come in yet. Not wanting to bother her, I didn't call her again. And since I was staying in a sublet in Manhattan there was no way she could know my number. That didn't stop Kate.

At the crack of dawn the next morning the phone rang. "Hullo," I murmured, half asleep.

"Fine friend *you* are!" snapped the familiar voice.

"Kate?"

"Yes. Kate. Why didn't you call me back?"

"Oh, well . . ." But before I could explain, she went right on.

"Jim, did you make many changes in the play?" she asked.

"I cut, cut, cut," I told her.

"*Really!*" She made it sound like a cannon exploding. "That much! Well, it certainly strengthened the play! Phyllis was moved to tears."

She didn't say *she* was moved to tears, but I think that, generally, she liked it. Back on Tower Road we had often played the casting game — she once tried to get me to go immediately to the telephone and call John Colicos, wherever he was in the world, to see if he would be interested in playing Robert Lincoln—and I was happy to hear that she approved my ultimate choices.

I asked her what she'd been up to and she told me she'd just returned from London where she had filmed Edward Albee's *A Delicate Balance*. Although my emotions about him were mixed—Edward was never lovable—his Playwrights Unit had established me in my profession.

"He's mellowed, hasn't he?" I asked her.

"Well," sighed Kate, "when people turn on you, you *have* to mellow." She'd thrown him off the set.

She was going back to Los Angeles, to settle into the St. Ives house again for a bit. Things to be done. But we would, she assured me, meet again.

1973

The Last of Mrs. Lincoln closed in February after a short but, I think, distinguished run. Julie would win the Tony Award in March, the day after I returned from a trip to Lisbon and the Azores. She invited me to accompany her that evening, but I said I'd rather watch it cozily at home on television. How dumb can you get? That was the night not only Julie won, but another actress in my production, Leora Dana, won as well. I made a mental note not to miss these things in the future.

I won a New York Drama Desk Award as "Most Promising Playwright," and at the ceremony upstairs at Sardi's I accepted and said, "Yes and when you think how long I've shown promise, this award becomes even more awesome."

But wasn't it time to move west? Joe Hardy said it was. He was moving to Los Angeles and urged me to follow, especially if I wanted to do more work in television. Translate that to read: make money.

In August, then, I settled into an apartment in West Hollywood, an apartment that I have to this day. It wasn't large—two bedrooms, two bathrooms, a terrace—but it was Hollywoody. One approached through a rain forest and across a wooden bridge over a waterfall. (The waterfall was turned off at midnight.)

Here I proposed to entertain the stars. The fact that I knew no stars, with the exception of Miss Hepburn, didn't stop me. I was a known commodity. By that I mean, people sort of recognized my name even if they didn't know why. I'd had two plays produced on Broadway and my little bit of fame had reached California, although they frequently confused me with Tom Prideaux, who was for years entertainment editor on Life, or couldn't quite figure out who I was. Still, it was a plus. My name was familiar enough that doors opened. The difference between that and being a total unknown in this town is like night and day. Ask anybody who's unknown.

Some of the stars were already in my apartment complex, only they weren't stars yet. I wandered into the recreation room one evening and came upon two of the most beautiful people I'd ever seen playing Ping-Pong. I fell in love with both of them on sight. And, as it turned out, the girl, whose name is Susan Sarandon, had the apartment just above mine.

Her young man was a tall, handsome, and wonderfully friendly chap named Barry Bostwick. I'm not clear whether Barry actually lived with Susan or not, but he seemed always to be there.

They took to coming downstairs to me at cocktail hour and we'd hang over my bar and discuss our futures. Neither of them were quite unknowns at that point. I think George Schaefer had already "discovered" Susan and used her in his television movie, *The Last of the Belles*, with Richard Chamberlain. But we could hardly have predicted that her career would take off as it did, despite the fact that she was luscious and obviously very talented.

Bob LeMond moved into the building, too. He was a theatrical manager I'd known in New York, a good old friend who had moved west, I suspect, to promote his favorite client, a young Italian-American named John Travolta. John moved into the complex, too, and Bob introduced us in the hall one day. And the next time I had a cocktail party, Bob asked if he could bring John. I said sure. After that, when Bob came by for drinks, he generally brought John. But John wasn't outgoing. Actually, he was dull. He merely stood around.

"Bob," I said one day, "I like John fine, but do you have to bring him every time? He doesn't add anything to the party." I knew Bob was bringing John because it might help his career. Now I'd like to go to John's house and help my career. We remained friends, although John no longer put a damper on the parties.

(A little time had passed—it didn't seem like much—and LeMond called to invite me to a screening at Paramount. It seemed John had made a movie and they were previewing it. I tried to get out of it—what kind of dull movie could it be?—but I couldn't. I went grudgingly. A full theatre and, oddly, an air of excitement in the audience. Franco Zeffirelli was sitting in the back row, and Franco Zeffirelli didn't generally hit the preview circuit in Hollywood. At the end, I staggered out in a state of shock. The movie was *Saturday Night Fever,* and John Travolta was the most electrifying young star we'd seen in years.)

As soon as I'd settled in, I called Kate to announce my arrival. It was a Saturday morning, and it was as if we'd talked to each other only ten minutes before.

"Oh, hello," she said. "Phyllis and I are going to the movies this afternoon. Want to come?"

I said sure. She said to be at the house by one o'clock because the movie started at two and it was in Westwood. Knowing Kate, who is always early, I planned to be there even earlier.

I'd never been to a movie with her and I thought it'd be interesting. We had once seen *Tom Jones* at a private screening that Irene set up when we were working on *Martha in Paris* because she thought it was an example of what we should aim for. It wasn't. Kate had heaved heavy sighs throughout the screening.

I had a sudden craving for pineapple as I was leaving my apartment and, in slicing the pineapple, I sliced my finger. I couldn't find a Band-Aid so I wrapped some Kleenex around the finger and, bleeding, went off to Kate's.

The house looked just the same, the foliage perhaps a bit higher and thicker. The only difference was that Lobo wasn't there. He'd died, of old age or possibly just loneliness.

I was greeted, again, as if we'd parted only the day before. Kate was all concern over the chopped finger and led me immediately into the bathroom, where she applied a Band-Aid to the finger with great dexterity.

"I'm not the daughter of a surgeon for nothing," she declared. Due to her father, she'd always had a keen interest in anything medical. Until he died she also, the dutiful daughter, sent her paychecks home to Hartford for Daddy to invest (wisely) for her. No wonder she felt her roots were still in New England — they were, at least financially.

Phyllis was puttering around somewhere.

I'd remembered that Phyllis had once mentioned wanting to read Margaret Webster's autobiography, *Don't Put Your Daughter on the Stage*, and my little surprise was that I'd brought my copy to lend her.

"Put it in on Phyllis's bed," said Kate.

"I don't know where Phyllis's bed is," I said.

"Really?" she joked, "I thought everybody in Hollywood knew where Phyllis's bed is!"

I put the book on Phyllis's bed, and that was the last I ever saw of it.

We piled into an aging convertible (top up) without a trace of distinction, Phyllis in the back seat, I in front with Kate. When with a man, Kate always asked if he wanted to drive before she took the wheel. I often wondered what would happen if I'd said, "Yes, thank you. I will drive." (This was years before her accident and the advent of drivers like Hilly and Jim, about whom more below.) She was a good driver who enjoyed driving, and I figured if it was her car, she drove.

As we headed for Westwood, Kate bombarded me with questions about my moving. How much stuff did I move? How much did it cost, coast to coast? For years, she said, she'd been contemplating giving up this Los Angeles house and shipping everything to the house in New York, but she could never make up her mind to do it.

"My friends all say they admire me so much," she laughed. "I'm *so* firm, *so* decisive. But all I do really is procrastinate."

For some reason we wandered onto the subject of "poor Mr. Nixon," and I was glad when Phyllis, perusing the newspaper in the back seat, interrupted to announce that the movie didn't start at two, it started at two-thirty.

"Good," said Kate, "that gives us plenty of time." Actually, that meant we were only an hour too early.

We pulled up in front of the theatre on Wilshire Boulevard, and Kate and I waited in the car while poor Phyllis, who lived solely for others, stood in line to get the tickets.

A young male hippie with long red hair, wearing rumpled old clothes, came by and Kate exclaimed, "My God, he looks just like *me!*"

We had a lot of catching up to do.

I wanted to hear about *The Glass Menagerie*, which she'd just completed filming for television in England. She had nothing but good to say about it and about the British director, her friend Tony Harvey. She claimed to have discovered a new star in Michael Moriarty, a fairly accurate prediction.

And what new worlds did she plan to conquer?

She didn't know. There were several possibilities, but none of them really excited her. The most interesting was a screenplay based on the life of Colette. I thought she'd make a stunning Colette and said so.

(But would she? She'd never had much success in biographical roles. "I'm sure nobody believed me as Clara Schumann," she once said. I certainly wouldn't have believed her as Mary Todd Lincoln. Nor, I might add, did I believe her as Amanda Wingfield when I saw it. She was more like Katharine Hepburn cuttin' up.)

I knew that Kate, like so many of the older movie stars, was snobbish about television, and it was to her credit that she was realistic and did the occasional television film. Later, I was to be very glad.

When she'd done the Dick Cavett interview, though, I was, like everybody else, really knocked off my pins.

"Smartest thing I ever did," Kate chuckled. "They're my pals," she said of ABC, "but it was sheer luck that it came off as well as it did."

She had visited the studio merely to look the place over, she claimed, not intending to do the show. (I've never fully accepted this. Never underestimate her sense of drama.)

"I told Cavett he could do the show then and there if he wanted to take the gamble. I knew perfectly well it would cost them $25,000 to tape it and I had the right to kill it if I didn't like it."

He took the gamble and everybody won.

"I could see that he was more nervous than I was so, of course, I tended to take over. It's very calming, isn't it, to have someone more nervous than you are?"

Poor Phyllis—one was always inclined to think of her as poor Phyllis—had now returned with the tickets and climbed into the back seat. Since we had so much time, Kate began driving around and around the block to find a place to park. The ladies began a heated discussion—the wait in line seemed to have made Phyllis a little testy—as to where the best place to park was.

We were finally, somewhat reluctantly, forced to settle on a lot, south of Wilshire and half a block from the theatre.

"I think Marilyn Monroe's buried in there," I said, pointing at a small cemetery that nestled, oddly enough, directly behind the theatre, within a stone's throw of busy Wilshire Boulevard.

"Let's go look," said Kate.

So we wandered among the tombstones, reading off the names and laughing because some of them were pretty funny. No sign of Marilyn, though.

"I'm sure George Cukor wrote in his book that she's here," I told them.

"Well, when we get home," said Phyllis, "we'll call George and *ask* him where Marilyn is."

We gave up. (Later I learned that she's in a vault in a wall, easily identifiable by the red roses Joe DiMaggio provided daily.)

We left the cemetery and walked up the street to the theatre. As two businessmen passed us, they smiled and said hello to Kate. She helloed back.

"Do people usually do that to you on the street?" I asked her. She said they did.

"Rather pleasant," I said.

"Very," said she.

Kate is generally friendlier to strangers than her reputation might lead one to believe. Autograph hounds have always annoyed her, of course, and with good reason. I can't blame her for giving them a hard time.

(Some years later, I was talking to her in a theatre at intermission when a man suddenly stuck his face between ours and demanded an autograph. "I'm sorry, I can't do that," she said more politely than I would have done.)

Now, like Albee, she appears to have mellowed.

"I have the feeling that one day I'll be saying to someone that I can't give out my autograph and they'll say, 'You old silly, why can't you give out your autograph?' and it'll serve me right. Why *can't* I?"

We hurried through the crowded lobby of the movie theatre. Famous people move fast through crowds. However, we got stopped not by autograph seekers but by a small boy who wanted change to make a telephone call.

Phyllis dug into her purse for it.

Nobody recognized Kate until we started down the aisle. The lights were up and an excited little buzz ran through the audience as they waited for the picture to begin. I think Kate enjoyed it.

We went through quite a ritual as we selected our seats, all to a fascinated audience.

According to Kate, we had to find three empty seats with two empty seats directly in front of them.

Kate finally found them. She sat in the center of the three seats with Phyllis and I positioned on either side of her. Protected, you see, from being seated next to a stranger. She plopped her bag down on the empty seat in front of her and instructed me to put my jacket on the one in front of me. I assumed this was to discourage any heads we might have to peer over, but it turned out that she wanted to put her feet up on the back of those seats.

The lights were still up.

"How many seats do you think there are in this theatre?" Kate asked me suddenly. I said I had no idea.

"Well, let's see," she said and she started to count the seats—so many across and—how many rows of them?

We were midway in the theatre and counting the rows necessitated her turning around and counting the ones behind her, which she did.

"I've lost count," she moaned and she turned around again.

I couldn't imagine why she was making such a fuss about the number of seats in the theatre. It then dawned on me that she was turning around so that the people behind us could see her. To this day, that is the only answer I can come up with. Shy she may be, as are many people who have developed forceful personalities. And her privacy is jealously guarded. And she purports to go to great lengths not to be recognized. But she's also an actress and a star, and a part of her wants to be recognized even as she pretends not to.

Kate chattered throughout the movie. It was one of those "new" pictures where the young lovers pop into bed and then have the courtship, thereby giving us a downhill ride.

"This is the *dullest* affair," sighed Kate.

I was ready to walk out, but she refused. "I never walk out on a movie," she said, "no matter how bad it is."

(Years later, I was reminded of this statement when she suddenly got up and walked out on a movie in Vancouver that she considered dirty.)

As we walked to the car, we discussed the actors. Kate loathed the tousle-headed, plain young man who played the lead. (This movie made him a star.) She also disputed my statement that the director-turned-actor, making a much-touted debut, was brilliant.

"He's one-dimensional," she declared, "all on one level." The minute she said it I knew she was right. I went on, though, to say I had liked the ingenue very much.

"She's got a lovely face, but she can't act and she's a lard ass."

"A what?" I asked, startled.

"A *lard ass*," said Kate again, loud and clear. Her voice rang over the parking lot.

Driving back through Beverly Hills, Kate, who'd been reading Arthur Rubinstein's splendid memoirs, appeared shocked and dismayed that in writing of his early loves he'd named names. That it happened some seventy years ago didn't seem to matter.

"Uncalled for," she said.

From the back seat, Phyllis informed me that Kate had been offered a vast sum—a million dollars, I think—to write her memoirs, but had turned it down. (She was to be offered much more in years to come. And accept.)

"What would I write about?" said Kate. "I'm certainly not going to talk about my personal life."

"Well," I said, "why don't you write about acting? Or your career? Or, I think a book about your family would be fascinating." I've often thought that Kate is only one of a family of remarkable people. Her parents were extraordinary, and the Katharine Hepburn the world reveres is basically a product of her upbringing.

I'd wanted to read what she had to say about acting, too.

I'll never forget an evening when we were discussing a current New York production of *Holiday*, which had been played as camp. The reviews were disastrous. Kate told me—and showed me!—how it should be played. You don't camp it up. You play it absolutely realistically, giving it more intensity, not less. And very fast.

We stopped for a traffic light and a small boy sailed by on a skateboard. Kate was enraptured. I could see she was itching to try it. She said proudly that a young nephew of hers had written a book on the subject.

An elderly couple in the car beside us waved frantically at her. She waved frantically back.

"Come in for tea," Kate said when we got to the house, "but I think what we need is hard liquor." We settled for tea.

A fire was blazing in the fireplace in the living room. No room was complete to Kate without a fireplace, and she meant a real fireplace, not those gas things we had in southern California.

While Phyllis and Margaret retired to the kitchen to prepare a high tea, Kate flung herself down on the floor and lay on her back with her head on the raised hearth. I remembered to sit in my customary chair.

We talked idly about the state of the American theatre. I maintained that Tennessee Williams was the greatest living American playwright (but I forgot Thornton Wilder, who was alive then and certainly in the running), having "done it" seven or eight times, a remarkable accomplishment.

Kate readily agreed.

Albee I put into second place, although far behind Williams with what I considered his one great play, *Who's Afraid of Virginia Woolf?*, and a couple of one-acts that seemed to me to be small masterpieces. Arthur

Miller was dismissed, with the exception of *Death of a Salesman*, as highly overrated—at least I dismissed him. Kate wasn't so ready to.

Phyllis brought the tea and Kate got up and went to the big, black chair, Spencer's chair. It was just like the old days when we were doing *Martha*.

"What other news?" I asked, remembering that Kate once advised me: "If you come into a room and you see a telegram or an open letter lying there, for God's sake read it—you get the news so much faster that way."

"Well, I got fired," announced Kate.

I couldn't believe it! Fire Katharine Hepburn? But she insisted it was true.

She had been led to believe by MGM that she would do *Travels with My Aunt*, a film she was eagerly looking forward to. Not only that, she had traveled, she said, "twice to Europe to scout locations!"

"How we enjoy scouting locations!" interrupted Phyllis. "When we get a script, the first thing we look for is where we get to go!"

Furthermore, Kate went on, she had spent probably $100,000, finally ended up writing the script herself (I took that with a grain of salt), and was ultimately done in by a chap at MGM named Thatcher and fired by James Aubrey.

And there was more! Once Aubrey had fired her, he had gone on to commit that most inabsolvable of sins: he had written her a letter in which her name was spelled *Katherine*! Nothing infuriated her more.

(I recalled, back in 1968, riding in a taxi from Manhattan to the Newark airport and passing a billboard in the Jersey swamps advertising *The Lion in Winter* on which her name was spelled Katherine. When I got to Los Angeles I told Kate about it. Immediately she shouted, "Phyllis! Call the lawyer!" When I passed the billboard going the other way five weeks later, the spelling had been corrected.)

"Fired!" I kept saying, "Fired!"

"Well, I sent a letter off to Mr. Aubrey in which I said there wasn't any point in taking anyone seriously, anyway, who couldn't even spell your name!"

It was slow going, but I gradually made my way, both socially and professionally, in unfamiliar Los Angeles. The mistake I'd made was thinking of it as New York West. It wasn't. Los Angeles was a whole new ball game, at least professionally. People in "the Industry" didn't think or act the way people in "the Theatre" did back east. And contacts were everything.

The first agent to take me to lunch was Georgia Gilly. She took me to a typical Hollywood restaurant, The Fish Shanty. It's long gone, but as I recall you entered the restaurant through a huge fish's mouth. I like Georgia and I liked being taken to lunch, but I signed with the William Morris Agency because I especially liked being taken to lunch by Peter Thomas.

It was from Peter's lips that I first heard that agency cliché: "We're going to do wonderful things together." I was naive enough to believe it. I signed with William Morris so that Peter and I could do wonderful things together, whereupon Peter left the agency and, indeed, the profession. I guess he was tired of doing wonderful things with clients. Michael Peretzian then took over and was to be my agent for the next seventeen years. He's still one of my best friends.

Julie Harris was in town, doing a curious sitcom about life in a pickle factory, and one balmy August night I went to the Hollywood Bowl for some sort of benefit at which, leaving the pickle factory behind, she did a scene from Shakespeare. Julie was wonderful, but the surprise of the evening was Jean Stapleton, who sang and danced in front of a chorus line and was simply dazzling. I couldn't have been more impressed, a reaction that would affect not only my life at a future date, but Elizabeth Taylor's.

George Schaefer was currently established at Paramount as executive producer of a television anthology called, bluntly, *Love Story*. The idea was that every week they'd air a one-hour love story. I went into his office to discuss my ideas for the series and, while waiting for George to be free, sat next to a very handsome chap also waiting. He was friendly and chatty, and I asked him if he was going to work on the series.

Overhearing this, Adie Luraschi, George's assistant, said quickly, "James, Michael is going to direct one." It was only then I realized that I was talking to Michael Landon, who was about as famous in television as you could get. Obviously, I had a long way to go before I even knew who anybody was in "the Industry."

George had a terrific story editor named Esther Shapiro, whom I liked a lot. (She and her husband later became multimillionaires when they created *Dynasty*.) The *Love Story* series, however, got cancelled after a few segments, despite top writers and directors like Michael and Glenn Jordan.

The writer Ellis St. Joseph, an old friend of Howard and Anne Koch, introduced me to Hermione Baddeley, then living at the Hotel Marmont. The Hotel Marmont was "old" Hollywood and looked it. All of the furniture was threadbare and the draperies were almost in shreds, but Garbo had stayed there at one time, and it was dear to the hearts of old-timers.

I was delighted to meet Hermione, an English character actress whom I'd admired ever since seeing her in *Room at the Top*.

"Oh, Joe, how could you do it?" she had said heartbreakingly to Laurence Harvey after Simone Signoret had killed herself over him, and I was hooked. She was now riding the crest of the Hollywood wave as Mrs. Naugatuck, a sustaining character on the television series *Maude*.

She was warm and funny and, I thought, far too generous. She ultimately left the Marmont and took a house in "Birdland," not far from Kate up Doheny Drive above Sunset. A perpetual party seemed to go on there, at least when I visited. She apparently operated an open bar, and every down-and-out Englishman on the West Coast hung out there. But she was making, I trust, a great deal of money, and continual partying amused her.

It was Ellis St. Joseph, too, who brought Vera Caspary around for drinks one afternoon. As she walked into the living room and saw the plants outside on the terrace, she exclaimed, "Oh, you have green!" And that's all I can remember of her conversation, despite the fact that the author of *Laura* was legendary and this was a momentous event for me. I have since been known to say to guests, "Vera Caspary sat right where you're sitting . . . in that very chair." I used to get a reaction; now nobody remembers her.

I had met Anne Seymour, the venerable character actress, a year or so before when I'd wanted her to play Mary Todd's sister in *The Last of Mrs. Lincoln*, but Annie hadn't wanted to leave the West Coast. I was later to twit her with, "Well, Leora Dana got *your* Tony Award!" It didn't damage our friendship. Nothing could. I loved her and she was a darling friend until her death.

It was through Annie that I met a smart, beautiful creature named Diane Baker. And Annie's house was always filled with interesting people. I met Greer Garson there. George Cukor was a frequent guest. Cathleen Nesbitt often stayed with her. Mercedes McCambridge would stop in. And a lovely British writer, Rosemary Sisson, who wrote so many sparkling segments of *Upstairs, Downstairs*. And Ethel Barrymore's aged son, Sammy Colt, who served as an amusing escort for older ladies.

I have a photograph of Annie and me sitting outside a garage in Frank Levy's backyard on his birthday. I'm with Jean Stapleton, but Annie's being kissed on the cheek by Rock Hudson.

And another photograph. I took it one evening in Annie's living room. It's of Jean Stapleton, spread out, clowning, over the laps of her husband Bill Putch and Melvyn Douglas and his wife, Helen Gahagan Douglas. I had never met the Douglases (nor had Jean and Bill), and it was a night to remember. Helen Gahagan Douglas was still one of the most beautiful women in the world. She was also bright as a button. (Her political career had been destroyed by the smearing Mr. Nixon.) Melvyn's looks were gone and he was cranky. But they were delightfully articulate on practically any subject and complimented each other perfectly.

I couldn't resist asking Melvyn, absolute awe in my voice, what it had been like acting with Garbo. Was it wonderful?

"Pooh," said Melvyn. "She couldn't act her way out of a paper bag. Furthermore, she let the whole of World War II go by and never noticed it." I got off the subject of Garbo.

Melvyn had come to the films from the New York theatre, and he told us about making his first movie. He'd been in front of the camera for a few days when the director quietly took him aside, lowered his voice, and said, "Mel, what are you doing out there?"

"What do you mean?"

"What are you doing out there in front of the camera?"

"Why, I'm *acting*," said Mel.

The director shook his head and sighed. "Oh, Mel," he said, "leave that to the ladies."

The Douglases and Bill and Annie are all gone now, but I cherish that evening. Melvyn signed a paper napkin for me on which he wrote, "The word is important still—go on." I look at it often.

Annie also took me to Sunday afternoon parties that Audrey Christie and Don Briggs gave in their little house on La Jolla Avenue. A lot of movie people were there, including Charles Walters, who had directed some of my favorite MGM musicals, only I didn't know it at the time. I didn't know who he was, and I can remember babbling on about Judy Garland and MGM as if I were a great authority. Until he stopped me cold.

"You don't know *what* you're talking about, Jim," he said, stopping not only me but all conversation. It was a humiliating moment, but he was dead right.

The first time I saw him I thought he was the handsomest man I'd ever seen. The last time I saw him he was almost skeletal and riddled with cancer. And then he, too, was gone.

An actress friend, Laura Stuart, came through in a play called *The Day after the Fair*, which starred Deborah Kerr. Laura invited me to the opening night at the Shubert Theatre and to the party afterward that Deborah Kerr was hosting across the way at the Jade West.

The play wasn't memorable, but the party was. Miss Kerr, gracious as always, made a point of going to every table.

"Are you having a good time?" she'd ask. I fell in love with her on the spot. She was very beautiful and exuded a warmth that permeated the entire party. Only Jack Benny and his wife Mary, sitting opposite me at the table, seemed unaffected by it. Indeed, he seemed unaffected by anything. For a funny man, he was the gloomiest gus I'd ever seen.

Brenda Forbes, who was in the play, sat next to me, although she doesn't remember it and neither of us could know our lives would become wonderfully enmeshed in later years.

I called Kate and Phyllis on Christmas Eve to wish them a Merry Christmas.

"Are you doing something gussy tomorrow?" I asked.

Kate laughed. "We never do *anything* gussy."

But I discovered what they did do, in those years, on that and every other important holiday. They cooked a splendid dinner, packed it in a basket, and spent the day with a lady who was once John Ford's script girl. After dinner, Kate sat and read to her—a million-dollar performance that was available to nobody else on earth.

When she was in California, Kate never forgot to spend the holidays with this friend, who was totally blind.

1974

It was the year of the hip operation.

Kate's operation was conducted somewhat like World War II, at least as far as tricky maneuvers and murky tactics were concerned. Rommel couldn't have done it better. When it was all over, I was invited up to dinner to see her snappy chrome crutches and hear all about it.

Kate was in the living room talking with her doctor on the telephone when I arrived, so Phyllis ushered me in to Kate's bedroom to wait.

"Oh, don't sit *there!*" she gasped as I started to sit on the edge of Kate's bed. So I perched on an uncomfortable little chair.

As we waited, Phyllis confessed to me that the recent hospital bout had exhausted her. At her age, which she proudly proclaimed to be seventy, she was no longer able to take it in her stride. But I was not to breathe a word of that to Miss Hepburn.

Kate appeared looking wonderful in white pajamas and demonstrating her prowess by swinging through the living room on the handsome metal crutches in no time flat.

Over dinner, I got the full story.

"You'd have been proud of me. I made the decision to have the operation quite quickly. I didn't procrastinate at all. I knew, you see, that if I waited until I was back in the house in New York I'd have stairs to climb."

She had told no one about it, not even her closest friends. Indeed, she was in the hospital for two weeks and had been operated on before her friends—or the press—even got wind of it. If you called the house, you were informed by Phyllis quite truthfully that Miss Hepburn was "out," but would call you back. The call back came from the hospital, but nobody mentioned that.

It was, Kate thought, a grand joke. And she had mapped out the entire expedition with the greatest of care.

First, she took her sister's name, Mrs. Margaret Perry, a name she borrowed for just such occasions as this. Well in advance of the operation, Kate—as "Mrs. Perry"—slipped into the UCLA Hospital to do a job of reconnoitering. She lurked about, checking out the rooms.

Now it so happened that Elizabeth Taylor was also in the hospital at that time, confined with one of her illnesses. As Mrs. Perry was poking into yet another room, a nurse entered and said casually, "Oh, by the way, Miss Hepburn, Miss Taylor would like you to stop up and say hello."

Kate whirled on her.

"How the hell does Miss Taylor know I'm here?" she demanded.

Cowed, and unable to admit that the whole hospital knew she was there, the nurse ran out of the room.

"Did you go up?" I asked.

"Oh, yes," said Kate, "I'm fond of Liz."

But when Kate walked into Elizabeth's room and looked around, she was horrified. It was small and dark, and Liz was supposed to be living pretty grandly. Ye gods, thought Kate, this wouldn't do for me!

And she continued her search for the perfect room.

The day she checked in, our Mrs. Perry walked up nine flights of stairs to avoid being recognized in the elevator—and this was a woman going in for a hip operation.

Even then, she was unhappy with her room and, looking further, found another one, larger and airier, which she immediately claimed.

They moved in, and Phyllis was busily opening the windows when a nurse rushed in and exclaimed, "Miss Hepburn! Miss Hepburn! I mean, Mrs. Perry! Mrs. Perry! You mustn't open the windows! It's against hospital regulations!"

"And why is that?" asked Mrs. Perry, unruffled.

"Because of suicides."

Mrs. Perry smiled knowingly. "I am *not* going to commit suicide, dear," she said. The windows remained open.

Mrs. Perry then discovered a directive that had circulated throughout the hospital that read: "Mrs. Margaret Perry is actually Miss Katharine Hepburn and is not to be disturbed." Even Kate had to laugh.

After the operation, she insisted Phyllis stay with her despite the three round-the-clock nurses.

"Lord, don't ever leave me alone with a strange nurse," Kate begged her. "We didn't live the way Liz did," Kate explained to me, "with waiters from Chasen's running in and out. Phyllis cooked in the bathroom. It worked out splendidly."

I could see why Phyllis was feeling worn out.

The hospital had a special buzzer installed for Kate. "They said I was a"—her eyes rolled heavenward—"*very* important patient and they weren't about to let me die."

She was very funny about the bedpan. It wasn't so much a question of getting on it—she could manage that pretty well—it was the worrying thought of the nurse going away and leaving her on it. She was aghast at the tale of a patient who had been stranded, high and dry, so to speak, on a bedpan for two hours. "I'd go *mad!*" declared Kate.

She was also horrified at the cost of it all. The nurses alone came to $150 a day. Later she telephoned me in further horror to report that she had received a bill for the whole thing that came to $6,000. "So?" I said. I thought that was fairly reasonable, considering that she had taken over practically the entire hospital. "And you can afford it. What about the people who can't?" It shut her up. (We won't dwell on what it would cost today.)

She was in the hospital for four weeks, two of those before the world got wind of the fact that she was there.

"But *then*," Kate said, lowering her voice conspiratorially, "Joyce Haber sent a spy!" Joyce Haber was a local gossip columnist.

It happened late in the day and Phyllis, standing guard—and probably bone tired—was a trifle lax.

There came a rap at the door. Phyllis opened the door a crack and a strange nurse stood there with an armful of flowers.

"These flowers are for Mrs. Perry from Agnes Moorehead," she announced.

Kate shot up from the bed, hip operation or no hip operation.

"Phyllis!" she cried, "I don't know Agnes Moorehead! That's a bogus nurse! Throw her out!"

So poor, exhausted little Phyllis attempted to slam the door on the bogus nurse, but she'd already gotten her head halfway in, and the damage was done. She had seen that Mrs. Margaret Perry was, indeed, Katharine Hepburn. The jig was up. The news was out.

When the time came for Kate to leave the hospital, the plot became even more cloak-and-dagger.

They waited until 4:00 A.M., when all was dark and still in the hospital.

"All right, Phyllis," whispered Kate, "now we'll go."

Phyllis got her into a wheelchair and placed the crutches across her lap. She opened the door, peered out, saw nobody, and pushed Kate into the hall.

"It was most gratifying," said Kate, "not a soul in sight."

They arrived at the service elevator and the doors opened automatically. Phyllis pushed Kate in. But before Phyllis could get in, the doors started to close. Quick as a flash, Kate thrust a crutch into the doors and forced them open. It was a tricky moment, but all was well.

They then rode down to the basement and made their way through the subterranean passages, as pre-mapped by Kate.

"There were some black people working down there, but they paid us no mind," said Kate, smugly.

However, they were almost at the outside door when suddenly they saw a man approaching from the outside walk and headed straight for the door. He was wearing a business suit and a fedora hat. Kate panicked.

"Crikey, we're caught!" she cried. As they stared in dismay, he fumbled at the door.

But then Kate looked down. "And what do you think he was carrying?"

"What?" I asked, breathless with anticipation.

"A white cane! He was blind!"

Phyllis helped him with the door, Kate passed silently through, and they made their way to a waiting car.

Mission accomplished.

Richard Chamberlain was starring in a production of *Cyrano de Bergerac* at the Ahmanson Theatre in Los Angeles, directed by my old pal, Joseph Hardy. I saw it and thought it was marvelous. As a matter of fact, it was so good I wanted to see it again.

I was, however, involved in filming my segment of a six-part series for television based on Carl Sandburg's *Lincoln* at Paramount. It was called *Mrs. Lincoln's Husband*—I was considered, erroneously, an authority on Mary Todd Lincoln—and starred two lovely and talented people, Hal Holbrook and Sada Thompson. The director George Schaefer had also brought in a young actor named Michael Cristofer, who padded after me to lunch one day and didn't leave for four years. (He turned to writing, hacking out nothing but a play called *The Shadow Box*, which won a Tony Award and the Pulitzer Prize.)

Anyway, it was difficult getting away, but I managed a matinee, and invited Kate and Phyllis to join me.

"Richard Chamberlain!" exclaimed Kate, making a slight moue. I think she thought of him only as some character on television. Like Dr. Kildare.

I assured her that Chamberlain was terrific and the production was terrific and they'd have a great time. Kate agreed to go, somewhat reluctantly.

Then she telephoned to say that Alan Searle was in town, staying with George Cukor. Mightn't he make a fourth? "He's very rich," said Kate. "We'll let him pay for the tickets." I told her no matter how rich Alan Searle was, I'd pay for the tickets.

She called again the next day to say that Alan wanted to take us all to lunch at the Beverly Hills Hotel before the matinee, and wouldn't that be a bore? So why didn't we lunch at her place? Fine.

I thought I knew what to expect of Alan Searle. He was the valet, but also the constant companion—for thirty-seven years, Kate told me—of Somerset Maugham. Indeed, I believe that Maugham at one point actually adopted him, thereby inspiring a famous *Punch* cartoon in which Maugham is seen running out of the nursery in which sits middle-aged Alan. "He said Dada!" Maugham is exclaiming, ecstatically.

I remembered, too, that Searle had once been described by Lytton Strachey as his "golden boy." I expected him to be tall, elegant, patrician and rather intimidating. After all, Maugham had left him everything, all rights, all royalties. I agreed with Kate that he must be very rich.

I arrived at the house only a moment before Alan, who had walked down the hill from Cukor's house despite some sort of foot difficulty. He was a complete surprise.

Short, chunky, ruddy-faced, and with a pronounced accent, he was your typical Cockney valet. Where was the golden boy? The day was humid, but Mr. Searle was attired like a proper Briton in a heavy tweed jacket and woolen trousers.

He was plagued by ailments. Aside from the foot condition, he claimed that the pollution had given him a sore throat, and he spoke so softly one had difficulty in understanding what he said. He also complained, upon entering, that the new high-rises where he lived, in Monaco, were shutting out the sun.

Kate ushered us out into the little patio behind the house. It had only one usable chair in it, the others being butterfly chairs without the canvas.

"What a beautifully furnished patio, Miss Hepburn," I said, gazing at the seatless chairs.

"Yes, isn't it?" said she, and, offering the one good chair to Alan, she perched on the metal rim of one of the butterflies. I perched on the other. It was good for a laugh, and then I brought out the dining room chairs.

Kate went off to check lunch. Seated as we were, Mr. Searle and I faced a large, ugly, octagonal cage made of chicken wire. We speculated on its function and when Phyllis appeared we put it to her.

"It was probably meant for vines originally," she said, adding thoughtfully, "although it might have housed birds."

"We kept ninety canaries on the Riviera," said Searle in his husky whisper, "but they refused to breed there." After Maugham's death, Searle gave them to a lady in England and, once there, "They wouldn't *stop* breeding."

"That would be the English climate," I said.

Mr. Searle looked at me strangely.

Kate returned and told us she had little feeling for birds, but Phyllis had a first-rate bird story.

"Tell it," she ordered Phyllis.

Well, it seemed that Constance Collier had kept a cockatoo when they lived in Hollywood, and one day it got loose and flew away. Deeply distressed, she and Phyllis went through the streets calling "Mimsy!" into the air. They got all sorts of responses, but not from Mimsy.

The scoundrel was finally located in the top of a tall tree. Dear little Phyllis—loyal as always to her employer—proceeded to climb the tree as Miss Collier remained on the ground and supervised in stentorian tones.

When at last she felt that Phyllis had gone too far out on the limb, she called, "Phyllis, dear, don't go further! You're more valuable to me than that bird!"

Phyllis grabbed Mimsy, scrambled down, and faced Miss Collier.

"It took *that* for you to tell me!"

We laughed dutifully.

Kate led us in to lunch, and I carried the chairs back in. Mr. Searle seemed incapable of carrying anything. He wasn't old, especially; he was simply lethargic.

The room was filled with enormous bouquets of flowers.

"Where did those come from?" I asked.

"Oh, they're for my birthday," said Kate. Alan and I both look startled. Had we been negligent? Was it her birthday?

"Of course not," said Kate. "Years ago the publicity department at MGM wanted to give out the date of my birth. Well, I wasn't about to give them the actual date, so I made one up. This is it. And every year people send me flowers. Those are from Abe Lastfogel. Aren't they beautiful?" She thought it a fine joke.

We sat down to a superb lunch. There was an excellent wine, too, which only I touched.

I noticed that beads of sweat were forming on poor Alan's face, and he hesitantly asked if he might remove his jacket. It was suddenly stiflingly warm. Kate leaped up and, checking the thermostat, discovered that the heat was on in the house. She turned it off, opened a window, and lunch continued more comfortably.

We got to talking about writers, Alan saying how crazy they were. He loathed T. E. Lawrence, thought him an odious little man, and didn't like D. H. Lawrence either, but felt that H. G. Wells was a pleasant enough sort.

"I'm sorry I never got a chance to meet Scott Fitzgerald," said Kate. Alan said he and Maugham had known Scott and Zelda very well on the Riviera.

Since we were on the subject of literary couples, the names of Eugene O'Neill and Carlotta Monterey came up.

"I'm fascinated by love turning to hatred, as theirs did," Kate said. She'd heard that he'd stormed out of the house one winter night after a ferocious battle, had fallen on the ice and broken his ankle, and Carlotta let him lay in the snow for two hours before doing anything about it.

We agreed that their relationship would make a strong play.

Alan informed us that Maugham, who had lived regally on the Riviera, once resided with a London slum family for four months "to hear the language" for a piece that he proposed to write, which he never did.

"Really!" exclaimed Kate. "I wouldn't have believed Willy could do that!" He was, after all, devoted to luxury. I was more interested in the reaction of the slum family who endured the fastidious Mr. Maugham in their squalid little parlor for four long months. I used this later when I wrote *Laura Lansing Slept Here* for Kate.

Kate talked about her own family, those enlightened Hepburns. Mrs.

Emmeline Pankhurst had come through Hartford, and Dr. Hepburn had said to his wife, "Well, let's go down and hear what she has to say." Mrs. Hepburn came back a fighting suffragette.

"There was always an unwed mother or two in the attic of our house," said Kate. "They'd stay with us through their pregnancies, treated like family. Father would deliver the baby, then they'd move on, and Mother would find immediate replacements."

As a consequence of the parents' liberated views, there were certain neighbors in Hartford who wouldn't permit their offspring to play with the Hepburn children. It had a lasting effect on the sensitive young Kate, who determined to show the world who she was.

But they were a wonderfully close and happy family.

"In the summertime, we thought nothing of sitting down to a table of twenty-three relatives. How my mother managed I can't imagine, but it seemed to take no effort and we all thoroughly enjoyed it."

It was getting on toward curtain time. We all piled into Kate's car, Phyllis and I relegated to the back seat, Alan in the seat of honor next to Kate.

Kate didn't take the freeway. She had experimented when she was playing *Coco* at the Music Center and formed an affection for Beverly Boulevard, which she found faster, especially at rush hour. Consequently, we passed through a series of diverse neighborhoods en route and in one of them were a couple of porno houses.

Kate hooted at them. "You know what they're *called?*" she asked us, incredulous. "They're called *adult movies!* They must be so depressing." She acted as if none of us could possibly have ever seen a porno movie. I knew I had, and I suspected Alan had, but neither of us said a word.

Howard Hughes's name came up. He had been a beau of Kate's.

"Was he always so eccentric?" I asked.

"Well, he was deaf," said Kate, "and that made him seem odd. But he wouldn't admit to it and apparently he didn't do anything about it. He just kept pretending he could hear, which didn't always work. We used to play golf together and he'd say that I could be a great golfer, why didn't I practice it more and concentrate on it? I asked him why he didn't concentrate on being an artist, as I did."

Concentration was perhaps Kate's favorite word. She found it, I think, the key to a great many things—and certainly it was Spencer Tracy's key to acting, which so impressed her.

Speaking of Hughes, Kate was greatly amused by Clifford Irving's hoax and felt that he shouldn't have been given a jail sentence at all.

"After all, he entertained the whole world," she said.

"Did you ever go to San Simeon?" I asked.

"You've asked me that before," she snapped.

"Well, I've forgotten what you said."

"I *said* I was invited one weekend, but I didn't bother to go . . . which shows what a fool I was."

Kate refused to park underground, so she drove in an ever-widening circle around the Music Center trying to find a place to park. Phyllis complained, gently at first and then vehemently, that we were getting farther and farther from the theatre.

"Remember Alan's foot," she said, pointedly. Alan said nothing.

"Aha!" cried Kate. She had discovered an empty lot with a barricade across the entrance to keep people like us out. She stopped the car and leaped out.

"What are you doing?" I yelled at her.

"I'm going to lift the barricade," she said, "and in we'll go."

"Let me do it!" I shouted.

"You stay where you are. I'll do it!" she shouted back. So the three of us sat in the car while the woman in her sixties struggled to raise the barricade. I felt like a perfect jackass as she huffed and puffed and heaved and groaned but couldn't budge the barricade at all.

"Kate! Kate, get back in the car!" Phyllis called, annoyed.

She had to. Finally.

"Well, that didn't work," she said, dusting off her hands. She started the motor again. "We'll let you and Phyllis out at the theatre," Kate informed Alan, "and Jim and I will find a place."

So we let them out near the box office and we continued our search through the streets.

Then Kate had an inspiration. Half a block from the Music Center was a large apartment building where she had kept a flat when she was doing *Coco*. There was parking in front of it for the tenants. Surely they would see reason.

We pulled up and parked as the black doorman came running down the steps to shoo us away. But Kate had already bounded out of the car and was rushing up to him.

"Do you remember me?" she asked. (I loved the question.) "Can't we park here?" He did, and we could, of course.

Then we started running up Beverly Boulevard to the Music Center. As usual, I was hard-put to keep up with her. But we didn't run on the sidewalk. Kate had stepped off the curb and into the street and I suddenly realized we were running right down the yellow line in the center of Beverly Boulevard. Fortunately, there wasn't much traffic.

"Why are we running down the middle of the street?" I asked as a car whizzed past my ear.

"I find it congenial," said Kate.

"Well, stop it," I said, "we'll be killed."

She immediately went over to the sidewalk.

"What did you do that for?" I asked.

"Because you told me to," she said. It was a moment to remember.

A young couple we passed pointed at us and laughed. We laughed back.

We found Phyllis and Alan seated on a bench in front of the Mark Taper Forum. There they were, heads together, the confidant of Somerset Maugham and the confidante of Katharine Hepburn.

"Look at them," Kate said as we approached. "Comparing notes, probably."

Richard, Kate's adored brother—she used to read his humorous letters to Irene and me—had asked her to take a look at the Mark Taper Forum. He was a playwright and he thought it might suit one of his plays. So Phyllis and Alan went on to the Ahmanson while Kate and I worked our way through the crowd going into the Taper.

I went up to the ticket taker.

"May we just take a quick look at the theatre?" I asked.

"No," he said, without looking up.

I glanced helplessly at Kate beside me. Without a word, she swept past the ticket taker and me and approached a young man in the lobby who appeared to be the manager.

"I'm Katharine Hepburn," she said, softly but firmly, "and I should like to look at your theatre. May I?"

His jaw dropped to his chest. He managed to nod.

We went in and walked through it, to the great delight of the assembled audience.

Coming out, I said that if you wanted something it certainly paid to be Katharine Hepburn.

"Isn't it awful?" said Kate.

"It's a convenience, that's all," I said.

"Yes, it's a convenience."

We settled into our seats next to Phyllis and Alan just as the curtain was going up. I knew Kate would enjoy the production, but her reaction was even better than I expected. In the middle of a dueling scene in act one, she began to applaud before anyone else.

"It's just so good!" she whispered.

"I'm going to promenade," I told her during the intermission. "Do you wish to promenade?"

"I *never* promenade," Kate said. Indeed, she never left her seat during intermissions for obvious reasons. Phyllis wanted to stay with her, naturally, and Alan had his bum foot, so I promenaded alone.

I was approached by one of the administrators of the theatre.

"Mr. Prideaux?"

"Yes."

"I'm Robert Linden. Now when the performance is over I'll meet you here and lead you through that private door to the backstage area. We're very excited that you're here."

"Oh?" I said. "This has nothing to do with Miss Hepburn, of course."

"Oh, *no!*" he said with a straight face. "The cast all knows about *The Last of Mrs. Lincoln.*"

When I got back to my seat, I had a serious talk with Kate.

"Now, look," I told her, "they're very excited that I'm here. They all know about *The Last of Mrs. Lincoln.* So I have to go backstage afterwards. You can come too, of course, but only if you stand in the back and don't say anything."

She whooped with laughter. (Later I heard that Chamberlain had told the cast, "Let's give the best we've got—*she's* here!")

At the end of the performance, Kate, moving fast as always, was ushered backstage with the rest of us in her wake. It was as if the queen mother had come to visit, not because Kate acted like that, but because she was held in such awe by theatre people. The entire cast, with one exception, stood by trying to look as if they weren't staring at her.

The exception was my old friend, Lucian Scott. Lucian had first seen Kate on Broadway in *The Warrior's Husband* in 1932 and had never forgotten the thrill of her marching up the aisle as the young Amazon warrior. He had always wanted to tell Miss Hepburn how he felt and this, I had informed him, was his chance. But he was in his dressing room scrambling to get his costume off.

"Get Lucian!" I hissed to somebody as we entered Richard Chamberlain's dressing room. Mr. Chamberlain was visibly nervous, but Kate put him at ease by telling him how terribly good he was and, having delivered that message, she headed out.

As we passed her dressing room, Kate offered her hand to Joan Van Ark, the ingenue, congratulating her.

Miss Van Ark was obviously moved.

"Just to touch your hand is enough!" she told Kate.

Our Leader was almost to the stage door, and still no Lucian.

"Kate, you gotta wait for Lucian!" I insisted. And so, somewhat to my surprise, she waited.

Fortunately, before long he came running up, breathless with excitement, and she listened intently as he told her of that moment so long ago and what it had meant to him.

"You keep that memory," she said, taking his hand.

It was dark when we got outside. Phyllis and Alan waited patiently while Kate and I ran to get the car.

"I was sorry to hold you up," I said, "but Lucian has waited forty years to say that to you, and I was determined he was going to get his chance." She said she was touched by it.

Again we jaywalked (or jay*ran*), which appeared to be the only way Kate knew to cross a street.

As we were getting into the car, the doorman came running up and started filling Kate in on what had happened to him since they had last met. He had hit the bottle, but he was off it now. He had also been in the hospital, where he had had a UTR.

"Really!" exclaimed Kate, "a UTR!"

I didn't have a clue as to what a UTR was, and I thought, God, isn't she wonderful! She knows everything!

After he departed, Kate turned to me and said, "What the hell is a UTR?"

I climbed into the back seat.

"Once round the park please, driver," I said.

On the way home we talked about how hungry audiences were for the kind of good theatre we had just seen. Alan was reminded of a restaurant story. (That's how his mind worked.)

It seems that he and Maugham had gone to a restaurant for dinner, and Maugham ordered an obscure something that he had never seen on a menu before. The waiter's eyebrows flew up, which, Alan said, should have been a warning. Other waiters seemed to take an unusual interest in him, too. They all watched as the dish was brought to him. Their waiter stationed himself near the kitchen door. As Maugham dug in, the waiter opened the kitchen door and they heard him call out, "Well, he's eating it!"

We dropped Alan off at Cukor's door, and Kate invited me into her house for a drink.

The fire was lit as usual, but Margaret was nowhere to be seen. At Kate's invitation, I made myself a vodka martini. Kate and Phyllis each took a drop of scotch and we went to our accustomed places.

I knew several of the young actors in *Cyrano* and I mentioned how tough an acting career was.

"Not for me," declared Kate. "I had it all handed to me on a silver platter."

"And you could really give it up?" I asked.

"Why not? I know I've had what some people think of as an important career, but what's all the fuss? Like that Van Ark girl today. 'Just to touch your hand is enough.' Nonsense!"

She told me about a newspaper clipping somebody had sent her that stated that Martin Luther King was right up there with such greats as George Washington, Abraham Lincoln, Christopher Columbus, and Katharine Hepburn. She howled.

We talked about her always going back to the stage or home to New England after every movie role. Phyllis swore that she could never go back to where she came from, and so did I, but not Kate.

"Clinging to my roots," she said, "was what saved me from Hollywood."

Somehow we got to talking about Max Beerbohm, whose work I love, and Phyllis recalled that famous meeting when Constance Collier visited her old flame, Beerbohm, in Rapallo after a separation of many years. Phyllis was in attendance as Miss Collier's companion.

"I hadn't realized that Max would have grown so old," said Miss Collier, forgetting that she herself had as well.

"He was very hard up then," said Phyllis, "and his clothes were from another era."

It was like another world to me, and that Phyllis could have been a part of it seemed extraordinary. I was to feel the same amazement when Dame Judith Anderson spoke of Arturo (Toscanini) or Alice and Gertrude (B. Toklas and Stein). Or when Christopher Isherwood spoke of Virginia (Woolf).

Kate said George Cukor was interested in doing a film on Virginia Woolf and had acquired the rights to the Julian Bell biography. I didn't mention the fact—even after a martini—that I considered myself something of an authority on Virginia Woolf and longed to write the script. She said George wanted Maggie Smith for it. I suggested Vanessa Redgrave. But Kate replied that Vanessa had already played Woolf on British television, and George had not approved.

"However," she explained, "when one is embarking on a project, one is apt to view the competition as a disaster."

Kate invited me to stay to dinner. "Have another drink while I do it," she urged.

So I made myself another martini and chatted with them in the kitchen while they quickly and efficiently put together a marvelous meal.

I asked Phyllis what her childhood had been like and she confessed that she, too, had acted.

"That's news to me!" exclaimed Kate.

Phyllis said yes, she had had a part in a play and had fallen in love with a boy in the cast, but unfortunately it was love unrequited. Kate pretended great shock at this revelation, but Phyllis smugly turned the broiling tomatoes and implied that she had a past.

I was instructed to set up three tray-tables at our chairs in the living room and open a bottle of wine for myself.

As we ate, I told them I had proposed a television special on Amelia Earhart to a producer at Universal.

"You know who could play her," I said, "Katharine Houghton."

"Well, I immediately thought of her when you mentioned it but, of course, I couldn't say it," Kate said. "And I could coach her. I met Earhart, you know. As a matter of fact, I almost played her myself once. It would have been, I felt, pretty good casting."

Kate went on to explain the Tomboy Girl to me, who developed in this country in the 1920s as never before. Kate was a good example of her.

"She flourished in an innocence and directness and honesty that we don't have anymore," said Kate. "It's been lost. The clue to Amelia's character was forthrightness." It was eventually filmed with Susan Clark. and I had nothing to do with it.

The subject of marijuana came up. They had, of course, never tried it. Had I? I sometimes felt Kate and Phyllis saw me, in those days, as a kind of cozy link to the underworld, someone to whom they could, given their comfortable conservatism, put such shocking questions.

I confessed that I had tried it once or twice, but it bored me. They refused to accept my argument, however, that pot was less harmful than alcohol.

Kate poured me another glass of wine.

And then she said, quite casually, that it was actually happening.

She would work with Laurence Olivier at last.

1975

We had often talked about the possibility of Kate's doing something with Olivier, an exciting prospect. I had, naturally, even kicked around a couple of ideas for them in my own mind.

But it was James Costigan who provided the property for them. He had written *Love Among the Ruins* years before and, indeed, George Schaefer told me he had optioned it at one time for the Lunts. And when the Lunts turned it down for some inexplicable reason, George had sent the script to Spencer Tracy in the hope that he would wish to do it with Kate.

"Really?" said Kate when I asked her about it. "I don't recall ever seeing it and I saw all the scripts Spencer was sent."

At any rate, George heard nothing from Tracy and ultimately dropped the option. Now, years later, Kate had gone off to London to do it with Olivier under the direction of her dear George Cukor.

When she returned to Los Angeles, I went up to the house for dinner.

She'd brought back with her some stunning stills of the production, which whetted my appetite for the real thing. The sets and costumes were gorgeous.

"And those wonderful British character actors!" exclaimed Kate. "Nobody like them!"

She and "Larry" had gotten along splendidly.

"Don't be a pig!" she told him on those occasions when he might tend to become querulous over small matters. Consequently, she felt they had a perfect understanding.

When I finally saw *Love Among the Ruins* on television, it was everything I could have hoped for. A brilliant script, two great actors, and exactly the right director had pulled it off.

I came to see less and less of Kate.

One night, as she'd walked me to my car after dinner, she told me she was planning to make a film with John Wayne. She had always wanted to; now was her chance. She had never done a western, she said, unless you called *The Sea of Grass* a western and nobody called *The Sea of Grass* anything.

I was less than enchanted with John Wayne, whom I thought a terrific movie star and a crummy human being. But who knew? Hadn't Humphrey Bogart been an odd choice for her as a costar? And just look at the chemistry they generated!

"Is it a good script?" I asked. That was the important thing.

"It's a wonderful script," she said and, believing her, I wished her well with it.

So she went off to do *Rooster Cogburn* with John Wayne in the wilds of eastern Oregon, and the press provided almost daily accounts of the filming. She was, as usual, bringing her extraordinary vitality and interest to the project. I thought the matching of Hepburn and Wayne might be dynamite, and I had high hopes for the picture.

When I saw it, however, my heart sank. It seemed to me a cheap shot, even to the point of parodying *The African Queen*. How could she have done it? How could she have thought it was a wonderful script?

And as for the teaming of Katharine Hepburn and John Wayne — well, I never brought it up.

She had done, by the way, a curious thing on a recent trip to New York. It was terribly unlike her and I couldn't understand it at all.

She and Phyllis and Tony Harvey had gone to a matinee of Hal Prince's production of *Candide*. There was no curtain, and before the performance was to begin, Lewis J. Stadlen, one of the actors, slipped into a bed on the stage prior to the lights coming up and the play starting. He lay there waiting for the play to begin. The entire audience then saw Miss Katharine Hepburn leave her seat, walk up on stage, and get into bed with him. She stayed a moment or two and then returned to her seat.

It was such an odd thing, I could hardly believe it. Kate was certainly not given to making scenes in public, and any unprofessional behavior would appall her.

What had gotten into her?

A week later she came out to the coast and invited me to dinner.

"Well, what's this about you getting into bed with Lewis Stadlen?" I asked her.

She laughed.

They had gone to a Saturday matinee, entered the theatre and were ushered not to seats, but to a kitchen chair, a box, and the end of a bleacher. It was that kind of production.

Having endured a hip operation and, furthermore, suffering from a back ailment, she was less than enchanted with the accommodations. Nor was she thrilled to pay eleven dollars to sit on a box.

"Ye gods!" she said to Tony and Phyllis, "at these prices I should be up there in that bed."

"I dare you," said wicked Tony.

"Kate, you wouldn't!" said Phyllis, alarmed.

So she did. And as she walked up on stage, she said the entire audience began to cheer.

Now, she had seen Stadlen get into bed and she thought he was an old character actor who would have a certain air of aplomb.

"I assumed I'd get into the bed and he'd say something witty to me and I'd say something witty to him and he'd push me out." Instead she found herself in bed with a very frightened and thoroughly shattered young man. So she mumbled something apologetic—not in the least witty—and hurried back to her seat. The audience, she added gleefully, went wild.

"Then it was a protest," I said, in her defense, "against the lack of comfort and the price of the seats. Why didn't the press report that?"

"Oh," she shrugged, "they called to ask me about it, but I wouldn't talk to them."

I struggled on with my own small career.

We taped *The Last of Mrs. Lincoln* for Hollywood Television Theatre, a thrilling experience in that Julie Harris's brilliant performance was captured forever. Michael Cristofer abandoned writing long enough to portray Robert Lincoln beautifully. Robby Benson was touching as Taddy. And a new young man named Patrick Duffy was hired by George Schaefer and me with some trepidation. He'd never been before a camera. Actually, he was driving a truck, delivering flowers for a florist shop. Dare we chance it? We did and, boy, did he come through! I spent the next year trying to find work for him, since he had a wife and baby to support.

I wrote a play called *The Housekeeper* and had three readings of it, as time went on. First with Sada Thompson and Michael Cristofer, then with Jean Stapleton and Howard Morton, finally with Zoe Caldwell and Leonard Frey.

In the end (years later), Cloris Leachman and Noel Harrison played it.

On a cool autumn morning, Frank Levy telephoned to say he was producing a benefit show at the Hollywood Palladium for the Beverly Hills chapter of Hadassah, and Joe Hardy would direct it. Was it possible that I could write it? No money involved, but it was to be a salute to Anthony Newley and Leslie Bricusse.

I leaped at the chance. I'd always been a fan of Newley's, and here, too, was an opportunity to try my wings at writing that sort of comedy: one-liners. I thought I'd be terrific at it and turn out all manner of hilarious jokes for the performers.

I was to learn a great lesson.

We gathered for a meeting at Tony Newley's house, high in the hills of Beverly. Tony couldn't have been pleasanter, and I liked him instantly. Leslie was a little more waspish, and a good deal less realistic than Tony. Frank was there, of course, and our musical director, Ian Fraser, but Joe Hardy was off somewhere, probably directing a television movie.

Leslie pretty much took over the meeting. Although we'd never met, any of us, I was "Jimmy" from the first five minutes.

And Jimmy had a great deal to do. Leslie explained that they proposed to use their "mates" as performers. These included Mike (Michael Caine), Pet (Petula Clark), Roger (Moore), David (Niven), Sellers (Peter), and, of course, Rex (Harrison). Jimmy was to contact them all and write material for them.

They'd all be glad to come, Leslie explained. Pet, for instance, owed him one. Mike would certainly be there, as would David and Rex and, of course, Sellers.

Tony wasn't so sure.

"If you rely on the Sellerses of the world, they won't be there," he said flatly. But Leslie was undaunted. He said he had double-checked and triple-checked with Mike, for instance, and "he'll be there."

My task was to be made easier because they'd give me telephone numbers and, too, Nivens and Sellers were in Los Angeles making a Neil Simon movie, *Murder by Death*. I sailed out of the meeting feeling quite elated. I would meet and work with all these fabulous people.

The next day I telephoned Michael Caine. He seemed somewhat

vague about this benefit for Newley and Bricusse, but at any rate he couldn't possibly make it.

Petula Clark was working out of town and unavailable.

I went out to the lot in the San Fernando Valley where they were filming *Murder by Death*, and chatted with David Niven as he came out of his trailer. He was really awfully sorry, but it was out of the question.

Peter Sellers was more cooperative. All he asked was that I write him some good material. I said I'd come back with it.

Roger Moore greeted me at the poolside of his Beverly Hills home, where he was sunning in his swimming trunks. He couldn't have been nicer, and was only concerned about what he could do. I said we'd work up some lovely dialogue, but in the end he pretty much worked it up himself. And he showed up on the night.

I can't remember why Rex Harrison was not available. I only know that he was nowhere near the Hollywood Palladium on the night of December 14, 1975. (I was to meet Harrison later at a dinner party in his honor at the home of the publicist Dale Olson. Jean Stapleton went with me and, I recall, we had to stop the car en route because a pack of coyotes were crossing the road. Where but in L.A. could you be stopped by coyotes on the way to a party for Rex Harrison? Anyway, he was fairly drunk. During cocktails, he was seated next to Sada Thompson, but didn't speak to her. I asked Hermione Baddeley why not. "Oh, my dear," she said, "he doesn't know who she is." He seemed interested only when Neil Sedaka came in with his gorgeous wife. That perked him up. Before dinner was served, he stormed out, and after that we had a fine time.)

For four solid weeks I attempted to write material for Peter Sellers. I'd present it to him and he'd say, "Oh, dear boy, I can't possibly do this." I assured him that I'd come up with something better and finally he accepted what I'd done. I heaved a sigh of relief. It'd been hard work, but it was worth it.

And on the night of the benefit, as Tony predicted, he did not show up.

Doing a benefit is a marvelous way to discover what stars are really like, to separate the good from the bad. Robert Goulet didn't show up, either, and we called Jack Jones in a real panic. That gentleman was down there in twenty minutes and performed like the trouper he is.

At our rehearsal, Tony Bennett came in, sat in the back, and said, "Jim, just let me know when you need me."

Gene Kelly, who had cataracts and had to be driven at night, never-theless was there, and he was wonderful.

Something went wrong with the lights while Florence Henderson was on, but I watched, dazzled, as that pro used it and turned what might have been a disaster into a triumph.

Marvin Hamlisch did a stunning turn at the piano that was the smash of the evening.

Now, I had written a routine for Tony and Leslie as they came out and started the show. It was a disaster. Joke after joke fell like a dull thud. I began to sweat. These were clever guys and I silently begged them to drop the lousy routine and wing it. But they didn't. I was sick about the whole thing.

It was all the more heart-warming, then, when I ran into Tony New-ley and his wife on the street one evening a few weeks later. He hugged me and called me Jimmy and was just as friendly as if I hadn't ruined his tribute.

I might also add that the day after the benefit—when none of those stars need ever see me again—two of them rang up to thank me and tell me what a help I'd been. They were Roger Moore and Gene Kelly, which is why I love Roger Moore and Gene Kelly.

Kate, meanwhile, had pretty much moved to New York, but she hadn't quite given up the Cukor house. She'd pop in to Los Angeles from time to time, and we'd have dinner.

Now it was in the works for her to do a play of Enid Bagnold's, that octogenarian original. It was, Kate said, a brilliant piece of work.

"What's the title?" I asked her.

"*A Matter of Gravity*," she replied.

"Lousy."

But I said it in a bantering way.

I was making a gradual discovery in my relationship with Kate. Whereas I'd always felt that I could be perfectly honest with her—tempered with a little tact—I now found that I couldn't do that any-more. She didn't want to hear the truth, she wanted reassurances and she wanted to hear praise. It seemed to me that with the growth of ego—and, perhaps, the natural vicissitudes of time—the legend of Katharine Hepburn had begun to take over the person Katharine Hep-burn. But the Katharine Hepburn I knew and loved was far removed from the public legend—every bit as remarkable, but different. "St.

Katharine" was not a saint, nor had she ever been. She was a struggling actress, a struggling artist.

She was, actually, a great deal more human than St. Katharine.

That was the last time I was to have dinner with her in that house. She was to give it up shortly thereafter.

I did have cocktails there once more when she lent the house, in her absence, to a young Australian actor, Noel Trevarthan. It seemed strange without Kate and Phyllis there, almost a violation, and I still didn't have nerve enough to sit in her chair.

We did maintain a sporadic correspondence, so sketchy that, as in the case of this one written to her when she was rehearsing *A Matter of Gravity* in New York, she simply added notes to my letter and sent it back to me.

20 August 1975

Dear Kate:

An actor came by the other day who had read for your new play. He reported that you rose, shook hands, greeted every actor as they came up to read, and shook hands and thanked them as they departed. The thrill of it he may never recover from. I asked him if it made them nervous and he said no, on the contrary it so buoyed them up they all felt they were momentarily a part of the finest and the best in theatre and gave their top readings. (NOTE: Oh-h-h, I'm so lovely, but still no girl—)

I've been reading your Higham bio and if you're upset in any way about it I suggest you don't bother. It's a splendid piece of work. God knows how he's done it, but he's certainly got you down on paper. What I particularly like is that he's captured your sense of *fun*, which nobody else ever seems to write about. I laughed and laughed. What a lovely life you've got, really! (NOTE: Shame on you—so *inaccurate*, but I'm glad you laughed—)

The Housekeeper is slated for fall rehearsals. No definite cast yet, though. I'm determined to have Sada Thompson. Maybe Alec Guinness for the man, if we can get him. Maybe we'll be on Broadway at the same time. (NOTE: Good for you) (MY NOTE: Ha!)

I'm staying in the old Cedric Gibbons house in Bel-Air for a few weeks, house-sitting for friends. You must have known Gibbons. His widow, Hazel Brooks Gibbons Ross, speaks of you so frequently and intimately as Katie, I'm beginning to think she never knew you at all. (NOTE: Some people called me that—)

Good luck with the play. Have you changed the title?
(NOTE: No, same title)   Love to you and Phyllis.

Jim

The Bagnold play opened on Broadway and, as always, Kate packed 'em in and cleaned up. The play was not well received critically, but, given Kate as the star, that seemed to make no difference at the box office.

When she played it in Los Angeles, I thought I might hear from her, but I didn't.

I arranged to take Jean Stapleton and her husband, Bill Putch, to see it, and I telephoned Kate to say that we would like to come backstage afterward to say hello.

Phyllis answered and made no move to call Kate to the telephone. I told her I was bringing Jean Stapleton.

"And who is that?" she asked. I explained that Miss Stapleton was rather well known because she played Edith Bunker on a popular television series called *All in the Family*.

"Oh, we don't watch television," said Phyllis, still snobbish about the box. "Now, Mr. Prideaux"—I was Mr. Prideaux again—"there's a little door to the left of the stage, a private door that leads backstage. I'll meet you there after the performance and take you back to Miss Hepburn."

She'd forgotten that it was the same door we had used when we saw *Cyrano*. I said I'd find it.

The play was very, very bad. It was a straight dramatic play, but Kate was bathed in a follow spot, something that hadn't been seen—outside of musicals—since Mrs. Fiske. Wherever she moved, the spot followed so that the other actors were suddenly struck by it when near her or plunged into shadow outside her aura.

The Hepburn magic, however, was intact. She took the stage in that inept play like the star that she was. Whether it was enough for those members of the audience who weren't dyed-in-the-wool Hepburn fans is moot. But it was enough for me.

After the curtain call, Jean and Bill stopped to chat with friends, but I hurried over to the little private door. Phyllis was standing there. Her greeting was cool. She told me that we would have to wait because Miss Hepburn was going to see Charlton Heston first.

Phyllis was facing me, her back to the door. At that point, a bearded Charlton Heston, with his son, came up behind her and tried to turn the doorknob. Phyllis swung around.

"What are you doing there?" she demanded.

"We're going back to see Miss Hepburn," said Heston.

"Indeed you are not!" said Phyllis, "Miss Hepburn has done two shows today. She's not seeing anyone."

"But . . ."

"It's out of the question. Miss Hepburn is seeing *no one!*"

"Phyllis," I interrupted, "Phyllis, this is Mr. Heston."

"Oh," she said, "*Oh!* Oh, well, won't you come right back, Mr. Heston?" she said, leading them in.

"You wait," she said to me.

The door closed on me as Jean and Bill came up.

"We have to wait," I said.

We waited perhaps ten minutes. The theatre had cleared out and we were all alone, standing there, waiting.

I suddenly thought, what's going on here? Here we are with Jean Stapleton, who's starred in this theatre, waiting like autograph hounds who can't get backstage. I was about to say something when Jean simply opened the door and we went backstage.

As we approached her dressing room, Kate was standing outside saying good-bye to the Hestons. Phyllis looked startled as we came up. I think she had forgotten us.

Kate was a shock to me. I had only admiration for her courage and stamina. She had done two shows that day, carrying the weight of that cumbersome play on her shoulders, doing a job that most youngsters couldn't have done. It was downright valiant. And onstage she had appeared vibrant and electrifying.

Now, standing there immobile in her little German cap, she looked very small and very old.

I reached out and put my arms around her.

PART TWO

1978

Joe Hardy and I had drinks one day and wondered, since we both knew and liked her, why we didn't put together a television movie for Jean Stapleton?

I remembered how she'd impressed me with her singing and dancing one night at the Hollywood Bowl, and I went home and outlined a story that very night about a lady college professor, plain and academic, who had a secret show business past. She took a misfit student into her home and he, discovering her secret, blabbed and forced her to go into the college variety show. I called it *Return Engagement*.

Joe was delighted with the idea, as was Jean, apparently. Joe and I pitched it to Tony Converse at CBS, following up the pitch with a lunch at the Women's Assistance League that included Jean. Everybody appeared to be ecstatic over the idea. It was a sure thing.

Except that it wasn't. It was purchased by CBS, but I sometimes thought networks purchased certain properties so they could control them and their stars couldn't do them. I suspected they had a vested interest in Jean remaining the dingbat in *All in the Family*. Maybe I'm being unjust. Maybe it was Jean who backed out. Anyway, a year later it hadn't been produced and reverted back to me.

Things were, on the whole, looking rather bleak. My career seemed to be going nowhere at all.

What I didn't know was that the biggest star of all was on the horizon.

Elizabeth Taylor was about to come into my life.

Joe Hardy called one morning and asked if I was sitting down. I said I was. He told me to think of the most unlikely star in the world to play the part of Emily Loomis in *Return Engagement*. I said I thought it was beside the point, that the project had been shelved. He said no, that his producers, Frank Levy and Mike Wise, had sent the script to the Hallmark Hall of Fame people and they liked it and would do it, but only if this particular star would play it.

"Who?" I asked, uneasily.

"Elizabeth Taylor."

Well, we laughed. And laughed and laughed. To go from Jean Stapleton to Elizabeth Taylor was so ridiculous, so Hollywoody—well, we laughed a lot.

"She'll never do it," I said, sobering up.

"Don't be so sure," said Joe. "She does want to do television."

There was then a small pause and I knew what we were both thinking. A little thrill went right through the telephone wires. Elizabeth Taylor! We were both old enough to regard her as the ultimate star. Elizabeth Taylor starring in my script! Elizabeth Taylor being directed by Joseph Hardy! We might joke, we might pooh-pooh it, but still the thrill was there.

Before we hung up, however, we concluded that the chances of her doing it were very, very slim. And in the weeks to follow I honestly put it out of my head, except for telling one or two friends that Elizabeth Taylor might star in my script, which seemed to me a shameful piece of pretension.

But then rumors began to filter back to me. Miss Taylor, living with her then-husband John Warner on his Virginia farm, had read the script and liked it. She was interested. I began to give some credence to the fact that she might actually do it.

And then I heard that she had asked Hallmark for $200,000 plus all those little extras that made her life worth living, like first-class air travel for her and her entourage, a chauffeured limousine at her disposal, the largest suite at the Beverly Hills Hotel. I might go to the set on the bus, but Miss Taylor never would. I assumed that Hallmark would never meet all her demands.

But they did. (And isn't it interesting how modest her demands seem now, though they struck us as exorbitant at the time? Now we deal in millions and it doesn't appear unreasonable.)

Frank Levy and Mike Wise called to say that Miss Taylor would, indeed, star in my film. Frank was on his way to confer with her in Virginia. I still couldn't believe it.

I studied the script again. Elizabeth Taylor as plain, unloved Emily

Loomis? Singing and dancing? There was, I felt nervously, work to be done. But I didn't do it because I still assumed that at the last minute Miss Taylor would pull out. She would see that the part wasn't right for her.

When Frank returned, I bombarded him with questions about the legendary Elizabeth. Did she really like the script? Was she actually going to do it? Could she honestly see herself in it? Would she really return to Hollywood, the first time in years, to do a picture?

The answer to all of these questions was: yes.

I prepared myself as best I could for the impending arrival of Elizabeth Taylor. I read every book I could find about her, including one called *Who's Afraid of Elizabeth Taylor?* When I finished it, I knew exactly who was afraid of Elizabeth Taylor.

Me.

In my local supermarket, I came upon a copy of the *National Enquirer* with the blazing headline: LIZ TAYLOR QUITS HER HUSBAND'S SENATE CAMPAIGN TO GO BACK TO HOLLYWOOD.

I couldn't have been more fascinated. One quote of hers in the article endeared her to me. In reference to my script, she was reported as saying, "I was too enchanted with it to turn down the opportunity." And Warner was quoted as saying, "I've always encouraged Elizabeth to do the occasional acting role. She feels that this one in particular is very important to her at this time."

I began to feel as if I were single-handedly saving Elizabeth Taylor's career.

As a result of the criticism that she was walking out on her husband, however, Elizabeth decided (I was told) that she must see Warner through his campaign before she could do *Return Engagement.* The production date was set back a month.

Oh, well, the writing was on the wall. Postponements. The next thing would be a firm cancellation. We were playing games. Hollywood games.

She came, though, finally. I had thought there would be a great hullabaloo among the press at her return—it'd been quite a while since we'd seen her in these parts—but, aside from a couple of comments by television newscasters that "Elizabeth Taylor is coming back to town," there was nothing. Being a dramatist, I had imagined hordes of her (aging) fans descending upon the Los Angeles Airport, perhaps rioting, possibly squads of cops called out.

But nothing.

She was due in from Washington at 7:00 P.M. on the evening of June 10, 1978. At that precise moment, I lifted a solitary toast to her in my humble West Hollywood flat. The biggest star in the world was mine and she was arriving, even as I poured myself another martini, to star in my picture.

I heard nothing all that evening, although I kept the television set on for news coverage. She had certainly slipped into town quietly. Was this the "new" Elizabeth Taylor, the shadowy helpmate of her politician husband? The Virginia farm wife? Was this the sensible Elizabeth Taylor who was adjusting to age, weight, and a declining career with a realistic and cheerful attitude? And no fanfare?

Everybody I talked to about her admired Elizabeth Taylor. Everybody seemed to feel that, whatever the endless husbands and flamboyant lifestyle, here was a real person.

"You'll like her," they said, "and she'll like you."

I was prepared to like her and for her to like me. After all, wasn't I a chum of Katharine Hepburn's? And hadn't I worked with stars before? I wasn't awed; I wasn't cowed. I assumed they would do their jobs and I would do mine, all of us professional and efficient and reasonably respectful and friendly.

And yet, she was different. I didn't feel nervous about meeting her, but I did feel an unusual excitement. She was such a legend. I had rushed out to see every movie of hers I could find, not easy in those days before VCRs. I sat through *Cleopatra*, the uncut version. I endured all of *Raintree County*. I watched her as an enchanting teenager in *National Velvet*, luckily showing on television, and I admired her as a mature Martha in *Who's Afraid of Virginia Woolf?* at a neighborhood grindhouse. I journeyed all the way across Los Angeles to catch her in *A Place in the Sun* and sat enthralled by her magic. I was not only ready to like Elizabeth Taylor, I was prepared to worship her.

There were, however, warning signals.

Some of them I knew from my own experience. Professional and efficient and reasonably friendly, yes, stars could be that. But stars were not people, a cold and perhaps callous observation, but very true. They were stars. Quite a different thing.

Anita Loos, hardly given to cynicism, yet wrote "The main tenets of film-star psychology are to be mysterious, difficult, irrational, and suspicious, thus bringing about confusion and giving the star the whip hand." I would encounter a bit of that later on, but not from Elizabeth.

I knew, however, that anything was possible with a star of Elizabeth's magnitude. But we live in hope.

Waiting for Miss Taylor that evening in suite 184 of the Beverly Hills Hotel was a large bath towel with an MGM logo on it and, at the bottom in small letters, the words "Stolen from the Prop Department." I know because I sent it, thrown into a quandary as I was by Mike and Frank, who had filled the suite with flowers, and by Joe, who'd ordered caviar and champagne to greet her. I couldn't compete with that, and the bath towel was my pathetic stab at humor and friendship. I didn't expect her to acknowledge it. Stars, with the unbridled exception of Joan Crawford, weren't especially good about acknowledging gifts.

I telephoned Joe early the next morning to see if she had actually arrived. She actually had. Not only that, Joe was to meet with her at 3:00, their first meeting. I resisted the urge to suggest that I join them. I had not yet attained the exalted status of producer, as I later would, and I knew full well that the director and his star, especially in movieland, didn't want the writer around at this first, wary confrontation. Miss Taylor would have been greatly startled had the writer, the lowest of Hollywood's creatures, appeared at so august an occasion.

But I insisted Joe call me the minute he was home. The minute. I wanted full details. I got them.

The door had been opened by a tall, gorgeous blonde. Her name was, oddly enough, Chen Sam, and I was later to learn that she had become Elizabeth's factotum as a result of nursing Richard Burton through some malady in her native Egypt. When I later met her, I liked her very much and admired her for the forbearance with which she served her illustrious mistress. No secretary to any star ever has it easy, and they deserve all our sympathy and understanding.

Chen Sam offered Joe whatever he wanted to drink and, unfortunately, he chose coffee, which he claimed was instant and undrinkable. Then John Warner came through in tennis togs. They made desultory and not very successful conversation. Senator Warner was obviously not a member of the profession and didn't have any of the easy camaraderie that show folks like ourselves recognize and enjoy.

But then Elizabeth Taylor entered the room. Sedately, was the way Joe put it. She was reserved and quiet, although he reported that her handshake had the strength of a dock worker.

One was always hearing rumors about how fat she was, but he said no, she didn't seem "like a big, fat lady" because she was so short. She seemed more "like a small, chunky lady." I didn't find that especially encouraging.

They had discussed many details of the production, primarily of a visual nature ("lady star time"), such as wardrobe, hair, and makeup. Joe asked if, as Emily, she might want to wear glasses? She had sensibly vetoed that, saying who would believe Elizabeth Taylor in glasses?

Joe suggested our friend, Noel Taylor, as costume designer and she agreed to that. (Indeed, Noel had already been approached and was hired. Alas, Elizabeth later said she must have Edith Head. So that was that. Noel sighed and said, "Well, Edith got to her.")

Joe was greatly heartened, as was I, when she said she hoped they would have "fun" with the production. It was what we all wanted.

They had even touched upon the delicate question of the "variety show segment," that segment of the production originally written so that Jean Stapleton could show off her stuff as a singer and dancer. Joe and I had kicked that one around endlessly and anxiously. He had devised a plan whereby Joseph Bottoms, playing opposite her, would actually do most of the singing and dancing and Elizabeth would kind of fake it. (I was *still* anxious.)

Elizabeth was delighted by this solution, and I hoped it would bury forever her suggestion to Joe, via an earlier telephone conversation, that instead of singing and dancing she might have been part of an acting team—"like Richard and me"—and would do dramatic scenes. She said she might do a scene from *Candide*. Joe said she meant *Candida*. And he actually felt that, if worst came to worst (and wouldn't it?), she could do the scene from *Candida* and get away with it.

"Or even *Candide*," I said, sweating.

She told Joe she would read from cue cards for her opening scene, a lecture in her college classroom, which didn't faze Joe.

"I don't give a damn if she reads from cards," he told me. But he did tell her he hoped she'd memorize her long monologue where Emily Loomis talks about her life with her former husband. She assured him she would.

(She didn't, of course, and the world was none the wiser. She read the cards brilliantly. She was a master of it. You'd never suspect.)

Joe had left after an hour. He felt it had gone well. She seemed enthusiastic about the project and eager to get started. I asked him if she had mentioned the script, if she had wanted any changes. She hadn't.

So far, so good.

The following morning Joe spent with Elizabeth and Edith Head at the hotel as Elizabeth tried on costumes, which she apparently enjoyed. She was, he reported, bubbling. They'd had a grand time going over the dresses and all was sweetness and light.

That afternoon she reported to Metromedia, where we were to film, only half an hour late for a reading of the script with Joseph Bottoms. Joe Hardy noted that she was wearing a blouse and jeans that Edith had suggested for the production, already getting into the role. I was not asked to this session because Joe felt it might make Elizabeth nervous to have the author there for the first read-through. I understood that.

It was only later I learned that nothing on earth could make Elizabeth Taylor nervous.

She read very well. Joe called and told me there was a bit of *National Velvet* in it, then *Butterfield 8*, then . . . and it was all quite exciting. He was greatly heartened. And we assumed that what he heard at that first reading was pretty much what we would get since she disliked rehearsing. She simply got up in front of the camera and did it.

Joe casually dropped the fact that John Warner had gone off in her limousine, so he had driven Elizabeth and Chen Sam back to the hotel. I detected a faint flush of pleasure in his voice. Well, why not? It wasn't every day one drove Elizabeth Taylor home. He added that they had passed a wooden fence surrounding a construction site and on the fence had been painted portraits of movie stars.

"Oh, look, it's me!" Elizabeth had cried, delightedly.

It was all very interesting. I couldn't wait to meet her.

But I had to wait, anyway.

The producers had arranged a week of rehearsal time, a luxury in television, but Elizabeth didn't feel up to it. She wanted to rehearse, she claimed, but she was not feeling well. On the first morning, she telephoned Joe to say that she had a strep throat and wouldn't be in.

"I'd better stay home, don't you think?" she had said. "I'll study my lines." Naturally, he agreed that she must stay home.

I was waiting at the studio to meet her and catch the rehearsal, but instead Arthur B. Rubinstein, the composer, and I worked with Joey

Bottoms on the songs we had written—I did the lyrics—for him and Elizabeth. Joey couldn't have been more cooperative and, while his voice wasn't trained, it was pleasant. And he was a good dancer. We had a great time and felt the morning hadn't been wasted.

In the afternoon, I went home to try to work out that pesky variety show segment in detail, at least as we now envisioned it. It was pretty peculiar. Emily Loomis would do practically nothing, and yet she was to get a standing ovation? It was a major problem and I wish we had solved it by killing the standing ovation, but we didn't. We kept thinking that Elizabeth would ultimately come across with something spectacular, star-fashion. Thus do we sometimes kid ourselves in show business, especially when it comes to stars. Miscasting is a common pitfall, particularly if you snag that Big Name. You convince yourself that they're right for the part, whether they are or not.

The following day, her throat was better. Joe Hardy went to her hotel in the morning and she opened her mouth and he stared into it.

"Is she really ill," I asked, "or is it psychosomatic?"

"Well," he said, "the throat looks ghastly. Really ghastly."

"Maybe it always looks ghastly," I replied, pettishly.

Days passed.

Every morning Joe talked with her on the telephone and one morning he said she had a suggestion for a script change. In the scene where Emily told the boy, Stewart, that they were going to do the variety show together, Elizabeth suggested she tell him that she was going to "work your frigging ass off!" She said she knew we couldn't use "frigging," but did we get the point? I got the point. I didn't think "work your ass off" was much of an improvement over "work your frigging ass off," and I think, after toning it down, what I ended up with was "work you until you drop."

She remained sequestered in her hotel suite.

Arthur and I went ahead and worked with the trio of girls who were to sing and dance the introductions in the variety show. We had to do something.

Joe Hardy and Joey Bottoms went off one afternoon at 4:00 to work with Elizabeth at the hotel. Joe had told me that if she was feeling well enough and agreed to it, he'd telephone me and I could finally stop by and meet her. I stayed by the telephone, but no call came. Later, Joe reported that she and Joey Bottoms were getting along famously.

The next afternoon at 4:00—that seemed to be Elizabeth's favorite time to work—Joe took Allyn Ann McLerie, who was to play her best friend, to the hotel to rehearse with Elizabeth. Again, I was to wait by the telephone and fly to them if summoned. I wasn't summoned. I began to think that every member of the cast would be an old friend of Elizabeth's before I ever met her.

But Joe said they hadn't worked at all that afternoon. Elizabeth's throat was worse. Hopefully, Joe would work with her over the weekend and she'd be able to start filming on Monday.

That night I went to a screening of Joe's television film, *Taxi*, at the Academy of Arts and Sciences. The star of it, Eva Marie Saint, asked me how Elizabeth was—all of Hollywood was asking how Elizabeth was— and jokingly added that she was "ready and standing by."

I managed to laugh.

Later that night, Joe Hardy and I sat on the terrace at Joe Allen's in semidarkness and engaged in what was to be our main avocation for the next few weeks: talking about Elizabeth.

We touched on loneliness. It was incredible to me that in this, her hometown where she had spent most of her famous life, she appeared to have few friends with the single exception of Roddy McDowall.

What was nice was that her kids kept dropping in. Elizabeth, I was to discover, tended to talk about them as if they were five or six years old, but Liza Todd and the two Wilding boys were adults (Liza, the youngest, was twenty one) and Elizabeth was a grandmother. Like Judy Garland, she appeared to adore her children and she was adored in return. These lady stars, we mused, did have a childlike quality that made them great companions for their children. They were all the same age.

However, the same immaturity that bound a star to her children could be infuriating when it came to working with adult professionals. She could be demanding, we suspected, and that could be tiresome. How demanding she would be—and how tiresome—remained to be seen.

In the meantime we agreed, sitting there in the shadows, that we were embarking on what would probably be the most exciting project of our careers. And, in two words, there was only one reason for that. Elizabeth Taylor.

It was a relief, on the first day of shooting, to see a long, gray limousine parked outside the sound stage. Miss Taylor had obviously arrived. We were actually going to make a movie.

When I entered, there was a great deal of activity going on. The college classroom had been constructed in the center of the sound stage and, under the hot lights, an entire roomful of college-age extras were seated, chatting, waiting. A large cluster of people were centered around the desk, prop people, lighting people, sound people, makeup people, hair people, the assistant director, and the director, Joe Hardy. And standing beside Joe was a short, middle-aged woman.

As I approached, she turned and suddenly looked right at me. The face was heavily made up so that one would have difficulty saying what was actually there, but when the eyes leveled on you there could be no doubt. She was a witch or she was a saint; she was the most beautiful woman in the world or she wasn't, but this was certain: she was one of the most extraordinary creatures on earth.

I went right up to her.

"I'm Jim Prideaux," I said. I didn't know whether that would mean anything to her or not. In the Hollywood of her day, the writer was hardly more than hired help. (Is it any different now?) Would she connect me with the name on the title page of her script? Would she care?

Much to my surprise, she squealed—the squeal didn't go with the face—and took my hand.

"Oh!" she exclaimed, "thank you for the towel! I'm having the logo cut out and framed and John loved it so much he went to the shop to get another one, but he didn't because they were too expensive!"

I was delighted by her reaction, although I mentally calculated that the price of the towel was something like twelve dollars.

She was then called to work, leaving me slightly dazed and terribly pleased. Why, she was warm and friendly and human! Loving her was going to be easy.

I tried to stay out of the way and at the same time watch Elizabeth at work.

She was positioned at the desk in front of the students.

"You've got to help me," she told those extras, "because I don't know what I'm doing." She wasn't accustomed to the two-camera technique. Behind the students and out of camera range, a couple of assistants at opposite ends of the room held up cards on which Elizabeth's lines were printed. She would read a line from one card, then her eye would travel to the card on the other side of the room for the next line, then back again. On camera, she appeared to be delivering her lecture thoughtfully, thinking out sentence after sentence, her eyes darting about the room and, presumably, looking at her students. It was wonderfully real, despite the fact that she was actually reading the scene.

They rehearsed the scene just once and it was all right, I thought, but Joe called me over to look into the monitor as they filmed it.

"Look at this!" he whispered, excitedly.

When the cameras were rolling an astonishing thing happened. The "all right" scene that Elizabeth had rehearsed became something else. It only happened when the cameras were rolling. And, oddly, Elizabeth seemed to be doing nothing more than she had done in rehearsal. But an extraordinary something happened, and it is almost impossible to describe or define. One hesitates to use the word *magic*, but, by God, it *was* magic. The cameras loved her. Day after day, week after week, Joe and I watched it and it never lost its fascination for us. It was a kind of cinematic miracle. How did it happen? How did she do it, while apparently doing nothing?

At one point that first morning, when I felt that we were going to be great friends, I went up to her and said, "Joe and I would like to take you out to dinner one evening."

"Great!" she said, "it's a date. Some night when I don't have to work the next day."

We were never to do that, though. The time would come when the strain was simply too much.

Mike Wise came by and told her we'd have lunch sent in for her.

"Oh, no," she exclaimed, "I want to eat with the peasants." And so he telephoned the Brown Derby on Vine Street—that was where the peasants were planning to eat—and reserved us a table.

That first lunch with Elizabeth! Elizabeth loved lunch—it was her favorite event of the day—and there was no such thing as a quick sandwich on a tray. She liked her lunches baronial.

There must have been a dozen of us at the table at the Brown Derby. Joe Hardy sat at the head with Elizabeth to his left and then Joe Bottoms. I sat next to Joe Bottoms. (Once again, we Show Folk understood the pecking order and moved automatically to our proper places.) Edith Head, Elizabeth's only old friend in that company of strangers, sat opposite her. The producers sat opposite me. Below us were the assistant director, Chen Sam, and Elizabeth's driver Harry. Each in his place.

It was at this lunch that I made a disturbing discovery. I discovered that I could not be casual or, indeed, quite at ease with Elizabeth Taylor. It was disturbing because it had never happened to me before. I became faintly alarmed. What was causing it? Was I so impressed with her? More impressed than with Hepburn, with whom I felt totally at home? Surely not. Or was it that we were just not on the same beam? Or was it . . . was it that she was a little scary?

Whatever it was, as we—all of us—struggled to make conversation that first day, I gradually became aware that I was working awfully hard at it. But Elizabeth created that. One felt that she had to be entertained, amused, that she had to be made to laugh. Her boredom, when I got to know her, was colossal. To amuse her became a part of one's job on the set. Not that Elizabeth ever said so or demanded it. In all fairness to her, she never demanded anything. She didn't have to. (At lunch that day, she said casually, "I've been in this business since I was nine and I've *never* had a red-headed stand-in." By the time we got back to the studio, a black wig had been slapped on the redheaded stand-in who was, by the way, Darlene Conley, now a soap opera star.)

For whatever reason, being with Elizabeth was work, at least for me. Hard work. And one went home drained.

Part of it, I learned early, was that we didn't share the same sense of humor. Hers was far broader, a hell of a lot earthier, and—I hesitate to say it—more vulgar. She screamed with laughter, in that Earth Mother way of hers, at rotten jokes that I could hardly smile at. There are, I admit, certainly worse faults in this world. She was a good sport, and her love of laughter was an endearing quality. She seemed to need it so desperately. What I hated was what it did to me. I found myself, in my fumbling attempt to be easy and palsy with her, saying the most remarkable things.

For instance, at lunch that day she and Joey Bottoms ordered "the special," whatever it was.

"You should be glad," she said to the producers. "It'll be quicker and . . . [she mimicked] . . . time is money . . . time is money!" We all laughed. When the special arrived, however, Elizabeth claimed it was inedible. It was getting late ("time is money!"), so she ended up nibbling on my sandwich, hardly more than a bite. The waiter was appalled, needless to say, and would have done anything for her, but she waved him away grandly.

As we got up to leave, I heard myself saying to her, "Shit, you hardly got anything to eat at all!" Now, that is a four-letter word I had probably never used to a woman in my life. Elizabeth shrugged and went on out, but Joey Bottoms grabbed me and hissed in my ear, "You shouldn't talk to her like that!"

I felt wretched. I watched as she walked alone to the front door, a middle-aged woman heftily crammed into a shirt and blue jeans, walking the length of that restaurant with every eye on her, head high, looking straight ahead. Had I offended her?

It bothered me all afternoon, and I even entertained the notion of going to her and trying to explain. But I didn't. And later, of course, it seemed ridiculous.

We filmed for a week, a week of revelations.

She arrived every morning on the dot at 7:00 A.M., Harry driving her from the hotel. On the second morning, Joe was ready to shoot after an hour, but she was still in her dressing room. She remained in her dressing room until 11:00. Down on the set, we were gradually panicking. Precious hours were going by—time *was* money—and if she wasted three or four hours every morning we'd be in serious trouble.

When she finally came on the set, she merely said to Frank Levy, "Eighteen years of penal servitude."

We all looked blank.

"That's what it was at MGM," she said, "eighteen years of penal servitude. They penalized you for everything. Even if you did something natural—like having a baby—they penalized you."

Why she had announced all this we had no idea, but we came to realize that the chip on her shoulder that was MGM was the size of a boulder. She had been a slave for eighteen years and we, and the world, were going to pay for it. Anything she could get she felt she was entitled to, having been so wronged in her youth.

(Rumor had it she said to Louis B. Mayer once as a very young girl, "You can't talk to my mother like that . . . and I'm never going to talk to *you* again!")

We all, in a way, symbolized Mr. Mayer.

One day Joe mentioned the overtime on *Cleopatra* to her and she replied, "So what? I made an extra million dollars."

I began to think of her as The Toughest Little Girl in the World.

We need not have panicked that second morning. Elizabeth, like Marilyn Monroe, put off going to work as long as possible. I would pass her dressing room at 8:00 A.M., where her door was always open with people running in and out, and she would be sitting in front of the mirror doing her face. I would pass again an hour later and she would be sitting in front of the mirror doing her face.

However, once she came on the set and started working, she worked so fast we were able to make up the lost time and more.

And once at work, she began to have fun.

She genuinely liked people and with no distinctions. She could be seen walking along in conversation with a grip, her arm on his shoulder. Or chatting with the extras. Or laughing with the wardrobe mistress.

Elizabeth never threw her weight around or lorded it over anybody. She was quick, though, to spot phonies and, I think, hated any pretension in people. Anybody pompous was given short shrift.

Once, at lunch in a restaurant, a bunch of executives from *TV Guide* came up as we were eating and paid court, rather too obsequiously, to Elizabeth, who was seated there with her usual entourage.

"If there's anything we can do for you, Miss Taylor . . ." said one of them.

"Sure," said Elizabeth, "you can pick up the tab for lunch."

Another time we were having our usual midday banquet in a restaurant when a suburban-type matron came right up to the table and, bending down, said into Elizabeth's ear, "I just want to tell you, Miss Taylor, that we all have loved you since you were a little girl and we will always love you."

After she left, somebody at the table said, "How pushy," and somebody else said, "Why can't they leave you alone?"

But Elizabeth looked at them with that steady, unflinching gaze of hers and said simply, "It was nice of her."

"Here's to the first day!" I had said at our first lunch at the Brown Derby, lifting my glass.

"Here's to the *last* day!" Elizabeth replied wryly, lifting hers.

She hated work, apparently, and yet it seemed to me that she was happiest when she was working. One had to be very careful, however, how one broached her on the subject. After work one evening, Joe made the mistake of telling her they had an especially strenuous day tomorrow and she looked daggers at him.

"What do you mean—a *strenuous day*!" she spit out, sarcastically. She could not be told to work harder. (Shades of Mr. Mayer?) She could not be even gently pushed around.

That first week was full of optimism and hope. On Frank Levy's thirtieth birthday, a terrific picnic lunch was served us all in Joey Bottoms's dressing room. Elizabeth made an entrance in one of her caftans (we all applauded, of course), sank into the sofa, put her feet up on the table, and told funny stories in her friendliest manner. When she discovered that wine was missing, she rushed off to her dressing room and returned with three bottles of chilled champagne.

"Now, this is my contribution," she said, making sure she got full credit. "These are on me." She signed a birthday photograph for Frank, who had requested it, and then reminisced about the old MGM days. (She might have hated them, but she certainly didn't mind talking about them.) She said when she was a little girl if anyone on the set ever used profanity in front of her, they were fired on the spot.

"What if you used profanity in front of *them*?" I said, thinking it would make her laugh. It did.

"Oh, I wouldn't," she said, demurely. "I was a good little girl — *then*."

"Did you really want to be an actress?" I asked her.

"Oh, yes, of course I did. Because my mother had been an actress. My dad was against it, but Mother and I got together behind his back."

Elizabeth, with her feet up like that, chatting away, sipping her champagne, was a delight and I felt a surge of affection for her.

I left the studio one day just after lunch. It was nice, sometimes, having no real function on the set and being able to go home for a cozy nap. Nobody minded. (Except, maybe, Elizabeth. She said accusingly one day to Joe Hardy and me, "You can go out and fart around all night. I have to stay home and learn my lines." Which she never did — learn her lines, I mean.)

About 6:oo that evening, I got a telephone call from Firooz Zahed: He was a member of a prominent Iranian family and Elizabeth's personal photographer. Everything she did was photographed by Firooz and censored, or not, by Elizabeth. He was everywhere, and immensely likable. Adoring her, he served Elizabeth in practically every capacity, and now he was telephoning in the role of secretary to Miss Taylor.

Miss Taylor wondered if I would join her for caviar in her suite at the hotel at 8:oo? I said I would be delighted.

I didn't know what to expect. Certainly, knowing Elizabeth, a crowd. And when I entered that enormous suite, I found Joey Bottoms was there with his friend and stand-in, Dirk, and Elizabeth's publicist, John

Springer, and Edith Head and Elizabeth's famous hairdresser, Sydney Guilaroff, and our Hallmark producer, Ron Hobin, and, of course, Chen Sam and Firooz, snapping away. And Elizabeth's children. And Joe Hardy.

Elizabeth was wearing what seemed to be a voluminous white nightgown and had no makeup on. She was relaxed and charming. I was wearing a T-shirt I had had made up that said ELIZABETH TAYLOR IN RETURN ENGAGEMENT on the front, and she squealed with delight when she saw it. (The squeal never quite went with the face.) Then she quickly pulled Joe Hardy and me into her bedroom and closed the door behind us.

"Look at these!" she said, excitedly.

She brought out an envelope and showed us some Polaroid snapshots of a piece of sculpture, a winged horse.

"Liza did it," she said, proudly. "Isn't it wonderful? Isn't it really good?" We could honestly agree that it was really good. And Elizabeth's pride in her daughter's work was touching.

"You mustn't tell her I showed them to you, though," Elizabeth said. "She's so modest about her work."

I then went into the living room and was introduced to her children for the first time. The two Wilding boys rose, like twins, from the sofa. They had their mother's extraordinary eyes and Michael Wilding's patrician nose. With longish dark hair drifting down their necks, they were quite handsome, had English accents, and were quiet and pleasant.

And then I met Liza Todd. She was, in a word, darling: a tiny creature with delicate features, dark, sensual, again her mother's wonderful eyes and, like her mother, with no pretensions. I was always to feel old in her presence because somehow she treated me as if we lived across a great crevasse of years, but I liked her. And her affection and concern for her mother was, if unsaid, obvious and endearing.

Somebody got me a large vodka on the rocks in what appeared to be an old jelly glass, and we consumed great quantities of caviar out of small tins that cost—it was whispered—a hundred dollars each. Knowing Elizabeth, they must have been a gift.

Joe Bottoms sat with Liza on the sofa and I sat cross-legged on the floor in front of them, the coffee table between us. Elizabeth came and sat on the floor next to me, also cross-legged. I noticed there was a large black-and-blue spot on her arm, an ugly blemish about the size of a silver dollar. It added to my impression that she was without sex appeal. Glamorous, striking, still beautiful perhaps—but not sexy.

And had she ever been? She was never a pin-up in the way that Rita Hayworth, Betty Grable, or Marilyn Monroe were. I doubt if soldiers fantasized sexually over Elizabeth as they did the others. They might have dreamed of walking into a nightclub with her on their arm, a plum prize certainly, but I suspect she was too aloof (or maybe just too beautiful) for casual dreams of intercourse. Looking at her now, I had to remind myself that her legend made her one of the most desirable women in the world, if not her physical self.

Despite Elizabeth's warning not to mention Liza's sculpture, the subject came up, I suspect because Elizabeth herself couldn't help talking about it.

"You should have a show, darling," she told Liza.

"Oh, Mother, I can't have a show," Liza said, "I'm not ready. I only have a few pieces and they're small."

"She's being realistic," I said to Elizabeth, who suddenly looked at me as if she was seeing me for the first time.

"Yes, she is," she agreed in a tone of voice that was the most honest I think I'd ever heard her use.

Liza went on to say she'd never even sold any of her work.

"Well, I don't see why you don't sell *me* one of them," Elizabeth said. Liza's reaction was that of any young person whose parent wanted to buy something they'd made: it didn't count.

Sitting there on the floor with Elizabeth, her "family" around her (and I put it in quotes because it included Chen Sam and John Springer and Edith Head, who cherished and nourished her long friendship with Elizabeth; John Warner had returned east), I didn't know it at the time, but I was having the nicest, most intimate moment that I would ever have with Elizabeth Taylor.

When I came on the set the next day, Elizabeth and Joe Bottoms were surrounded by photographers snapping them for various publications. The moment they were finished, Elizabeth came over to me and patted me affectionately on the stomach. She was wearing jeans and a loose man's shirt.

"You look so cute in that," I said.

"If I had my way, I'd dress like this all the time," she replied. I thanked her for the evening and mentioned what a nice family I thought hers was.

"Isn't it?" said Elizabeth. "Wherever I am, the kids are always running in and out of the place."

I asked her about her husband's senatorial campaign, and she launched into a discussion about the workings of politics that left me dazzled. She knew exactly what she was talking about, and since then I have never thought of Elizabeth Taylor as being in any way unintelligent.

Ever after, though, it was pretty much downhill for me with Elizabeth.

A day or so later I watched her on the monitor do a scene so movingly I rushed down to the set and stopped her just as she was coming off.

I took both her hands in mine and said, "That was really wonderful!"

"*What* was really wonderful?" she replied in a very businesslike voice.

"That *scene!*" I said. "I've got tears running down my cheeks."

"Why have you got tears running down your cheeks?" she said, as if I were the village idiot, and she moved on. I stared after her.

Was it really all technique? No heart? Could she turn it on and off like a faucet? No thought of creativity or art?

I asked Joe Hardy whether she cared anything about the work she did and he said, "Oh yes, she does." But I didn't think so. I really believe she thought I was crazy to react as I did. And, also, I was to see her turn the magic on and off exactly like a faucet. A great deal of what Elizabeth knew she learned at MGM. And at MGM she was trained to do a job.

Elizabeth wasn't feeling well the next morning, but she managed to do an hour's work. I escaped to have lunch alone (entertaining her at lunch was an awful strain), and when I returned to the set I found a very shaken Joey Bottoms.

"Elizabeth's sick," he told me, ashen. "She's gone to the hospital." I stared at him, aghast. "She was crying," he went on. "I think she was scared. And you know what she said? She said, 'What about all these nice people depending on me?'"

The report came from the hospital that she had "a mild case of pneumonia."

We all behaved splendidly, I felt. There was none of that "she can't do this to us" business. The producers calmly announced that the production was closing down for a week.

We put signs on the set reading, DO NOT SIT OR DRINK ON THE FURNITURE. Joe Bottoms said he was going to visit her in the evening, so I wrote a note for him to deliver telling her not to think of the production, only of herself and getting well. I then went out and bought a small ceramic box in the shape of a heart. On top it read, "If you need anything, just whistle" and inside was a tiny whistle.

I left it for her the next day at the hospital reception desk.

That night there appeared in the local papers a small item that we have all grown so accustomed to seeing over the years: Elizabeth Taylor was ill and confined to the hospital.

Over the next day or two, those of us who were a part of the production spoke of her with admiration. Joe Hardy recalled that she had admitted to feeling strange and unsettled the first couple of days, but then she began to relax and enjoy the work and the people. We agreed, all of us, that she was cooperative and funny and professional and wonderful.

As the days passed, however, our attitude experienced a subtle change. We got conflicting reports of her condition, the most prevalent being that she was simply "resting" in the hospital. How sick was she?

John Warner didn't bother to fly out, which led us to believe that her condition couldn't be *too* serious. Nonetheless, the producers urged her to spend the entire week in the hospital and get fully rested before coming back to work.

There wasn't much speculation as to whether she would actually finish the film, not at first. People kept saying that there were always interruptions with Elizabeth, but that she always finished the production.

And then Warner did fly out to, as Elizabeth reportedly said, "get me out of this place." However, he didn't immediately get her out. The Fourth of July weekend came along, and she was still up there on that top and exclusive floor. We were told that she was studying her lines, but whenever you didn't see Elizabeth you were told she was "studying her lines."

I began to despair. Should I kiss the production good-bye? And there was a new kind of talk among the producers about replacing her, an option I had considered unthinkable. But at that precise moment, she left the hospital.

I am sometimes asked by people what it was like working with Elizabeth Taylor. I reply that her world is nothing like ours, that she exists in air rarer than any we will ever know. Rather like British royalty.

I can only speak from a professional point of view, but I might illustrate by saying that she has only to mention something and it is done.

(Like the black wig on the redheaded stand-in.) She must be kept happy at whatever cost. I had never before worked on a set where food and drink were as available as at a bacchanalian feast. Champagne was kept chilling in a refrigerator. The coffee table in Elizabeth's dressing room was piled high with cold cuts, cheeses, and fruit from the moment she arrived in the morning until she departed at night. Like most stars, she was very careful about the quality of what she ate, and so only the finest (and most expensive) caterers were employed.

The most childish whims were treated as important, like the morning when she claimed she couldn't work because she was hungry and (despite the piles of food on the coffee table), she had to have a peanut butter and jelly sandwich for breakfast. (In all fairness, I should mention that I never saw her eat much. However, I rarely saw her without a glass in her hand, or nearby, at whatever time of day or night, which surely accounted for the weight problem.)

All of this — the food and drink — may well be in her contract, but the point is it is there without her having to ask for it. If I tried that, I'd starve to death.

On the first morning after her return from the hospital, Elizabeth arrived with John Warner at the studio for her call at 6:45 A.M. We then waited the usual three hours for her to come onto the set. That gave us time to look John over, which was quite a surprise. He seemed remarkably awkward in social intercourse. To this day, I'm not sure he understood who I was or what my function on the set was.

We were glad he was there, though, because Elizabeth tended, for whatever reason, to be a happier person when he was around. He was forever surprising her with silly little presents that sent her into squeals of delight. (So unlike Kate Hepburn, whose ego may be greater than Elizabeth's, but whose need for presents was nil.)

We waited, that first morning, because Elizabeth wanted to tint her hair before facing the cameras. (She was forever tinting her hair.) And then, we heard, she'd started coughing. I finally left the studio in a state of frustration. When I called in around noon, I was told that she had done one scene and they were preparing to do a second. Once she got going she was, as always, fine.

But there came a time when even patient Joe Hardy lost patience with her.

We were on location at a small house in the Los Angeles suburbs and the scene had been set for two hours. And for two hours Elizabeth, in her trailer, had been informed that they were waiting for her. Joe, exasperated, finally sent word that if she wasn't on the set in five minutes, he was going home.

She came on the set immediately, walked right up to Joe and said, accusingly, "You hurt my feelings." The message was clear. She must never be in the wrong, could never be put in a position of having to apologize. (Typical star stuff.) It was his fault, he had hurt her feelings and she was the one who should be apologized to.

He put her right to work.

Normally she wouldn't work on weekends, but she agreed to come to the studio at noon one Saturday and rehearse her songs and dances. At last. She would give a full hour to it.

I couldn't have been more worried. However, I didn't want to be there because I didn't think I could face it, and, although I was the lyricist as well as the screenwriter, I didn't feel that I had the right to be there. I left her to the choreographer, the composer, and the director. But I waited, as always, for a detailed report. How bad had it been?

The report I got from Joe was good. She'd worked for three full hours, instead of one, and caught on to the dance routines quite quickly. She was interested, Joe said, and worked hard.

I began to see her as a perfectly acceptable musical comedy star—a grave mistake that we all made.

The following Monday we convened on the campus of Whittier College and spent the morning shooting exteriors that Elizabeth wasn't needed for. Her call was at noon and at noon she appeared in the school cafeteria, where we had all gathered for lunch. And when I say "appeared" I mean just that, as, for instance, the Virgin Mary appeared to dear Bernadette at Lourdes. She did not come in; she did not—contrary to the impression one has of stars—make an entrance. She was suddenly just there.

It was a knack she had. With most celebrities you do sense that a "presence" has entered the room, and every head turns. With Elizabeth it was different. She continually astonished me by appearing, spectrelike, as if from nowhere.

"How are you all this morning?" Elizabeth said, passing among us with Chen Sam in attendance. Her natural friendliness made her perfectly comfortable in this cafeteria filled with extras, but she balked when she saw the food. It had been catered, but by a local firm and was no more than ordinary. She took one look at it and turned on her heels.

"We're going out to get some food," she announced as she and Chen Sam exited. God knows where she went in Whittier for food that would suit her, but she came back fed. Possibly she had stored something in her trailer, which was loaded with luxuries. Including air conditioning. It was hotter than Hades in Whittier on that July day in 1978, but only Joe Bottoms had access to Elizabeth's air-cooled trailer. The rest of us sweated it out.

I had created a very long, rather complicated walk across the campus for Elizabeth that was to open the picture under the credits. It was right up front so that viewers could get a good look at her figure and, if they were in shock, get over it by the time we cut to her remarkable face as she lectured her class in the next scene.

She did it in the heat cheerfully. And I think she understood why I had done it that way. Which leads us to her realistic attitude toward herself.

Joe Hardy, one evening, decided that her long monologue needed cutting. Elizabeth and I agreed. We all went home that night and cut separately, coming back the next morning with our new versions. They were almost identical. But Elizabeth had done an astonishing thing.

In the original monologue, written for Jean Stapleton, the character of Emily Loomis alluded several times to what a "plain" girl she had been. I didn't quite know what to do about that, but Elizabeth did. In every instance, she had crossed out *plain* and written in *plump*. She knew that audiences would never accept Elizabeth Taylor as plain, but she also knew that they would now accept her as plump.

As it turned out, neither word was used in the cut version of the scene, but Elizabeth had gained a new respect in our eyes.

We soon moved to the Bancroft Junior High School in Hollywood, where we were to film our variety show in the auditorium. And, once there, the equipment broke down and a delighted Elizabeth was sent home at noon. New equipment would arrive the following morning. In the meantime, various members of the cast who performed in the show rehearsed all day and far into the night. I wandered in after dinner and watched until, hollow-eyed, they called it a day after 1:00 A.M.

Because of the cast's hard work, I was annoyed the next day when Elizabeth appeared "so tired" and was in her pouty "little girl" mood.

Her disposition wasn't helped by the air conditioning breaking down in her trailer (everything seemed to be breaking down at that point in the production), making it, as reported by Edith Head, like a bad Turkish bath.

Elizabeth got grumpier throughout the day. She pouted and sighed and was bored and obviously wanted us to commiserate over her great suffering. But she didn't take it out on anybody. I never saw her be unkind or pull rank on anyone working on the production.

The next day was better; Elizabeth appeared in midmorning in a cheery mood to shoot the variety show.

And it was here that we made our fatal mistake with *Return Engagement*. (One of them; the other was in not prerecording the songs.) Jean Stapleton could sing and dance very well, as I knew when I wrote the script. The entire school handing her an ovation at the end of her act would have made perfect sense. But when they gave poor Elizabeth an ovation, you asked who was kidding whom?

I suspect we lost our viewing audience right there, and I doubt if we ever got them back. I should have rewritten the script. She should have gotten through the act, but not triumphed. And they should have loved her for trying, even if she fell on her face. Or *something*.

At the time, however, I guess we thought we were getting away with it.

There were many sides to Elizabeth, or, perhaps, many Elizabeths. One never knew when one looked into her violet eyes which Elizabeth one was seeing. Or which Elizabeth was seeing you.

In the course of the production, Joe Hardy grew a mustache, and Elizabeth came up to him one day and said, "I love your mustache." She then proceeded to do ten minutes on his mustache, how he should shape it, how he should maintain it, how it flattered his face. Her interest in his mustache seemed all-consuming.

The next morning she came in and exclaimed in utter surprise, "You're growing a mustache!"

Now, what was that?

The worst moment I had with her was on a very hot day. She stepped out of her air-conditioned trailer into the street, where fifty extras had been waiting hours in the scalding sun.

"I'm hot," she said.

I said the nicest thing I could think of. "It's cooler than yesterday."

She looked squarely at me and said, in the hardest voice I have ever heard and in front of everyone, "Why are you always so chipper? It's annoying."

She moved right on and I stood, as embarrassed as everyone else, among the extras. I stormed off the set and swore I wouldn't see her again until the wrap party. And if I did see her before that, I would do something that was very badly needed: I would put her over my knee and spank her.

I did see her the following night, but she didn't see me.

Michael Cristofer and I had had dinner out and were driving home. He was dying for a look at Elizabeth, so I drove him past the little corner bar on Melrose Avenue where they were doing some night filming. Crowds had gathered, and a cop motioned us on, but not before Michael had glimpsed Elizabeth and Joe Bottoms doing a scene on the sidewalk. It was, thank God, a drunk scene—they were helping each other to get into Joe's car—and she seemed drunk, all right.

But she was doing it.

On a Sunday afternoon, Elizabeth completed her final scene and it was a wrap. As she walked off the set, everyone applauded her.

I had never seen her more relaxed and happy. (I was to observe the same thing with Kate Hepburn at the end of the films we did together: absolute elation at the finish. Because they had done it. And they had proved once again that they could still do it. There's no happier moment for a star.)

We all gathered for a group photograph, Elizabeth and Joe Bottoms seated in the center, with Joe Hardy and the producers and me standing by, surrounded by the entire crew and staff. It was a bit of a hassle with the hair people and the costume people and the prop people all trying to get as close to her as possible.

We then moved into a large rehearsal hall for a whale of a wrap party. I'd seen wrap parties in my time, but nothing to match this. Two bars were set up at either end of the hall and, running one entire wall between them, an enormous buffet of really wonderful food.

Elizabeth reappeared in the usual jeans and loose shirt, and with her was her mother, Mrs. Sarah Taylor, in from her home in Rancho Mirage for the occasion. Chen Sam followed with a stack of 8×10 glossies of Elizabeth.

We had all indulged in idle speculation as to what sort of presents Elizabeth would give out at the conclusion of the production. The general consensus was: none. She gave us, however, what all of us really wanted—personally signed photographs of herself. On mine, she wrote, "To Jim, It was lovely, Thank you, Elizabeth (Taylor)."

I had also kept a poster for the film, *Casablanca*, which had figured in our movie, and I asked everyone to sign that. On that she was more effusive: "Dearest Jim, I love you always, Elizabeth."

Not true, but she was playing the game.

I managed to spend a little time with Mrs. Taylor, a lovely lady. Liza was also there and being charmingly solicitous toward her grandmother. Firooz reminded me that they had no picture of Elizabeth and me together, so we remedied that, and there is now in existence a photograph of James Prideaux and Elizabeth Taylor, heads together, hand-in-hand, grinning at the camera.

Elizabeth circulated and couldn't have been nicer to everybody there.

After that party the hierarchy—meaning all of us who were "above the line"—went home to dress up for our big wrap party, a dinner at nine in the patio at Chasen's. It was a surprisingly large gathering of nearly a hundred people, including spouses, offspring, and significant others. All of the Bottoms gang were there, the various brothers and mother Betty and father Bud, seated at a table nowhere near Joey, who was with Elizabeth. (I don't mean to suggest that there was a romance between Elizabeth and Joe Bottoms, but I do think she was setting him up for a fling with Liza, which they ultimately flung.)

Tennessee Williams, invited by either Elizabeth or Joe Hardy, came with four young men and took over a table in the center of the room. He was pretty plastered, appeared to think he had written the film, and was soliciting congratulations, which annoyed me. When Joe Hardy asked if I didn't want to meet him, I grandly and foolishly said no, thereby denying myself the privilege of shaking the hand of our greatest living playwright. I could kick myself.

Elizabeth had appeared—magically, as always—in a stunning emerald green gown, the exquisite Liza beside her. Curiously enough, on occasions such as this when you might think Elizabeth had the right to be smashed, she appeared not to drink.

We had dinner, followed by speeches and presentations. The producers had purchased for Elizabeth a beautiful saddle for her horse in Virginia, which set her squealing. They then gave Joe Bottoms a valise. Elizabeth said it was "just the right size for the clothes I stole from wardrobe."

Goaded on by the inebriated Tennessee, who called out, "Make a speech, honey," Elizabeth then rose and said a few words. She told us that in all her career she had never had a happier experience and that she loved us all. It was exactly what we wanted to hear.

We were all introduced, and when my turn came, I said appropriate words, I hope, although I can't remember. As long as I live, however, I will never forget that Elizabeth applauded with the others as I stood up, but as she listened to me she looked at me with the coldest and most penetrating expression I have ever seen. It sent chills through me. Whether it was herself or some demon looking out from behind her eyes, it was a look I hope never to see again. In the Middle Ages, a look like that could have had her sent straight to the stake.

And then she was leaving.

She hugged Joe Hardy tightly, and I'm sure they tried to cry a little. She even hugged me and whispered in my ear, "Write me more words."

Everyone began to applaud as she strolled out of the patio and through the restaurant. We didn't stop applauding as we watched her, through glass doors, traversing the length of the restaurant. We continued to applaud until we were sure she was out of the restaurant and at the curb. A sudden silence then fell over us.

"Well, she's gone," said someone.

And somebody else said, "Thank God!"

We were just terribly tired.

When *Return Engagement* aired the following November, it was with surprisingly little fanfare. Nobody seemed to care very much. I had thought Elizabeth would be on the cover of every TV supplement of every major newspaper on the preceding Sunday, but she wasn't. I'm afraid those television editors who had advance screenings were less than enchanted. Nor were the reviews especially good, although they were no worse than "mixed." I can't even remember the ratings, which means they can't have been memorable.

And people were fairly unkind about Elizabeth at that time. Her being fat was considered a national affront. I had never encountered such shocked outrage as greeted Elizabeth's appearance in that film. (I would get something of the same thing with Ryan O'Neal later.) Women especially took it as a personal insult. It was as if she had epitomized all their dreams and she had let them down.

They climbed back on her bandwagon later, after she dumped the booze and slimmed down at the Betty Ford Clinic, but who ever claimed that the American public isn't fickle?

Given all that, there was a certain quality in the film that some people responded to. "It wasn't love," said the ads, "it wasn't friendship, but it changed two lives forever." What I was trying to illuminate was a love built not on passion or sex, but on affection. An affection that is perhaps more durable than love. Because, as Joe Bottoms says in the last scene, "love dies, but this affection goes on forever." I'm proud of that and happy that people sometimes tell me how much they liked *Return Engagement.*

That doesn't mean, however, that I don't think of it as my big flop.

1984

We did write, Kate and I, during those long years, and sometimes I would simply pick up the telephone and call her, but we'd drifted apart. There was nothing much to hold us together. And we had our own projects.

Cloris Leachman and Noel Harrison toured in my play, *The House-keeper*, only eight years after I'd written it.

Julie Harris and Geraldine Page joined Rip Torn and Michael Higgins to do my *Mixed Couples*, which I'd called *Slightly Delayed*, but the producer, Frederick Brisson (a real Hollywood monster of the old school), changed it. I first learned of the change by reading it in the *New York Times*.

We played it at the Kennedy Center and then on Broadway to devastating reviews, but I wouldn't have missed it for the world. Julie I knew about — a great actress, no star temperament, warm, loving — but Geraldine Page was a revelation. It was my one brush with true genius. Even in rehearsal, one was aware that one was seeing genius at work. Where did it come from? It was magical. Rip's no slouch, either, nor was Michael.

For some time, George Schaefer had wanted to do a series of short television plays, all of which would be talk. No action, only dialogue. Each would take place in a booth — telephone, restaurant, toll — and, indeed, the series was to be called *The Booth*. He finally made some sort of deal with PBS, and he and Merrill Karpf produced a pilot of three plays. One, about an aging actress trying to get a job out of a young producer, I wrote for Julie Harris and called *Bread*.

George liked it, but he could only see Judith Anderson in the part. Years before, I had seen Dame Judith play her Medea on the stage and had been thrilled. The mere thought of Judith Anderson playing in a work of mine was exciting. I didn't suppose that we could get her, since she was semiretired and living in Montecito. And if we did, what then? She was eighty-seven. Was she up to it?

Whatever she was, she agreed to do the part and, on the first day of rehearsal, Noel Taylor and I took her to lunch at a nearby restaurant.

That day began a new and wonderful period in my life. Knowing Judith, late in my life and later in hers, was a gift. We were to have five years of postcards and letters and telephone calls and visits, every one of them memorable.

Judith was a creature larger than life. Like Medea, she believed that the essence of life was in being generous to one's friends and merciless to one's enemies. She had plenty of both; her world was composed of great loves and terrible hates.

I happened on one of the terrible hates that first day at lunch. In the course of conversation, I chanced to mention the name she hated most in the world. It was, of all people, Helen Hayes. Instantly, she threw down her fork.

"You've ruined my lunch!" she cried in tones that shook the restaurant. I thought she was joking.

"Helen *Hayes*?" I said innocently.

"Don't! *Don't!*" she cried again in agony, as if I had tied her to the stake and was approaching with a torch.

I can assure you, she wasn't kidding. She meant that I had ruined her lunch and implied that her day was destroyed as well. The reason, as I later ascertained, was nothing more than that, in her book, Miss Hayes had gently criticized Dame Judith's performance as Hamlet. Not hard to do, given that Judith was well into her seventies at the time, clearly the wrong gender, and was giving us perhaps the greatest example of miscasting in the history of the theatre.

(Later, when I was in New York, they were tearing down the Helen Hayes Theatre, and there was a postcard with a photo of the wrecking ball crashing into the walls. I sent it to Judith. "Let me make your day," I wrote on the back.)

At her age, Judith had trouble learning lines, and filming the little twenty-seven-minute piece took twice as long as it should have. At the end, though, Judith was applauded not only by her fellow actors, Peter Coyote and Mary Kay Place, but by the crew as well. She tried to stop the applause. She didn't feel she had earned it.

Her performance is pure gold. It has a clarity and beauty that breaks your heart.

Later in her life, at ninety-three, she wanted to see it again, so I took a cassette up to Montecito and ran it for her on the VCR in her bedroom. She was very frail, tiny, and quite bedridden.

When it was over, I was quite surprised to see her struggling to get out of bed. And she did, making her way slowly to me and kissing me on the cheek.

"Thank you," she said.

I treasure that moment.

Somebody at the William Morris Agency had the idea that Jane Fonda, one of their clients, should host a series of television dramas. It was to be called *Unsung Heroes*, an anthology of dramas based on the lives of people who had faced incredible challenges and defeated them.

I was brought into it because, as Jane said when I met her, she'd seen *Lyndon* and thought I was the best.

I had never met her before, so I drove out to Santa Monica one morning to meet her and talk about the project.

In those pre–Ted Turner days, she was married to the politician Tom Hayden. They lived in a surprisingly modest house on Alta Drive, but hidden by shrubbery and protected by an electric gate. As a consequence, once we were buzzed in (I was with a lady agent), we found windows and doors of what looked like a large English cottage wide open.

We entered the living room and sat. Around it ran an upper balcony that apparently gave onto the bedrooms. There seemed to be activity somewhere in the house, but there was no sign of Jane or Mr. Hayden.

We waited the proper amount of time for a star entrance. At exactly the right moment, Jane Fonda appeared on the upper balcony. It was well worth the wait.

It's difficult not to gush. I expected her to look good—after all, what was all that aerobics about if not looking good?—but I wasn't prepared for the magnificent creature that looked down at us and said, "Good morning." She was attired in some sort of tight-fitting exercise clothes and she looked simply glorious. This was a remarkable woman—or, at least, the body was. She came down the stairs like a lioness. Not since Brigitte Bardot had I been so struck by the thought that God did, indeed, create Woman.

We sat casually over coffee as Jane told us about her recent tour around America, promoting a line of clothing. Because of her famous anti-Vietnam sentiments, she'd been heckled and harassed at practically every stop. Some of her outlets, like Saks, had pulled out. She seemed resigned, not embittered, almost amused. This was a strong lady, I said to myself as I gazed at her in admiration. I was dying to work with her.

We discussed the project. Somebody had made up a list of potential "heroes," some more sung than unsung. Margaret Mead, for instance, was on it, as was my favorite, Rachel Carson, and Cesar Chavez, and Sojourner Truth. Two had been crossed out as "too controversial/ flawed." These losers were Margaret Sanger and Anna Ella Carroll, a nineteenth-century political writer and military strategist.

As we talked, we were suddenly distracted by a hummingbird that had come in the open window and was flying around the ceiling, madly trying to find a way out. In a panic, it was also doing something that seemed remarkable to me in so small a creature: it was defecating all over the room.

We started running around.

"Why, it's . . . it's . . ." I didn't know how to phrase it for Jane, but she did.

"It's *shitting*!" she said.

It broke up the meeting and we were soon out the door, but not before Jane and I had exchanged a hearty handshake and expressed our admiration for one another, not to mention our enthusiasm for the project. Nothing, I felt, could stop us.

Two weeks later, Jane Fonda left the William Morris Agency and the whole idea was never heard of again.

Kate wasn't having a great time.

She did a film called *Olly Olly Oxen Free*, memorable chiefly because she drifted into the Hollywood Bowl in a balloon, very Hepburn, and it died at the moment of release. It's known, at least to me, as Hepburn's "lost film."

She and Cukor went to Wales to remake *The Corn Is Green* for television — it was the last time they would work together — and they got away with it, I guess, but I still find it painful to watch when it shows up on the tube. She just wasn't Miss Moffat.

Help for Kate was on the way, however, and his name was Ernest Thompson.

I had met him first in June 1974.

Charlotte Rae was in town doing a play at the Ahmanson, *The Time of the Cuckoo*, and David Richards and I ran into her at the Farmers Market. She was new in town, didn't seem to know anyone, so I said I'd give her a party. She could ask anybody she liked.

So she invited a young couple who were acting in the play with her, Ernest Thompson and his girlfriend, Patty McCormack. Patty had been the awful child on Broadway in *The Bad Seed*, but she had grown into a beautiful, lovely woman.

Ernest Thompson was very tall and handsome—and cold. A veritable stick. I made a mental note not to ask him back.

Actually, it was Melina Mercouri who caused a sensation that afternoon. I'd invited her as a surprise guest and, indeed, Charlotte's mouth dropped open when Melina swept in in a white pants suit, dazzlingly dramatic.

She wasn't much fun, though. She was currently exiled from her native Greece and if you asked her, casually, how she was, she'd say, "I'm in a malaise for my country." Whatever you asked her—or wherever— she'd sigh and reply that she was in a malaise for her country. Not a barrel of laughs.

Anyway, a year passed and I was at the checkout counter of the Arrow Market and there was Ernest Thompson.

"Oh, hi, Jim," he said. "Say, I've been doing some writing. Would you read it?"

What could I do? I said, of course, you have my number, call me. I could imagine what kind of writing this guy would do.

Another year passed. Literally. I was in the Arrow Market again and there he was again and he said the same thing. And I said the same thing.

And again nothing happened.

Fade out, fade in.

My agent Michael Peretzian and I were at the Mark Taper Forum and at intermission I saw Ernest and Patty headed my way.

"Oh, my God, Michael," I said, "here comes that guy. And you know what he's going to say? He's going to say 'I've been doing some writing. Will you read it?'"

Which he did. Too boring.

But the next day he telephoned me, at Patty's insistence I later learned, and dropped off three one-act plays he'd written.

I was floored, because they seemed to be everything he wasn't: warm, human, very funny.

"You know what you are, Ernest?" I said. "You're a playwright."

He seemed very surprised.

"Well, nobody ever said that!" he gasped.

I got the three plays, called *Answers*, to George Schaefer, who optioned them for something like $150 a month. I took Ernest to Joe Allen's for lunch by way of celebration.

Ernest really started writing then.

He appeared one evening with a big play for me to read, a full-length play. It was in three acts, rather long and rambling, and I took it to bed with me. I wish I could say I loved it, but I didn't. It seemed unstructured and nothing much happened. What I failed to realize was that he had created two wonderful characters.

It was called *On Golden Pond*.

But he didn't have an agent, a play agent anyway, so I called Michael Kasdan in New York and asked if he knew anyone who could represent a play a friend of mine had written.

He suggested Earl Graham, exactly the right man. Ernest sent the play off and almost immediately, it seemed, it was done at the Hudson Guild. He was on his way.

Things happened very quickly.

They moved the play to Broadway, where it wasn't exactly a hit, but by this time there was talk of a movie, and Kate had been to see it. Ernest was dying to have her for the movie, of course, and called to ask if I would call her and see how she felt about it.

So I did.

"Shoot, I'm not going to do *that*," she said.

I duly reported this unhappy news to Ernest, who believed it, as I had. We should have known better. Miss Hepburn had every intention of doing the film version of *On Golden Pond*.

Driving to Joe Allen's for lunch one day, Ernest asked me what I thought of Mark Rydell to direct if the movie came to pass. Wrong again, I said that it didn't seem like a good idea. He'd done my friend Howard Koch's *The Fox* and Howard hadn't been happy about it. Happily, nobody listened to me.

One day Ernest called to report that the miracle of miracles had happened: he was going to write the screenplay for his own play. What did a screenplay look like? Could I give him one, just to see the form? I did.

I heard nothing from Kate during the filming in Vermont, although I did meet Ethel Thayer in the form of Ernest's mother, who was in Los Angeles and wanted to see my musical, *Jane Heights*. I took her and she was Ethel, all right.

I suspect Kate had a grand time working with Henry Fonda and Jane, but Ernest sent me repeated cards saying he wanted to "kill" Hepburn. She wasn't easy and she almost drove Ernest mad, but the result justified everything he went through.

On the night he won the Oscar for his screenplay, Ernest graciously thanked the likes of George Schaefer and me for believing in him before it was popular to do so. It's great fun, I might point out, to hear one's name on that remarkable occasion.

One sidelight: Kate later told me that Jane Fonda invited a friend of hers, a little black singer, up to visit on the set in Vermont, but then ignored him for a week. So she and Phyllis took over, of course, fed him, and entertained him. Had I heard of him? His name was Michael Jackson.

A chap named Martin Zweiback had thrown a screenplay of his called *The Ultimate Solution of Grace Quigley* over the fence into Kate's yard. That was the sort of thing that appealed to Kate, and she'd been trying for years to get it made.

Unfortunately, under the ultimate title of *Grace Quigley*, she did get it made in 1984 and—especially following the glorious *On Golden Pond*—it was everything about Katharine Hepburn that nobody wanted to see. She was shabby and dowdy and it was all about old people, not particularly ill or suffering, who killed themselves. Very unpleasant. The only thing to remember was Kate riding on the back of a motorcycle behind Nick Nolte, who reportedly called her "a cranky old broad who's a lot of fun." I thought that pretty much covered it.

I later asked her why she'd done it.

"It made me laugh," she said simply. I'm afraid she was the only one who did.

Meanwhile, I wrote a play called *Upper Broadway*, which Nanette Fabray starred in on the eastern straw-hat circuit. Directed by Porter Van Zandt, it was a completely happy experience made all the happier by two great young actors, Haviland Morris and D. B. Sweeney.

And I was spending the six summer months of every year in a magnificent Victorian house called the Casino on an estate in Stone Ridge, New York. It was very grand. Owned by Lord and Lady Margesson, who lived in the Manor, it was exquisitely set in vast green lawns. My living room had once been a ballroom and my back "guest wing" had originally housed three bowling alleys. Prideaux was moving up in the world. I was no longer at the corner of Twenty-seventh Street and Eighth Avenue.

People were frequently sending me things that they hoped I'd adapt "for your friend, Miss Hepburn."

George Schaefer had something called *The Dream Watcher*, a book about an elderly lady and a young boy and how she inspired him to "dream" and . . . well, you could write the rest yourself. Nevertheless, I sent it to Kate, perfectly willing to dramatize it if she wanted to do it.

She sent it right back saying she thought she'd seen it before—it had that effect on one—and that the old lady was a "bore" and the boy was a "wimp."

George dropped the project. He was dying to work with Hepburn, however. Who wasn't? What else could we come up with?

Then it occurred to me that I might write something for her myself. Something original.

1985

"Anything Hepburn says okay to," Merrill Karpf told me, "the networks will do."

I was in the office he shared with George Schaefer and the three of us were trying to think up a project for Katharine Hepburn. I gazed out over the Los Angeles smog.

"Well, let me see if I can come up with something."

It was so enticing. There are few stars whom the networks will accept without reservation, no matter the story, no matter the other actors. Hepburn was enough. She'd guarantee an audience and—this was all it was about—ratings.

That was early February.

On March 15 I delivered to them what they would call a treatment, but I called a short story. I wrote it just as if I were writing for the *New Yorker*. It was long, over fifty pages, but I didn't want to skimp. I wanted them to see exactly what they'd have on screen.

I gave it the temporary title of *Mrs. Delafield Wants to Marry*. The Delafields had been the earliest settlers on Leggett Road in Stone Ridge, but the only remnant left of that illustrious family was a lovely old house called Delafield House. I loved it. And wasn't that the perfect name for the Wasp lady Kate would play?

But what would the Wasp lady do?

Well, at Kate's age, why not assume she was a widow? And what if she wanted to marry again? And what if he turned out to be somebody considered totally unsuitable? Black? Well, no. Not Kate. Why not Jewish? A man of the right age, intelligent (a doctor?), attractive, perfectly suitable, but Jewish.

Fine.

I wanted a narrator, though, someone to tell the story, or at least weave a narration through it, holding it together, as seen through his eyes. But who?

Living in my house at the head of the drive on the Margesson estate, I was fully aware that they could see everything that went on at my place and I could see everything that went on at theirs. How about that? A nosy neighbor, even maybe with binoculars, watching—disapprovingly, as it turned out—everything that was going on with Mrs. Delafield.

And what if it wasn't all one-sided? What if the Jewish family didn't want her any more than her family wanted him?

Love would, of course, conquer all in the end, but wouldn't it be fun along the way? And, hopefully, stylish? Worthy of Kate?

It was lots of fun to write.

I gave it to George and Merrill, who were very happy with it, but I didn't call Kate and tell her about it. Let it come to her officially. She didn't know George and she didn't know Merrill, but a little checking on her part would show her that they had a whale of a track record.

She received it on March 22.

On April 4 I got an excited call from Merrill. Kate loved it! Would I come to the office tomorrow? Much to be discussed. Much to be done. We were on our way!

Now I called Kate.

"Well, what's this? What's this?" I said. "You like it?"

"Well," she said, "it's good. It's romantic."

That was the clue to the whole thing: it was romantic. I wanted to give Kate a love story, perhaps her last love story. I wanted to see her fall in love at her age. And why not? People did fall in love at that age despite the eternal emphasis on youth and its apparent monopoly on amour. And it wasn't unseemly, it wasn't wrong, it was absolutely valid and perhaps a damn sight more sensible than a lot of the love affairs the youngsters were coming up with.

Nor did I find it difficult to believe that somebody would fall in love with Katharine Hepburn at that age. She was still dynamite, still beautiful, still desirable.

"Now, here's what will work," Kate went on. "The fun is that it's seen through the eyes of the neighbor. Don't lose that when you're writing it."

I promised I wouldn't.

There was renewed warmth in her voice. I recognized it for what it was. There's nothing that so endears one to a star as coming up with good material.

We met in the office the next day and George and Merrill and I went over the plot, point by point. I like that. Film is a collaborative effort. It's only a fool who doesn't listen to every suggestion, but then he must use what helps and discard what doesn't, and on that the writer is the final authority—until it gets to the director.

They would then propose it to the network, in this case CBS.

I flew east and opened the house in Stone Ridge for the summer.

The first week in May, Merrill telephoned and asked me to meet him and Peter Frankovich, then head of motion picture development for CBS, for breakfast at the Park Lane in New York. I drove in and, seated at a table overlooking Central Park, had the pleasantest, easiest meeting I've ever had with a network executive. Peter had read the story, loved it, and with a handshake the deal was made. Naturally, CBS was thrilled to have Katharine Hepburn. All I had to do was go home and write the screenplay.

It was a snap, really. I know writing is supposed to be hard work and suffering is the order of the day, but this was a piece of cake. It simply flowed. From the first moment, it felt "right."

On June 3 it was finished, and to celebrate I drove up to Woodstock and had an ice cream at Papagallo. I thought I'd earned it.

I couldn't resist calling Kate.

"Well, it's done!" I said.

"Really!" I could tell she was as excited as I was, but she played it cool. "Are you pleased with it?"

"I think it's terrific," I said, modestly.

"Bring it in tomorrow."

"Oh, I can't tomorrow, Kate. It isn't even Xeroxed yet. And George and Merrill haven't even seen it."

"Bring it the day after tomorrow then. Come for lunch."

"All right."

But a strange thing happened on the day after tomorrow. The rains came. Torrential rains.

I set out in the car, but I got about a third of the way to New York and the rain was so heavy you couldn't see. Cars were stopped on the thruway.

Now, there are two things I'm cowardly about. One is driving on ice and the other is driving in the rain. I panic. And I panicked then, and turned around and went back home, despite the fact that I knew Kate was expecting me for lunch. How in God's name was I going to find the courage to tell her I turned around and came back because of rain?

But I called her, trembling.

"Rain?" she said. "You're not coming because of *rain*? You turned around? You went back home because it was *raining*?"

"Yes, Kate, yes. Torrential. Couldn't see a thing. Dangerous. Cars stopped on the thruway."

There was a terrible pause.

"*Rain*?" she said again.

"I'm sorry. Listen, I'll bring it in tomorrow."

"Do that," she said. "But not lunch. Come for dinner. That'll give the rain more time to subside."

"Yes. Thank you. Lovely. Sorry."

But she had hung up.

Kate's little house in Turtle Bay, situated on Forty-ninth Street, is wedged in between a house that once belonged to Garson Kanin and, on the other side, the home of Stephen Sondheim.

Her relationship with Sondheim is precarious, partly because she doesn't appreciate his music (or anybody else's) and partly through a series of unfortunate happenings.

For instance, his fireplaces abut her fireplaces, and his smoked into her rooms, or some such. She spent $10,000, she claims, to rectify this situation, and the minute he lit a fire it still smoked. (Or was it her smoke going into his house?) At any rate, an uneasy relationship.

She has been known to go out into the back garden and peer into his windows, presumably because of "noise" (a.k.a. music), and at all hours.

"Kate," I said, "you've got to stop that or you're gonna get picked up by the vice squad!"

Mr. Sondheim's "man," a charming fellow, is devoted to Kate and will serve at her infrequent parties or surprise her with delicious little desserts of a rich and satisfying nature.

I arrived with my script, which I flung down casually on a settee by the front door. Kate eyed it, as had Irene all those years ago, but led me into the kitchen before going upstairs into the living room.

Phyllis was there, the same Phyllis, a little older, but still protective of her Miss Hepburn and still a sweet woman.

I also met Norah Moore, the round-faced, cheery Irish cook, the mother of a flock of children. She managed to raise the children and serve Kate, too, and appeared to have not a worry in the world.

And then Hilly, the famous Hilly.

It is difficult, even now, to describe Hilly. I don't suppose he was yet forty then, tall, white, rather Prussian looking with cropped hair, and muscular. He'd been recommended by Kate's masseur, Rod Colbin, as a driver and cook. He did both sensationally. That he was scattered—unfocused—didn't seem to matter much. He had never held a job for any length of time in his life, that I knew of. He was brilliantly witty, quick, aware. He had a marvelous talent as an artist, or could have been a writer of humorous stories, but Howard Hildenbrand, during his short life, couldn't get his act together.

He was perfect for Kate. They thoroughly enjoyed one another, although a strong female was the worst thing in the world for Hilly.

On his first day, Hilly said, he was ordered to report at 9:00 A.M. He arrived at 9:00 A.M.

"Let's get something clear," Kate informed him. "When I say 9:00 A.M. I mean 8:45. What's that I smell?" He was wearing cologne. "Well, don't wear it again." Kate hates perfume in any form.

("I smell perfume," she is fond of saying, gazing at one accusingly. "Well, don't look at me," I'd say. "Must be coming in the window.")

As I followed her up the stairs to the living room, I wondered how her foot was. She'd had an accident while driving her car and run into a telephone pole.

"Damn near lost the foot," she said, settling into her chair. "Severed it. They had to sew it back on. Are you pleased? No, sit there."

She meant was I pleased about the script, and now I will instruct you where you're to sit when you come to visit.

"Very pleased," I said. "I hope you'll like it. But don't let's talk about it until you've read it. Yes, a little vodka, I think, on the rocks."

She had her scotch and Phyllis came up to sit and sip a scotch.

I suddenly sighed and relaxed. It was like the old days. The only thing missing was Irene.

Kate no longer cooked; that was now the domain of Norah and Hilly, and it was Hilly who brought the trays up to us. I had never, at that point, known Kate to sit at a dining table like a normal human being. She reclined in her chair with her feet up on a stool and the dinner tray in her lap.

It was hot in New York, but the air conditioning wasn't working, which upset Kate. Actually, I was surprised that there wasn't a fire in the fireplace, with the smoke pouring into Stephen Sondheim's living room.

"Now, who is this George Schaefer?" asked Kate. "And Merrill Karpf, who is he?"

She tended to think that anybody she hadn't heard of couldn't be anybody, forgetting that she'd been a bit out of the Hollywood scene in the last few years. I launched into a vivid description of the venerable George Schaefer and the energetic Merrill Karpf. I assured her that she'd adore them. She grunted at that.

(When the time came, she did adore them. They became her professional family, I think.)

"And where will we do it, do you think?" she asked.

"Well, as you know, it takes place in Philadelphia, but . . ." One never knew about things like that. If it was cheaper, one might well end up filming in Pasadena, avoiding the palm trees. Kate wanted to go to an interesting location. She wanted an adventure. So I hedged.

It was one of those delicious meals that one came to expect at "Kate's Place," as she called it. (She said she was thinking of putting a sign outside the house that said EATS.) A light meal and yet substantial, always a soup, always fish or meat, always lovely vegetables, and always ice cream and cookies to end it. And then go home.

She would, however, see you down the stairs and to the door despite the bum foot. She might even open the door and walk you out into the busy street, where passersby would smile knowingly at her.

I gave her a peck on the cheek.

"Enjoy," I said, referring to the script.

"Hope so," she said.

It was only a day or two later that she called me in the country.

She was very pleased with the screenplay, and she had dozens of suggestions for changes. I took notes as she talked. I said I would take them all under consideration.

CBS also had suggestions, as had George Schaefer and Merrill Karpf. We had conference calls. None of the changes were major, but they were work. I still wasn't up to using a word processor, and painstakingly retyped and retyped.

In late July, I was thrilled to take George Schaefer to dinner at Kate's. George had worked with practically every major star in the world, but not Hepburn, and I was delighted to be the one to bring them together.

I came to the house early and had a drink with Kate before George arrived. We were both, possibly, a little nervous. What if she and George didn't hit it off? I needn't have worried. I shut up and let them get acquainted. I could see that George was already working his magic, that even at this early stage Kate felt she was in good hands. Safe hands.

One matter concerned all of us, even then. It had to do with casting.

Yes, it was romantic, and Mrs. Delafield was going to fall in love and marry a Jewish doctor. The burning question was, who would play the doctor?

We all agreed that there would, of course, be somebody, some star who'd be right for it, but not a single name came up. We were at a loss. It would have to be resolved later.

As to where we would film—a question foremost in Kate's mind—George, for the first time, mentioned Vancouver. He and Merrill would go and scout locations, but he believed there were parts of Vancouver that might serve very well as Philadelphia. (They had good crews, too, and it would be cheaper, I was later to learn.) I could see that Kate was enthusiastic about Vancouver. British Columbia sounded exactly like an adventure to her.

August was hot and humid in Stone Ridge, and they were scraping and painting my house, but on the fifteenth I finished a complete second draft of *Mrs. Delafield Wants to Marry* and, half dead, poured myself an enormous vodka martini.

I took a boat trip up the Hudson.

One evening I read the whole of *Delafield* to Howard and Annie Koch in Woodstock. They couldn't have been more excited. Howard had been my mentor—the movies he'd written and cowritten, like *Casablanca*, were hardly chopped liver—and I was delighted by his reaction.

Merrill Karpf called to say that CBS "loves, simply loves" the revised script.

And it was now my turn to take Merrill to meet Kate.

"*You* could play the doctor," she told him, admiring his trim build, his clipped beard, his handsome face.

Merrill is a class act, and I think Kate sensed this immediately.

We discussed casting.

One thing was clear in my mind. I was going to give Kate a screen kiss—a real sexy kiss, not just a peck on the cheek—and my criterion for the actor who was to play the doctor was this: did I want to see him kiss Katharine Hepburn?

"The doctor can be younger," said Kate.

We didn't argue it at that time, but that was a can of peas I definitely didn't want to open. Being Jewish was enough; I didn't want to add the "younger" thing to it.

I went back to Stone Ridge and did more little rewrites on the script, but in the back of my mind was the nagging question of the casting.

Our casting director, the splendid John Conwell, put together a list of possible actors for the role of the doctor. I called the William Morris Agency and asked them to pull together whatever videocassettes they had on these actors that Kate and I could see.

They sent them over to her house and I drove in, meeting her one morning at 11:00 A.M. We had a little difficulty with the VCR, of course, but finally Hilly got it going for us.

We looked at Danny Kaye, a favorite and old friend of Kate's. No. Nothing romantic about Danny Kaye.

We looked at Ed Asner. Did I want to see Ed Asner kiss Katharine Hepburn? Not much.

Sam Wanamaker? A definite possibility, but wasn't he in England, and was he available and was he warm enough?

We broke for lunch and then I took Kate and Phyllis to a matinee of *I'm Not Rappaport*, which my friend, Chuck Kindl—known to all as Chuckles—was stage managing. It had gotten dreadful reviews, but Judd Hirsch was in it, and Kate loved Judd Hirsch.

As it turned out, it was wonderful. (It was to have a long run and ultimately win the Tony Award, causing the author, Herb Gardner, to announce that there was "life after the critics.")

We went backstage and Kate was photographed with Judd. In the car, she said it was a pity Judd wasn't available because he'd be perfect as the doctor. I began to wonder how old she saw herself.

We went back to the videos. We looked at Robert Preston. Romantic, yes, but who would buy Robert Preston as a Jewish doctor?

We looked at . . . oh, I can't remember who, but it turned into a very depressing afternoon. I drove home with a real sense of doom. What if we couldn't cast the doctor?

And then an extraordinary thing happened, proving that miracles can occur in show business.

The very next afternoon I wandered into the little Stone Ridge Library. Along with the books, in the corner they had a small shelf of videocassettes. I glanced at them and was surprised to see that there was a video of a production of Wilder's *The Skin of Our Teeth* at the Old Globe in San Diego. Why they had that I couldn't imagine, but I knew that my friend, Sada Thompson, had starred in it, so I took it home.

That night I looked at it and my head nearly blew off, because acting with Sada was Harold Gould.

I had found my Dr. Elias.

I tried to control my excitement. He might not be available. He might not be a big enough "star" for the network. He was perhaps a little younger than Kate, but not enough that it would become an issue.

I telephoned George and Merrill on the coast. They didn't say no. They'd look into it. They'd check his availability, and check with the network.

I couldn't resist calling Kate, although I knew what her reaction would be.

"Who's Harold Gould?" she said. She'd never heard of him, and if she'd never heard of him, of what use was he? I assured her that he was the perfect Dr. Elias.

"How tall is he?" was her next question. I said I didn't know, but I'd find out. (I still don't know whether that meant she hoped he'd be tall or not too tall.)

Three days later George and Merrill flew into New York and, video-cassette in hand, I drove down to Manhattan.

We met at Kate's house to look at *The Skin of Our Teeth*. Harold Gould was available and interested. The only difficulty was Kate's VCR, which wouldn't work at all.

"Come on," she said, "We'll go over to Bob Gottlieb's house. His VCR works."

We followed her out the back door of her house and through the communal garden and in the open back door of a house facing Forty-eighth Street. There were painters and workmen, but no Mr. Gottlieb, which didn't stop Kate for a moment.

She led us straight into a kind of study, lined from floor to ceiling with videocassettes and housing a magnificent television set and working VCR.

We started watching *The Skin of Our Teeth* and I began to sweat. At the end of act one, Kate said she didn't want to see any more.

"I think I ought to meet him," was all she said.

Merrill went straight to Mr. Gottlieb's telephone and called the coast. (Putting it, I trust, on his calling card.) Would Mr. Gould be free to fly in to New York this evening? Would he meet tomorrow with Miss Hepburn? He would.

The next morning I picked up Mr. Gould at his hotel and walked him over to Kate's house. I liked everything about him, his look, his walk, his talk. He was an intellectual—a former college professor, as it turned out—but he was in great physical shape for a man of his years. And he was sexy. Did I want to see him kiss Katharine Hepburn? The answer was sure. Mrs. Delafield would be lucky to get him.

Kate liked him, too, from the very first, although she wasn't about to say so outright. I shut up and let them get acquainted. They chatted amiably. Mr. Gould, a terrific actor but an unassuming man, handled himself well. I think he was thrilled to meet Miss Hepburn and excited at the prospect of playing opposite her (otherwise, why would he have sat up all night on the red-eye?), but he wasn't overwhelmed. He was good, solid Hal and, as we were to learn, a dear man.

I heaved a sigh of relief.

There was another tricky piece of casting. Kate had recommended Brenda Forbes for the wife of the nosy neighbor, and we were all delighted with that. But what about the neighbor? Very important.

George wanted Michael Hordern. But Sir Michael didn't wish to travel to the far reaches of Canada, where we were now planning to film.

We then went after Sir John Gielgud, but Sir John, after his splash in the film, *Arthur*, wanted $200,000. (I was later to learn that he also said he didn't feel he was up to working with Miss Hepburn, however he meant that.)

George's next suggestion was Denholm Elliott. I was dead against it. "He's got no snap, crackle, pop," I told Kate and then I heard her repeat to George that Denholm had no "snap, crackle, pop."

George ignored us. I'd heard that Elliott was in Marrakesh, so no danger of his getting the script. But George did get the script to Denholm in Marrakesh, and I was very annoyed to hear that he had read it, accepted, and been cast.

Kate and I were both put out. Now we'd have to work with somebody who had no snap, crackle, pop. Hard to imagine now, given the exquisite, absolutely perfect performance Denholm came up with. He was almost as important to the final production as Kate herself. Or Hal.

The rest of the casting we left to George and Merrill and Conwell, who cast it both in Los Angeles and Vancouver. It turned out, with one notable exception, to be perfect.

And then there was the question of Noel Taylor.

Like any lady star, Kate was deeply concerned about the way she'd look. Who would design her clothes?

"We're getting you the very best," I said. "Noel Taylor."

Long pause on the other end of the telephone.

"And who is Noel Taylor?"

"He's the very best, Kate."

"If he's the very best why have I never heard of him?"

"I don't know," I said, adding jokingly, "you really should get out more." She didn't think that was funny. And she didn't want Noel Taylor.

I reported this to George and Merrill, who decided that the best thing to do was have Noel fly in from Los Angeles to New York and meet with Kate. They thought it would be a good idea if I called and broke this news to her.

"Kate," I said, sounding enthusiastic, "Noel Taylor is flying all the way to New York just to meet with you."

"Why is he doing that," she said, "if I don't want him?"

"To meet with you. Who knows? You might hit it off."

"I don't see any point in my meeting Noel Taylor. Good-bye."

We took a chance and had Noel fly in. I called her again.

"Kate, guess what?"

"What?"

"Noel Taylor is in New York! He could come and see you this afternoon."

As Kate has often said, she knows when she's licked.

The outcome was that Kate was "thrilled" with the designs Noel showed her. And she was big enough to say so.

"He's the best I've ever had," she called and told me.

It was only the middle of September and, if the schedule remained as it was, we wouldn't arrive in Vancouver until the third week in October.

Plenty of time for perfectionist Kate to fiddle with the script.

I took the train into New York—it must have been raining—and lunched with her and spent the afternoon going over every word of the screenplay. I gradually watched Katharine Hepburn become Margaret Delafield, or was it the other way around?

She was very helpful.

"You must keep the screen alive," she'd say, which meant I must work a little harder, search a little longer for the unusual setting, the extraordinary situation, the surprise.

I had, for example, a scene in which Denholm, as the nosy neighbor, came by at breakfast time to have a talk with Kate. It was set, most unimaginatively, at a table in a kind of breakfast nook.

"Why not this?" suggested Kate. "She sees him from an upstairs window coming across the lawn and says, 'Come on up!' She's just finishing her breakfast in bed, reading the newspaper. He comes up and sits by the bed. Moves around it, actually. Isn't that more interesting?"

It was.

Or she would tell me, "You can't say 'bring the satin pillow, she'll want that.' No *lady* would have a satin pillow. She should say 'bring the *lace* pillow, she'll want that.' You see?"

I saw.

"When are you going back to the country?" she asked.

"I thought I'd stay overnight with Chuckles and go back on the train in the morning."

"We'll drive you. We'll pack a picnic lunch and then come back in the afternoon."

I was thrilled. The thought of entertaining her in my home was exciting. How often did Katharine Hepburn come to call?

I telephoned the Margessons, who were at their camp on the Canadian border.

"Oh!" said his Lordship, Frank. "You must use the Manor. I'll call Ida and have it opened for you. Show Miss Hepburn the house. Use the dishes. What a pity we won't be there!"

I then had a conference call with George Schaefer and CBS. Everything was falling into place. George and Merrill had scouted out some terrific locations in Vancouver and hired actors locally. George was very pleased with Vancouver. It was providing everything he needed.

The next morning I presented myself at Kate's door fifteen minutes before expected, which was what she expected.

Phyllis and Hilly were packing wicker baskets with cold chicken and salad makings and a fresh soup and plenty of cookies.

Kate's car was leased from Hertz, a couple of blocks away, and always at the ready for her. It wasn't anything like a limousine, but was large and roomy and black.

Hilly brought it to the front door and we packed everything in the trunk. Then Kate took her accustomed place in front beside Hilly, the better to monitor his driving. I think of myself as an awful back-seat driver, a terrible nag, but I'm not a patch on Kate. She was forever firing instructions at Hilly, often contradictory.

"Turn right here. No, left! No, *right!*"

It was no wonder that Hilly sometimes went mad and had what Kate called "fits."

I feel about Kate the same way I feel about Virginia Woolf. After reading Woolf I find everything heightened, enhanced: the grass is greener, the sky is bluer, life is more interesting. The same thing happened when I spent time with Kate. She found everything so interesting. Although it could get to be a bit much.

"What is that?" she'd say, as we drove.

"That's a barn, Kate."

"Really! How fascinating! And what is that?"

"That's a hill."

"Fascinating!"

Everything was fascinating. She'd spent her life making Katharine Hepburn fascinating—to bore was the inabsolvable sin—and everything about her had to be fascinating, too. I wasn't sure that a herd of cows standing in a pasture were all that fascinating, but her interest and enthusiasm were appealing. And, on the whole, contagious. Maybe a herd of cows standing in a field is fascinating.

I took them on the scenic route, through New Paltz and up over Mohonk Mountain, which houses a thousand acres "forever wild, forever free," as well as the famous Mohonk Mountain House, a vast Victorian hotel two or three miles off the road.

Kate had to see it, of course, so we turned off the road and presented ourselves to the guard at the gate. He wanted ten dollars before he'd let us go in.

"Show your famous face," I advised Kate.

"We just want to drive through," she said, smiling out the window at him. It didn't mean a thing. I don't think he'd ever seen a movie.

Phyllis, meanwhile, had found her purse and peeled off a sawbuck. Like the Queen of England, Kate never carried money. That was Phyllis's job.

We drove through the wilderness, up to the formal gardens, past the enormous hotel with its astonishing view of the countryside below, out through the wilderness again.

"Fascinating," said Kate. "Fascinating."

As we drove up the curving drive to my house at Ridgely—"my" estate—they were enchanted.

"Oh, how lovely!" said Phyllis.

I knew Kate would love everything about the place. It was the real thing—not bogus, as Kate would say—built by Frank's grandfather, an American merchant prince of the nineteenth century. The great oak trees, the sweeping lawns, the Prophet's Pine—a sacred tree planted by one of the Swamis at the turn of the century and considered, by me, to be magical—the beautiful manor and my own rambling Casino House, all combined to form a special place that seemed removed from time.

Kate swept through my house, investigating every nook and cranny. I knew she'd be crazy about the huge living room with its thirty-foot stone fireplace.

"Gore Vidal made his last political speech in this room," I told her, "at least, I assume it was his last political speech."

"Really!"

She wasn't above criticizing, of course. "Get rid of that," she'd say, pointing to a vase of artificial flowers. Kate hated artificial flowers, whereas I, having stayed in Julie Harris's house in Cape Cod where she made marvelously effective use of artificial flowers, liked to mix the real with the, er, bogus.

When she came to the master bedroom in the guest wing—out at the end of the former bowling alleys—she said, "This is where I'll sleep when I come to stay."

And it was.

I closed up the house in mid-October and went into New York to have lunch with Kate and George and Merrill before flying to the coast.

By that time, they were all very cozy. Kate bombarded them with questions, about the coming production, having apparently learned at MGM to check everything out in case no one else had.

It was all so friendly and so optimistic, I began to get nervous. Despite Kate's intruding into every aspect of the production—"I'm a buttinsky," she would cheerfully admit—we were all enjoying it and, so far, all having fun. Forgive me, but I think it began with the script.

Everybody seemed to feel very secure with the script, despite the endless suggestions for improvements and additions. It was solid. It was romantic. It was stylish. It was tailored to Kate — perhaps shamelessly — as I knew her. It was something we all felt we would be proud of.

There was, however, the day Kate came up to Stone Ridge for that picnic lunch.

They were in the car and about to go down the driveway, when Kate suddenly rolled her window down and, looking out at me, said, "Are you satisfied with the title?"

"Well, I guess so," I said, "unless you've come up with something better."

"You don't think," she said, "just *Margaret Delafield?*"

Without realizing what I was saying, I said, "You mean like *Grace Quigley?*"

"*Drive on*, Hilly! *Drive on!*" she cried and down the road they went.

There was no further discussion about the title.

In the week I stayed in Los Angeles before flying to Vancouver, I had ample time to ponder what I had wrought.

The production of *Delafield* would ultimately cost somewhere between three and four million dollars. Lives were being uprooted. Katharine Hepburn reported by telephone that she and Phyllis were in a state of "frenzy" getting ready for the trip and perilously close to "madness." People were arranging itineraries and closing flats and seeking plant-waterers.

Sitting alone in my corner in upstate New York, I had created this "thing." One had, I concluded, to be pretty careful what one created: it might get produced.

On the other hand, I thought of the work I was providing for cast, crews, technicians, publicists. Nor did I exclude myself with my healthy stipend as writer and coproducer. All rather pleasant. All to the good, so long as we came up with a decent picture.

A limousine pulled up on the evening of October 23. The driver leaped out and helped me with my luggage. I sank into the cushy back seat, stretched my legs out, and sighed contentedly as the luxurious car took me to the airport. Whatever else might happen, it was time for a little luxury. We were television folks and we were "in production."

Adie Luraschi, George Schaefer's venerable assistant of many years, joined George and Merrill and me as we flew to Canada, consuming several congratulatory cocktails en route.

It was raining when we landed in Vancouver—only a soft, poetic drizzle, really—but, dark and damp though it was, I knew I liked Vancouver.

As we pulled up outside the Pacific Palisades Hotel, I saw an old friend, Kevin McCarthy, coming out of the lobby. When we got to the reservation desk, Don Ameche was standing there chatting. And Jayne Meadows stepped out of the elevator as we got on. I felt as if I hadn't left Hollywood.

There were, I was to discover, twenty-four productions in the works at that time in Vancouver. One could hardly go to a restaurant without running into a famous face.

Miss Hepburn's face, however, was not to be among them, at least for a couple of days—not that she ever went to restaurants. Kate and Phyllis's later arrival gave us time to pave the way for her entry into Vancouver.

She wouldn't stay in a hotel. Going in and out of hotel lobbies was a "nightmare" for her, she said. Consequently, we—I mean, the staff— had located an apartment in a small, select apartment building in the attractive West End, close to Stanley Park. The greatest difficulty had been, oddly enough, finding one with a fireplace in Vancouver. I would have thought all apartments in Vancouver had fireplaces, but apparently they were rare.

Kate's apartment had to be large and airy and sunny, with two bedrooms and two bathrooms, since Phyllis would be living with her.

Kate had also sent a list of things with which the lodgings must be equipped upon her arrival. It was a practical list that covered everything from cooking utensils to tea to toilet paper. I added a bottle of scotch on my own.

When I saw the apartment, however, I knew it wouldn't do. It was smallish and looked right into the windows of the neighboring apartment building. She wouldn't have had a moment's privacy. Luckily, there was a second apartment on the same floor, actually larger and with a view of the mountains. I made an instant decision and had her moved—cooking utensils, tea, toilet paper and all. It was chancy. If she came and liked the first one better, I'd be in the soup, but I thought I knew Kate. Even I wouldn't have stayed in the first one.

I called her that night in New York and told her what I'd done. She wasn't entirely happy about it, probably not trusting anyone's judgment other than her own, but she'd see what the situation was when she got there.

I told her we'd done the final casting and found the last of the locations and it was all wonderful. I knew she'd see about that, too, when she got there. She'd see about everything.

"Have a good flight," I said, but she'd already hung up. Kate's telephone calls often ended as abruptly as they began. "Hello" seemed to her superfluous and a terrible waste of time. She launched right into whatever she wanted to say. God help you, too, if you called "just to chat." None of that. Have something important to say or don't call.

(She was one of three actresses I knew who sounded terrifying on the telephone before you identified yourself. Martha Scott was another. And, strangely, the warmhearted Julie Harris was the third. They all sounded like Gorgons until they knew who you were and what you wanted.)

Lesser mortals, meaning the other actors, were transported from the airport to their hotels by minibus, but Miss Hepburn and Phyllis were greeted with a white Rolls-Royce. Miss Hepburn wheeled her luggage out by herself, accepting no help. I expected her appearance to make more of a stir in the airport, but apparently, distinctive as she was, people couldn't believe that the little old lady (forgive me, Kate!) pushing her own luggage cart could be Katharine Hepburn.

"You follow us," she told me as she and Phyllis got into the Rolls. "We'll see you at the apartment."

By the time I got there she had already checked out the other apartment and was satisfied with what she had, thank God!

We had a drink.

"Dead!" Kate kept saying, "just dead!" She was referring to their condition and, at the same time, she was building a fire in the fireplace and laughing.

The next day was Sunday and I thought she might like to rest up, but not Kate. She wanted to check out all the locations—her house, the neighbor's house, the doctor's apartment—everything. We would meet in the morning and get an early start.

I met Denholm Elliott and his wife at the airport, too, and was surprised by my reaction to him. I had been a fan of British films for decades and, I might add, of Denholm since first seeing him in *The Holly and the Ivy*. Why I had thought he had no snap, crackle, pop I can't explain. Coming upon him, face to face, I felt a lovely link with all that was fine and good in English theatre and film. I felt proud that he had come.

They moved into the suite above me at the hotel and through the night I could hear their footsteps on the ceiling. Vancouver was hardly just around the corner from Marrakesh, but they didn't seem to be tired.

Indeed, they seemed to be dancing.

"I don't rehearse," Kate had told George. "Spencer and I never rehearsed." Hard to argue with her, given the work she and Tracy turned out, but George had the luxury, rare in television, of four days of rehearsal time and he proposed to use them. Kate protested, but then gave in gracefully and thoroughly enjoyed, I think, those four days.

But first came the reading of the script with the cast assembled for the purpose of meeting one another and Miss Hepburn.

It took place in a "rehearsal room" of the Ryerson United Church in Vancouver. Churches have large rooms that serve beautifully for rehearsing, and they don't mind at all taking a lucrative bite out of the television pie.

These first readings are always a bit nerve-racking, especially for the author, but when they involve a major star there is an added electricity to the occasion. Stars like Kate know they're stars and understand exactly how to behave in this situation, which is to be reasonably friendly and (in Kate's case) funny and utterly professional. At the table, they know who sits where.

"You sit next to me," she told me when I started to sit someplace else. I had hoped to sit apart, removed, as it were, as if I had nothing to do with it.

So we sat together and looked over the cast. They were all pretty excited. To sit in a room and hear Katharine Hepburn read a role for the first time is an event. You feel you're with the Big Time, some of them for the first time, some for the last. At any rate, it is a moment to remember.

Kate and I whispered to each other, huddled, as the cast watched every move we made. I'll never forget David Ogden Stiers watching us, amused, his eyes twinkling.

George took over, introducing everyone including Miss Hepburn, which got a big laugh. He started the reading and it was going very well until we got to the part of Chipper, Kate's son in the film. I had described him as a "blond, blue-eyed Wasp." It was being read by an actor named John Shea, who read beautifully, but he was as dark and Semitic-looking as John Pleshette, who was playing the doctor's son. There was no contrast at all.

Kate and I exchanged a glance. And then another. As the reading continued, we became truly alarmed. By the time it ended, we were in a state of panic. John Shea, good as he was, was all wrong!

"Call me when you get home!" Kate hissed at me as she rushed for her car.

I hurried to the hotel. The reading couldn't have gone better and I knew the script would work, but this piece of casting was a disaster and could sink us.

Kate was right by the telephone.

"What shall we do?" I asked her.

"You call Merrill and I'll call George. Then you call George and I'll call Merrill. I've got cast approval. This won't do. He looks more Jewish than the Jewish kids do. How could they have done this? What in the world got into them?"

I called Merrill.

"Merrill," I said, "Kate and I feel that . . ." I always prefaced any argument with "Kate and I feel . . ." I wasn't born yesterday. I knew who had the clout. "Kate and I feel that John Shea won't do. He looks more Jewish than the Jewish kids do."

"He isn't Jewish," said Merrill. "He's Irish."

"Black Irish!" I said, "Practically a gypsy! We need a blond, blue-eyed Wasp!"

"Well, we couldn't get Charles Frank, the one we wanted. The network wouldn't let us use him."

"Why not?"

"He was in some flops."

God, I thought, the networks punish the actors for the flops they put them in!

We went back and forth with our little debate. Merrill, I could see, was wavering. If Miss Hepburn wasn't happy . . .

George was more stubborn. He assured me that John Shea was perfectly cast and would be splendid in the role. He was Irish.

I had dinner with Adie Luraschi and the Conwells in Puffins, the hotel dining room, my mind in turmoil. My movie was about to be destroyed before it began by one horrible casting error.

Hilly wandered in.

Kate and Phyllis retired early, about 9:00, so after that he was free and had the car. Did I want to go for a ride? See Vancouver at night?

"She's really beside herself," he said of Kate as he drove. "Some kind of casting problem."

"Really?" I said.

I was awakened the next morning by an early call from Merrill.

John Shea was out and Charles Frank was flying up from Los Angeles this morning, and I wouldn't believe how it had come about.

As it turned out, I didn't, and I still find it hard to believe.

When Merrill got back to his suite after dinner, he'd had a call from John Shea's agent, who had terrible news. There was a conflict in John's schedule and he had to go to Paris right away and—John felt awful about it—he wouldn't be able to do our movie.

"Oh, come on, Merrill," I said. "You're making that up. He saw that he was wrong for the part at the reading and he's . . ."

"No, no, I think it's really true. I talked to the network right away and said we're in a bind and have to have Charlie Frank so they gave in."

"Sometimes," I said, "there's God so quickly!"

"Ain't it the truth!" sighed Merrill.

At rehearsal that morning, there was John Shea all apologetic and so sorry he'd let us down. A really nice man.

"It's all right, John," I said, managing to look only slightly pained. "You must go, of course. You had a prior commitment. I understand the mix-up. I know what agents are."

"You're swell," he said.

Kate was delighted, but she was wary. She had yet to see Charles Frank. She needn't have worried.

Just before we broke for lunch, in walked a blond, blue-eyed Wasp named Charles Frank. She and I exchanged a look and I think we both heaved a great sigh. And even the network apologized to us when they saw his wonderful performance. I hope they apologized to him.

George always napped during the lunch hour.

Merrill went off to do business.

Kate disappeared into her dressing room. (She would not have a trailer, like other stars, and much of her interest in locations had to do with a proper dressing room and hideaway for her. Preferably with a fireplace.)

I found myself walking down the street toward a shopping area and ran into Denholm Elliott. We chanced upon a small neighborhood restaurant and lunched together.

Denholm told me that he had first taken up acting as a prisoner of war in Germany during World War II. The prisoners were unshackled in the wings, went onstage to perform, and then were reshackled as they came off. It seemed to me there must have been easier ways to catch the acting bug—Lee Strasberg wasn't that bad—but it had done the trick. Denholm couldn't wait to be released and get into the profession.

I told him about my friend, Iggie Wolfington, who was an aspiring actor and also caught in the war. Iggie says he was known as "The Fat Boy of Company B" and became something of a whiz as a soldier. And one day he was advancing against the enemy, firing away, bullets flying all around him, when he became aware that something was nagging at the back of his brain. What was it? And then he realized what it was. He had to get into Equity!

Denholm, unlike Gielgud, was delighted to be working with Miss Hepburn and also with his compatriot, Brenda Forbes.

Brenda was our socialite cast member. She was very picky about her quarters at the hotel, moved a couple of times, loved to entertain, considered her dinner parties every bit as important as her daytime work. She also had a husband—"a darling man," Kate said—back in Sneden's Landing who was dying of cancer. He had insisted she not miss this job, knowing she loved her acting, and she would fly back east on weekends to be with him. Despite her worry, she was cheerful and every bit as brilliant as Denholm in front of the camera.

They did drink a lot, those Brits, and would appear a bit fuzzy on the set the following morning and then casually do the most dazzling acting. God knows how they do it.

Dr. Kievel came into Kate's life.

Dr. Kievel owned the large, white mansion that we used as the Delafield house. Dr. Kievel was self-made, many times a millionaire, we were told, from (I think) copper mines. We were duly impressed.

Dr. Kievel also had something like ten children, all grown up and away, apparently.

"Just think of that, Kate," I kidded her. "Ten little mouths waiting to be fed, ten pairs of eyes looking up at you."

It was fun to tease Kate about Dr. Kievel, but there was no way his attraction for her could be lessened.

Because Dr. Kievel had something Kate valued above all else on earth. Dr. Kievel had an indoor swimming pool.

And he gave her carte blanche.

I suspect he really had a yen for her, as who wouldn't? He was separated from his wife, and why not go about Vancouver with Katharine Hepburn on your arm? It was never to come to that—Kate kept him at a respectable distance—but he could dream, couldn't he? He remained, as it were, dangling.

Kate's regimen was very strict during that short rehearsal period and into the filming.

The rest of us might go out partying—and there was scarcely a restaurant in that city of good restaurants that we didn't hit—but Kate went to bed with the chickens, although she liked to unwind at the end of the day's work with a little talk and a drink before the fire.

I often joined her, but only after I'd viewed the dailies with Phyllis. Kate never looked at the dailies and Phyllis was her spy. We'd sit, Phyllis and I, clutching each other and laughing or crying over the dailies as the occasion warranted, and then, as the lights came up, she'd say, "Miss Hepburn looks so young!" Or, "Oh, isn't she lovely!" Or, "My, isn't she good!" This would be reported to Miss Hepburn, who consequently was in a state of continual euphoria.

One night, I remember, I got busy and neglected to inform Kate of my reaction to the dailies.

I got a very strong phone call.

"What's the matter? Why didn't you call me? What's *wrong*? Aren't the dailies any good?"

I had to reassure her that the dailies were great. Happily, the dailies did always seem to be great.

She got up at the crack of dawn and lay in bed with her breakfast tray going over the day's work. She was always prepared when she came on the set, having worked out every gesture, every nuance of the scene. I never knew an actress who did her homework more thoroughly.

Kate didn't have to tell me the script was good—otherwise would she have been there?—but we both felt there was something missing as the film went on.

When she had an afternoon off, I went home with her and we sat in front of the fire trying to figure out what was lacking. We kicked some ideas around, but they didn't seem right. And then it hit me.

"You know, Kate," I said, "I'd like to see a scene where Margaret Delafield isn't so damn fabulous, so damn sure of herself. I'd like to see her a little vulnerable."

We both thought that was it, and I went home to write just a scene. It was a joy to do. And, as it turned out, it became a sort of love letter from me to the legendary Katharine Hepburn:

Dr. Elias is talking to a scared Mrs. Delafield, who's appeared unexpectedly at his apartment. She'd made her big decision, decided to marry him, announced it to her family, was ready for a new life—but now she didn't know who she was. She was scared.

He tells her he was scared, too, but then, "I decided there was something more important to me than Dr. Marvin Elias . . . even more important than my work, which is important."

"What?" she asks.

"Your needing me. I happen to know that the elegant Mrs. Delafield . . . the strong, remarkable Mrs. Delafield . . . I know that she needs to be held by arms a little stronger than her own . . . kissed with a certain regularity . . . and told not that she is remarkable, but that she is loved."

That was exactly what I felt about Kate.

Where was Spencer Tracy when she needed him?

Not unexpectedly in Vancouver, it rained a great deal, and at one point we got a little behind schedule—but on the whole, *Mrs. Delafield Wants to Marry* was a charmed production.

As Kate was later to say on a documentary made about the filming, "When someone in a commanding position is having a good time, then everybody tends to have a good time."

And the someone in our commanding position was apparently having a good time.

It's difficult to tell, though. I thought Elizabeth Taylor, for instance, was having a fairly miserable time making *Return Engagement*, but she later thanked me profusely.

I wasn't sure that Kate was having such a wonderful experience. She was a terrible busybody—poking into everything, rearranging this, changing that—and it hardly seemed like fun. What I'd forgotten was that I was providing her with something she had, perhaps, thought never to find again—a romantic lead. She was a woman being courted. She was a woman in love. She was as giddy and excited as a girl of sixteen—Margaret Delafield, I mean. She felt desirable and sexy and youthful, our Miss Hepburn. It was a great gift. And when, to this day, she signs something for me it's "with affection and gratitude." The word *love* Miss Hepburn doesn't toss about lightly.

She had no trouble remembering lines—a terrible curse for aging actors—in *Delafield*, although she sometimes revised a little.

I remember an afternoon we were filming a scene and she left out one small phrase—not important really, except to me—and I went right up to her.

"Kate," I said, "Kate, you've left something out here and, you see, if you leave that out it ruins the rhythm of the line. You see?"

She looked daggers at me.

"God forbid," she said flatly, "I should ruin the rhythm of the line!"

And I thought, what am I doing? Who do I think I'm talking to? I'm explaining to Katharine Hepburn about the rhythm of the line?

But playwrights are like that.

One of the many reasons I love Julie Harris is that she never alters so much as a syllable of the playwright's words. The continual battle to get one's lines spoken as they are written can be wearing, I assure you.

A case in point is an almost hysterical letter that Enid Bagnold wrote to Dame Judith Anderson. Poor Enid in her home in England was several thousand miles removed from Los Angeles, where Norman Lloyd was producing her play, *The Chinese Prime Minister*, on Hollywood Television Theatre. Judith was starring in it.

But Norman had gotten to Enid with the appalling news that Dame Judith couldn't possibly say the word *fornicated*, which was importantly placed in her last line of dialogue. Poor Enid (as I always think of her) rushed to the typewriter and fired off the following to Dame Judith Anderson.

June 22, 1974

Dear Dame Judith—

You remember you came to see me here with Cathleen? You got your stockings wet in Brighton in a storm and Cathleen popped you onto the electric blanket in her room so that you should meet me *dry*. I am taken aback to hear how naughty you are about *fornicated*. You mustn't take away words like that, my dear—you a great actress. Edith made the same rumpus over *violated* in *The Chalk Garden*—but I said (and I say again) "Can't you *feel* that it has four syllables—it's charming—say it like your favorite sweet—slowly—with all your beats equally stressed—but gently—as though you loved it." And she did. Edith is both a genius and a goose (as she says herself—at least the "goose") —but from what I remember of your penetrating eyes and the way you spoke you are not a goose. Alas I haven't seen you ever on the stage. I *hope* you are a genius. I am very much banking on your being one because I have another play coming.

I would never have put *fornicated* in the last line of the play without weighing it with all the minute care I give, so slowly, painfully listening with my ear cocked—if I hadn't *deeply* wanted it. Listen—think of saying it sweetly—regretfully—over the lost poet—Bent—slowly—a requiem— with all four syllables drifting out—"Ah Bent—Oh Bent"—(slight pause as she weighs up the sadness—the sweet sadness because at the same time she knows how the world fails to make its great points through the frailties of its faults) —"if you hadn't drunk and you hadn't fornicated (all in one go, and gently) what a poet you'd have been!"

Don't say "Oh, these damned authors—how they think they can teach us—who have been all our lives at it!" because, God knows, I am *not* trying to teach *you*—I am only explaining to you how *I* dwelt over the lines. If you were to throw out that word I could hardly believe it of you—who must know the poets so well. This play—perhaps you have found already—is written in a hidden poetic form. Dear Dame—please—for my sake—who am no Dame—but am eighty-four and have dealt with words since I was nine (in the coffee bushes of Jamaica) —please don't belittle my last line—please—I trust you to carry the whole play—and many many people in America have seen it on Broadway and would get to know that the word was funked as once dear Gladys nearly funked the false teeth line in the opening nights of *The Chalk Garden*—and then *didn't*.

Yours *most* anxiously, Enid

Whether Dame Judith's heart was touched and she complied, I can't remember. But you see the lengths to which we desperate playwrights will go to keep our dialogue intact.

I was later to engage in the same battle with one of my favorite people, that other dame, Wendy Hiller. She was preparing to do my play, *Laughter in the Shadow of the Trees*, on the BBC, but claimed she could not possibly utter the word *lesbian*. I toyed with *sappho* and other unlikely alternatives, but ultimately the director and I decided to give that line to her costar, Sir John Gielgud. He said it with relish.

We didn't have a Halloween party because it was the night before the first day of shooting, but we celebrated everything else.

I gave a party in my hotel suite for the cast and crew to which Kate didn't come.

Merrill had a birthday so a few of us joined him and Suzy at the Georgian Court Hotel for a rather grand dinner. Kate went home to bed instead.

Adie Luraschi had a birthday and we celebrated that without Miss Hepburn. (Kate, needless to say, wasn't big on birthdays.)

Kate did, though, like to have a few people in for drinks and dinner if she wasn't too tired and the day ahead didn't look too exhausting. We'd have drinks in front of the fire, of course, and I'd slyly urge her to tell about MGM and the "early days." She told the stories so well and they were what we all wanted to hear. Hilly and Phyllis would whip up a splendid meal and then cookies and coffee and out. Hilly would drive anyone home who needed transportation and then, I suspect, go out on the town in search of much-needed recreation away from The Boss.

Hilly was, by the way, the cause of the only blowup I ever witnessed from Kate, and it was terrifying.

Kate was very fond of Hilly and certain that he was extremely talented as a painter and a songwriter. She was right. And when I came up with a kind of hippie wedding for Dr. Elias and Mrs. Delafield, I wanted all sorts of "entertainment" outside the church as family and friends gathered for the wedding: jugglers, belly dancers, a rock-and-roll singer.

Hilly wrote a song for the rock-and-roll singer.

Kate said, "You must hear Hilly's song. It's great!"

I heard it and it was. We decided to use it. Kate was excited and I was excited and Hilly was, as always, indecisive. He wasn't sure it was that good and did we really want to use his song? We did.

So we went into a recording studio one morning while Kate was filming at Casa Mia, the enormous house we'd rented that served (internally) as her house, her church, the doctor's synagogue, and a gentlemen's club.

I stayed in the recording studio long enough to see that it was going well and then waved to Hilly and went out to the Casa Mia. Kate, working away, saw me come in, but we didn't get a chance to talk. She assumed, apparently, that the recording session was over. Her eyes were bothering her, as they often did, and she needed her eyedrops. Hilly, however, had her eyedrops with him.

When he finally appeared an hour later, she exploded. I mean, literally exploded. I have never heard such a voice. I have never witnessed such power out of a human being. The very walls of the house shook and everybody, everybody disappeared instantly as she laid into Hilly.

She said, where had he been? She said, she was fed up! She said, I'm not going to put up with it anymore!

Hilly, ashen, ran from the room, presumably to get the eyedrops.

I'd run from the room long before that, scared to death. We all huddled outside, that's how incredible was the explosion. It was impossible when one considered that it came from a woman pushing eighty years of age.

I thought that might be the end of Hilly, but later in the day he was his old self—as was Kate.

"When she gets mad," he said, "she's always sorry after."

Kate told Merrill she wanted to give a party for everybody after work on Thanksgiving Day, the day before she completed filming.

An invitation was circulated that read: PLEASE COME AND JOIN ME FOR A DRINK (ON SET, AFTER WORK) BEFORE YOU GO HOME TO CELEBRATE THANKSGIVING! —KATHARINE HEPBURN.

She wrote a check to cover it for $400. The party, Merrill later informed me, came to something like $1,200, but who was about to point this out to the star?

I got there late, for some reason, having assumed that Miss Hepburn wouldn't even be there, but there she was, and a bit put-out that I was late. She was drinking and mingling and generally having a fine time. That the cast and crew adored her goes without saying. Would they ever have another such experience in their lives?

After that, the rest of us went to a dinner party at a place called Hy's Mansion for a proper American Thanksgiving dinner. Kate popped in early and popped out early, not drinking or eating, anxious to get to bed.

At noon the next day, we broke to have a group photograph taken of cast, crew, star, producers, all of us. This is always a heartwarming moment, the moment when we are closest as family, I think. Everybody wants that picture on their wall.

But there was a further surprise in store for the cast and crew.

Merrill had conferred with Kate and they'd come up with the perfect present for us all. Kate chose her favorite still from the shoot—Margaret Delafield in ragged clothes doing the weeding in her garden—

and signed them individually for each member of the cast and crew. They were put in gold frames and were to be handed out at the wrap party. It was additional work for Kate, but she didn't hesitate.

On that final afternoon, we shot her last scene in the doctor's kitchen. I got teary. As she said the last line and George said, "Print it!," I rushed up to Kate and kissed her on the cheek. So did George. So would everyone, had they dared.

As she went up the stairs, she said something I didn't understand at the time.

"Now, don't ruin it," she said. I was only to learn later in the editing room that she knew what she was talking about.

And then I heard her voice coming from her dressing room.

"I just think we've had a lot of fun," she said.

Kate and Phyllis flew to Victoria while Hilly and Kate's hairdresser, Ray Gow, drove the car down the coast to Los Angeles. They would all meet there, where Kate was planning to film a documentary at MGM on Spencer Tracy.

The rest of us finished filming and had a whale of a wrap party at Jonathan's Seafood Restaurant on a pier on Granville Island, a party that had an oddly Christmas motif given that it was only November 30.

Robert Sidley, who played Digby in the film, appeared as Santa Claus and handed out the photographs, thrilling even the drivers with their personalized "thank you" from Katharine Hepburn.

We all got very drunk and congratulated ourselves on a job well done.

I flew to Los Angeles and immediately came down with a sore throat and various ailments I couldn't give in to while we were in production.

I arose a week later to escort Dame Judith Anderson to a large Christmas bash the producers of her soap, *Santa Barbara*, were throwing. Dame Judith had an uneasy relationship with them—most of her relationships were uneasy—but she liked her fellow cast members and we tried to have fun. As entertainment, they had a pickpocket who was terrifying. He handed me my wristwatch, which he'd taken without my noticing. Why he wasn't out working Hollywood Boulevard I couldn't imagine.

Kate, meanwhile, had spent time with friends in Victoria and had flown down to Los Angeles with Phyllis. They were housed in the Hal Wallis mansion in Holmby Hills, while Mrs. Wallis was off in Palm Springs.

"Come on over for lunch," she said. "I've got something I want to read to you."

The Wallis mansion was impressive, to say the least. I entered, as instructed, through the kitchen, ushered in by a Chinese couple who appeared to speak no English.

Kate was in fine fettle and enjoyed showing me around the house, pointing out the art collection on the walls, which was awesome.

She and Phyllis gave me a glass of wine and then Kate sat down to read me the "something."

"It's a letter I've written to Spence," she said. "Tell me what you think of it. I thought I'd open the documentary with it."

She sat at a small table, as I remember, and I stood over her as she read the letter.

I was in tears at the end. It was so personal and so loving, I found it hard to believe that Kate would share that with anyone, let alone millions of television viewers. But she was opening up more these days.

"I think it's wonderful," I said, "absolutely wonderful. But you can't open with that, Kate. That's what you close with." Which is what she did and for anyone watching that terrific documentary, it was an extraordinary moment.

After lunch, prepared by the accommodating Chinese, we went over the stills of *Delafield*. Kate had picture approval and was crossing out the ones she wouldn't permit to be circulated.

"Here's a good one of you and me," she said, handing it to me. "Take it now or you'll never get it."

Hilly had the day off—a much-needed (every day off for Hilly was much-needed) day with friends—but the next day he drove them on a nostalgic tour of Los Angeles. Kate wanted to see the various houses she had lived in from her first days in Hollywood. She surprised several current occupants in the process.

Noel Taylor invited Kate and Phyllis to dinner a few nights later— that is, he invited us to his friend Adnan Karabay's place for dinner.

I'd been to Adnan's apartment several times. It was in a very middle-class neighborhood around the corner from the May Company on Wilshire Boulevard, and it was a very ordinary apartment, but Adnan is a great decorator and the place was so fabulously decorated and furnished it was ultimately photographed for *Architectural Digest*. I knew Kate would like it, although I couldn't imagine her eating his food.

Adnan would always disappear in the middle of the cocktail hour and return a few minutes later with a large parcel from the Chinese restaurant next door. He would then empty the cartons in the kitchen and serve them at table in exquisite bowls.

"You can't do that to Kate," I told Noel and Adnan. "You know how careful she is. She isn't going to eat food out of cartons from a Chinese restaurant." I thought that might stop them.

It was arranged that Hilly, who had yet another night off and looked a full ten years younger, would drop Kate and Phyllis at my apartment, and I'd drive them in my car to Adnan's.

We passed Rage, an enormous gay bar with all the doors thrown open, music blasting out, red lights, and hundreds of young men milling about.

"What's that?" asked Kate.

"It's an intimate little supper club," I said.

"Oh, yeah?" said she.

She was crazy about Adnan's apartment. "Fascinating," she kept saying, of course.

I was horrified when Adnan excused himself and went next door.

Well, she loved it. She just loved it. She didn't mind sitting up at the dining room table like a real human being, and she dug right in to the Chinese food. It was a very successful dinner party.

As we were leaving, one of the tenants from upstairs was coming in the front door. He found himself face to face with Miss Hepburn.

"Oh, my God!" he said. "My *God!*"

"Nice to have seen you," said Kate, sweeping out.

1986

Early in January I saw a rough cut of *Delafield* and decided to kill myself.

It couldn't have been worse. What I didn't know at that time was that all rough cuts look terrible. *Citizen Kane* probably looked awful in rough cut.

I almost called Kate in New York, but why depress her? George, however, seemed quite happy and was now settling down to some serious editing. A young man named Andy Blumenthal would be the editor. I wondered if he could save the mess I'd created.

I tried to go on with my life.

One night I again escorted Dame Judith, this time to Emlyn Williams's performance as Charles Dickens at the Westwood Playhouse.

We had dinner with Williams later at Louise Sorel's. He was well into his eighties and she was almost ninety, but at 1:00 A.M. he had a tumbler of gin and she had a tumbler of vodka and they were merry as grigs. I, who wasn't drinking at all, was so tired I was weaving as if in a high wind.

A couple of weeks later, they showed me a new cut of *Delafield*. It was a different film, but there was still something wrong. It seemed to go backwards at one point. Then George and I realized that a whole segment had to come out.

I had a long scene with Kate and Hal coming out of a movie house and going to his car, which wouldn't start. She fixed it, just as she had fixed Spencer's. But what the scene was about was Kate trying to get him to propose to her. "See," was the gist of it, "you need me and why don't you ask me to marry you?" It made him look foolish and her look bossy. And we had already gone beyond that. We cut it.

(It was a very funny scene, though, and they played it brilliantly, so I hope it's preserved somewhere.)

The next time I saw *Mrs. Delafield Wants to Marry*, I came dancing out of the screening room. "It was great!" I shouted.

Peter Matz had created his usual beautiful musical score, and I defy any screenwriter to see his movie being scored, to hear that full orchestra under his scenes for the first time, and not get a thrill.

We mixed the score and the sound effects for four days at 20th Century-Fox, and on the evening of February 21 I came home and opened a bottle of champagne, but not before I had called Kate in New York.

"It's finished!" I told her, a little tearfully.

"Are you pleased?"

"Oh, Kate, Kate!" I said, "It's wonderful! You're wonderful!"

"Well, you wrote the script," she said.

Invitations were sent out, and in mid-March we rented the Directors Guild Theatre and had a screening for eight hundred people. Kate didn't fly out, but she sent her emissary and great friend, Cynthia McFadden, a lovely young woman whom we looked upon as the "new" Barbara Walters.

Brenda Forbes flew out, too, and we partied at the Bel Age Hotel before going to the theatre.

At this time I'd had three plays produced on Broadway, and had played the Kennedy Center three times, twice in the Eisenhower Theatre, and once in the Opera House, but I can honestly say that the evening we showed *Mrs. Delafield Wants to Marry* at the Directors Guild was the one evening in my career I'd like to relive over and over again.

Everybody I cared about was there, from "little" Patrick Duffy—now a big star in *Dallas*—to Dame Judith Anderson and Charlotte Rae and Ernest Thompson, and Dr. Frederick Elias, on whom I had patterned Kate's betrothed. (I was especially concerned that Freddy like it and he did; alas, he died shortly thereafter.)

I called Kate the next morning and described every lovely moment. She had her own smaller screening in New York, not that she attended it. (She claims never to have seen her films, and I almost believe her.) But she did invite every member of the audience to her home after the showing for a party. I couldn't believe it. The Margessons, Lord and Lady and the Honorable Sarah, were among the guests, and said that everybody on the warm evening walked crosstown to Kate's house on East Forty-ninth Street. Stephen Sondheim's man had done the food, and there was plenty of booze and a very sociable Katharine Hepburn wanting to hear all about the film. They lavished her with praise.

"You should have been here," she told me on the telephone the next day. "They seem to think the movie's good!"

It was good, and when it aired on Easter night, I think everybody loved it, with the exception of the *Los Angeles Times* critic Howard Rosenberg, who wrote the only bad review of *Delafield* I ever read. He seemed to resent the Jewishness of it.

(This was fascinating to me. I'd thought I was striking a blow against prejudice, but in Vancouver the Jewish religious hierarchy hated the screenplay and wouldn't let us film anywhere near the synagogue. And the Salvation Army said "no way!" when I wanted the wedding ceremony performed by a Salvation Army captain. Who's prejudiced now?)

The ratings were sensational, in the top ten for the week, and CBS was delighted.

But what was I going to do next?

I wanted to do a television film called *The Hollywood Girls* using ex-MGM stars like June Allyson, Debbie Reynolds, Cyd Charisse, and Ann Miller, but I couldn't seem to get a network commitment.

I had breakfast with Richard Dreyfuss at Le Moustache in Westwood. I loved Richard Dreyfuss and was dying to work with him, but his somewhat vague idea about something having to do with the Constitution of the United States of America never came to anything. (He'd forgotten his wallet, and I wanted to pick up the tab, but he wouldn't hear of it. The restaurant staff seemed to know who he was, and would trust him.)

Peter Frankovich, who was now head of miniseries at CBS, called me in, sat me down, and brought out a large notebook.

"What would you like to do?" he said. Was I interested in John Wilkes Booth's story? They could maybe give me the Carradine brothers. I shrugged.

Or Sean Connery in a western series? I shrugged.

Or rewrite a script called *Conquistador*? About Cortez and Montezuma? I told him I thought it was one of the great stories, but not for me.

Well, how about Raquel Welch as Libby Holman? I perked up. I'd wanted to do the Libby Holman story for a long time. I told him I was interested. Good, he said. Would I meet with Raquel when I was in New York? I said I would.

But who knew if that would ever lead to anything?

Merrill Karpf and I pondered my future over an expensive lunch. We discussed and discarded any number of ideas about future films.

"Why don't you do another one for Kate?" he said finally, sticking a fork into his arugula.

I flew east and spent a couple of days in Manhattan with Chuckles. Before going up to open the Stone Ridge house, I spent an evening with Kate.

After dinner, I'd talked her into going to see Lily Tomlin's new one-woman show. It had just opened on Broadway to glowing reviews and I thought she'd like it.

She wasn't keen on it.

"Lily Tomlin is your kind of woman," I told her.

Hilly drove us to the theatre. There were an awful lot of paparazzi outside the theatre, and later we learned that Meryl Streep and Barbra Streisand were also seeing the show that night, although we didn't see them.

Kate whipped through the crowd into the theatre, with me scurrying behind and Phyllis even further behind us. (We were captured on the front page of the *Daily News* the next morning, Kate holding her hand in front of her face and me in the back looking like a frightened rabbit.)

I was a great Tomlin fan and I'd loved her first one-woman show, but as the first act unfolded I gradually realized that Kate was beginning to squirm. (The rest of the audience, I might add, was screaming.) I looked at her anxiously. Had I steered her wrong?

She sighed heavily.

"Do you want to leave?" I whispered.

"I never leave," she said. (Streisand did, though, I was told, at intermission.)

Phyllis nodded off.

When intermission came, we sat quietly. The rest of the audience spent the time watching us sitting quietly.

A lady stage manager leaned over us and said, "Miss Hepburn, Miss Tomlin would be pleased, if you'd like to, if you'd come backstage after the show."

"Oh, yes, yes, of course," said Kate.

The second act was even longer than the first, and we moaned a bit.

I couldn't imagine what Kate would say to Lily Tomlin, but the minute the curtain was down we were whisked backstage and up some steps and there was Lily Tomlin coming out of her dressing room.

"Oh, Miss Hepburn," she said, "I'm so thrilled that you're here."

"Well, I'm thrilled, too," said Kate briskly, "because I did my first play in New York in this theatre . . . the Plymouth Theatre . . . it was in 1928 . . . and I'll bet I had the same dressing room you've got. Good night!"

And with that we were out, leaving Miss Tomlin standing there with a little frozen smile on her face.

In the car, on the way home, I confessed to them that I might have a new project for Kate.

"Have you got an idea?" she asked.

"I'm working on it," I said. "Wouldn't it be fun to do it again? To go back to Vancouver?" I smiled.

We all smiled.

A workman was replacing a broken windowpane somewhat noisily at the Casino House, but I didn't care. I was on page twenty-six of the treatment for the new Hepburn project.

Merrill loved the idea.

Kate would play a celebrity who for some reason must spend some time with a normal family in a normal town . . . and what would happen? (Shades of Somerset Maugham with the London slum family. It also smacked of *The Man Who Came to Dinner*, but why not steal from the best?)

I'd thought of it one day as Kate had just gone down the driveway in her car, Hilly at the wheel honking the traditional thirteen times, Kate with her hand out the window waving until they were out of sight. As always, I was exhilarated while she was there and exhausted when she'd left. I collapsed in a heap. If she could do that to me, what would it be like if Katharine Hepburn visited a "normal" family?

Kate would play Laura Lansing, a famous novelist, who makes a bet with her agent that she can spend a week with that normal family outside of New York. Levittown? What happened then, I didn't know, but I was typing away.

The family would be Mr. and Mrs. Gomphers (too obviously funny?) and I thought they'd have a girl of thirteen, a boy of eleven, and a baby. I slyly used the name Laura because of Kate's closest friend, Laura Harding, just as I'd called her Margaret in *Delafield* because of her sister, Peg. Names she liked. Subtle, but one did what one could.

I was up to page ninety—this was a long treatment—and I got lost. (I was often to get lost on this one, unlike *Delafield.*) I came to a dead stop in the plot. Introduce a new character?

I went across the lawn to the Manor House and had dinner with Lord Margesson. Frank was an astute gent when it came to the literary. I explained my plight and, as he banged his chicken breasts with a hammer on the kitchen floor, he got me back on the track.

A memorial service was held in Manhattan for Clinton Wilder, but I missed it because I was at page 112—more pages than I should have had—and the end still wasn't in sight. Why didn't I do three- or four-page treatments like sensible writers? It did help, though, I felt, to have a movie so full and detailed. When the time came, it'd make the screenplay a snap.

Television executives, however, weren't famous for their attention spans. Shorter was probably better.

I had some difficulty in coming up with a title, always an indication, I think, that there's trouble ahead. If a title comes easily, generally the piece is solid.

My friend, Bradley Slaight, finally came up with it. He suggested *Guest Appearance.* I said that was great and wondered why I hadn't thought of it. I sent him a check for $500, which surprised the hell out of him, but he was young and struggling and could use the dough and the encouragement.

When it was finished, I telephoned Kate.

"Are you pleased?" was the inevitable question. I said I was, but actually I wasn't so sure.

I drove into New York and gave a copy to my agent, Ed Robbins, as we lunched high up in the Trump Tower. I had arranged to have dinner with Kate and deliver hers, but something strange was going on in my viscera. I was feeling queasy. And then downright sick. (I should point out, lest Donald Trump die of humiliation, that it had nothing to do with lunch at the Trump Tower; it'd begun in the car driving down.)

Nevertheless, I wanted badly to see *A Room with a View*, so I trotted over to the Plaza Theatre. I became deathly ill, went twice to the men's room and upchucked and, on top of that, thought the film made no sense at all until I realized that they had shown reel one and then reel three before reel two. At six bucks a ticket it seemed a bit much.

I finally gave in completely to my illness and went back downstairs to the lounge and telephoned Kate's house.

"Phyllis," I said when she answered the telephone, "I'm ill, really ill! Can I come right over and lie down?"

"Oh, yes," she said, "yes, you must!"

I honestly didn't know if I could make it, but I walked down to Forty-ninth Street and across to Second Avenue, head down, looking neither right nor left, determined not to disgrace myself.

Phyllis and Norah let me in and gave me ginger ale to settle my stomach. We sat in the kitchen while I bemoaned my terrible fate. God had given me the Curse of the Writer: a sensitive constitution. Could they understand how I suffered?

Kate's masseur was just leaving, and she was resting up in her bedroom, but when she heard I was there and ill she shouted for me to come up. I struggled up the stairs and spread out on a sofa in her bedroom as she lay in her bed and we chatted. I began immediately to feel better.

There was a framed photograph of Spencer Tracy in polo togs on the table by her bed.

I said I hoped she'd understand, but I couldn't possibly stay for dinner—the mere thought of food was too awful—but here, I thrust it at her, was her copy of *Guest Appearance*.

I kept looking at the photograph of Tracy. With the exception of an early photograph of her father, this was the only photograph of a man in her bedroom. They both looked young and fit and vital. The two men in her life.

"Hilly can drive you home," she said. "You'd better go to bed."

As I got up and stumbled out, she was opening the manila envelope.

Poor Chuckles had a sick houseguest on his hands for a day, but then I managed to drive back to Stone Ridge the next night.

Kate rang me up the following morning.

Her reaction to *Guest Appearance* was guarded, and mixed.

"I want to read it again," she said, "and then we can talk." I wasn't surprised at her reaction. I always expected, with *Guest Appearance*, to be stopped at some point. Kate would say no, or the network would say they weren't interested, or George wouldn't want to do it, Merrill wouldn't like it . . . somewhere along the line I would be stopped. We were all so eager to repeat the happy experience of *Delafield*, however, nobody ever said the expected no, even when the going really got tough.

George liked it. Merrill liked it. Even NBC, the network we were now dealing with, liked it, with some reservations. At any rate, the important thing was that Kate liked it.

I was too sick to care while the flu bug had me. I just wanted to die.

Merrill flew into New York, conferred with Kate, and then came up on the bus partly to discuss *Guest Appearance* and partly to see Ridgely, "our" estate.

We sat on the porch and discussed *Guest Appearance* as Rusty drove around us on his mowing machine. It was a given there that if one had guests and wished to sit on the porch and talk, Rusty would appear with his deafening mower. Rusty was one of the locals whom God had put on this earth, apparently, just to mow. He seemed to love it. He mowed in a state of bliss.

Kate, I discovered, had been a bit more blunt with Merrill than she had been with me. She "hated" the ending, she didn't like Laura's relationship with the old man—I had given her, in my desperation, a kind of relationship with an old neighbor—and she thought that Melody Gomphers was the better part.

I expected that.

We clearly didn't have a "go" with her.

When they'd parted, she had said exactly what she'd said to me: "Let me think about it and reread it again."

Kate was no fool. She was being cautious. And yet she wanted to go back to Vancouver as much as the rest of us.

But my heart sank.

I also knew there was something else in the works as far as Kate was concerned. She had written a screenplay called *Me and Phyllis* and Merrill, in tandem with Joe Levine, was a part of that. It was their other project.

Kate had given me the script to read. It was odd, very odd. It was All About Kate and she would play herself, but they wanted another major star to play Phyllis. And Kate, always thinking big, meant it as a feature film. Very odd.

I called her and said as tactfully as possible that I thought there was an awful lot about *Me* and not very much about *Phyllis*. She took it well, and actually wrote a couple of new scenes in which we would learn a little something about Phyllis's feelings, but it still seemed to me a kind of vanity production.

However, it had top priority with her and I knew it. There were rumblings that ABC was interested, and she might consider doing it for television, but that ultimately fell through. Joe Levine continued to treat it as a feature and offered the role of Phyllis to the likes of Maggie Smith. The likes of Maggie Smith, however, knew a lousy part when they saw it.

George Schaefer, Kate's choice of director, saw it as a kind of PBS thing, a day in the life of Katharine Hepburn as peeked at on the small screen. That made perfect sense to me, but not to Kate or Joe Levine, who continued to think big.

It was pretty steep competition, though, and I kissed *Guest Appearance* good-bye until one July morning when Kate suddenly telephoned and said she'd be coming up for lunch. That wasn't as pushy as it sounds. She'd bring delicious food, prepared by Phyllis and Hilly, knowing that, unless the Margessons fed me, I probably wasn't eating "properly." Why not give the poor old bachelor a decent meal?

Her visit also meant, I figured, that *Guest Appearance* wasn't entirely dead. An excursion into the country was pleasant for Kate, but she generally had a purpose in mind.

I rushed around cleaning the house a little and trying to gauge when they'd arrive, which was, as Kate had predicted, on the stroke of noon.

The big, black car turned into the driveway and there they were: big Hilly at the wheel, birdlike Phyllis in the back seat and, beside Hilly, Kate's wonderful face peering up over the dashboard and grinning happily.

But not so wonderful at the moment. She'd had the skin "burned off" her face, as she had to do from time to time, and it had left black scabs. The scabs looked dreadful, but Kate didn't seem to mind except that they itched and she didn't dare scratch them.

Hilly and Phyllis disappeared into the kitchen with their baskets of goodies while Kate prowled the house, approving and disapproving, and then settled on the front porch. She was hungry, as always, and in no time the four of us were at the table on the porch. "Never eat inside if you can eat *out*," is Kate's motto and I agree, if out is screened-in, as this was.

Kate never lifted a finger and was delighted to be waited upon.

"Shall I come by for lunch?" I'd call and ask in New York. "Is it easy?"

"*Everything's* easy," Kate would reply, having arranged her life so that everything was taken care of. Her comfort and a certain serenity (although she would cry, "I'm being driven *mad!*") were assured so that she could then go on to the adventure of making motion pictures.

After lunch Hilly and Phyllis disappeared back into the kitchen and Kate and I sat, in the hazy summer afternoon, and talked lazily—a little too lazily, I thought—about *Guest Appearance*. She was quite clear as to her reservations. She didn't think it was "right." I told her I didn't think it was, either, but we'd work on it. I suddenly wanted to go to Vancouver desperately. I wanted to relive the fun of making *Delafield*.

She didn't quite say it, but I could see that Kate's heart and hopes were with *Me and Phyllis*. She was counting on Joe Levine to come through.

I had to return some books to the Stone Ridge Library and thought, considering the state of her face, Kate might not want to come, but she did. If there's anything Kate loves it's going places, and she thoroughly enjoys the flurry of excitement she causes. The ladies at our charming little library—an eighteenth-century stone structure furnished with splendid oriental rugs, huge paintings of "ancestors" and gleaming antique furniture—had been at me to bring Miss Hepburn in ever since they got wind of her visits to the area.

Their excitement, as we trooped in, was everything I expected and most gratifying to Kate. And she loved the library. I could hardly get her out. She sat in every old chair until she found one she deemed "extraordinary" and planted herself there as the ladies fussed while trying to appear not to. They would talk of little else for weeks, I suspected.

I was struck again by her amazing fame. Everyone from teenagers to octogenarians knew her and loved her.

"It's so strange being me," I've heard her say. It must be.

By 2:00 P.M. she had begun to make noises about "getting back." She always had a schedule, was always anxious about being late, was always ahead of time.

As an alternative to the thruway going back, I suggested Hilly take the Taconic Parkway, a very attractive road.

The minute she was home, though, I got an irate telephone call from Kate.

"Don't *ever* put me on the Taconic Parkway again!" she said sternly. "It's *two feet* too narrow!"

Merrill began to explore other avenues where *Guest Appearance* was concerned. Maybe Melody was the better part, as Kate contended. So he went after stars for that part. Shelley Long had a new deal with Disney to do feature films. Maybe *Guest Appearance* was really a feature and Shelley would do it.

Shelley wanted to see a completed screenplay, however, and Merrill said, "No deal, no screenplay. Mr. Prideaux doesn't write on spec." (Ha!)

He then sent it to Goldie Hawn. I adored Goldie Hawn and wanted to work with her, but Goldie had readers; she never read a script for herself, we were told. When stars have readers, you can be pretty sure that even if you're sending them the script that will get them their Oscar, the answer is no. Readers are underpaid and bored and not that bright to begin with. If Vivien Leigh had had a reader, she'd have turned down *Gone with the Wind.*

In late July, Merrill called to tell me that *Mrs. Delafield Wants To Marry* had won three Emmy nominations: one for Kate, one for Harold Gould, and one for us as producers, although not me as writer. I was a little hurt, having honestly felt I deserved a nomination for the writing, but I was delighted to be nominated at all. (Is there a single person in the entertainment industry who wouldn't crawl on his knees over glass for an award?)

I didn't think we stood a ghost of a chance of winning, but I nevertheless spent the entire morning rehearsing my acceptance speech. I thanked Katharine Hepburn, from whom all blessings flowed. It was quite humble and terribly moving.

She came up again for lunch in September, a couple of days before I flew to Los Angeles for the Emmy Awards show. Her interest in that appeared to be minimal. I suppose when you have all those Oscars, an Emmy doesn't mean much. She might have suspected, too, that she'd lose, and Kate didn't care for losing.

It was a bit early for the fall leaves, but we were easing into autumn, and the grounds were especially beautiful. She walked over them, oohing and ahhing over every flower, shrub, and tree. I felt inadequate and numb, compared to Kate. Why couldn't I care that much about everything?

She had never been to Woodstock, so I suggested that Hilly could drive us up. (Phyllis hadn't come this time; it was just Kate and Hilly out on a lark.) Kate was game, of course.

Once we'd driven up and down Tinker Street, the main drag, a couple of times, there didn't seem to be much else to do.

"Let's drop in and see my friends, Howard and Annie Koch," I said. That went over like a lead balloon.

"What for?" she said.

But she grudgingly agreed.

As we got out of the car, she said, "Now, we won't stay long." I assured her that we wouldn't. One look at Howard, however, and she was bewitched.

The house is beautifully situated in the woods over a stream and we stood on the deck and those two old pros chatted like magpies. Annie was out shopping, unfortunately. Howard may have been somewhat surprised, but he wasn't at all ill at ease with her. They were pals from the very first. (And later they corresponded.)

We went inside and sat in the living room while they talked about old Hollywood. Howard expanded on *Casablanca*, and Kate got into *The African Queen*, about which she was doing some writing.

Annie was somewhat startled to come home and find Katharine Hepburn sitting in her living room, but she curled up beside Howard and listened. I couldn't get Kate out.

"We really should push on," I kept saying, but she wouldn't budge.

When we were finally in the car, she said, "I've never been so nervous. Why didn't you shut me up?"

"Why were you so nervous?"

"Well," she said, "he's so attractive!" Not bad, thought I, for an eighty-five-year-old man.

Later in the afternoon, before she started making noises about getting home, I took her to check out a house down the road that was for sale. Should I buy it?

"Not for you," said Kate firmly, having gone over every inch of it. Just as well, considering the price.

And what about *Guest Appearance*?

We touched on it, but only lightly. She wouldn't come out with a flat no, but neither was she enthusiastic. Her mind was full of *Me and Phyllis*. If that were to fall through, then I thought we had a chance.

A friend drove me from Stone Ridge to Kennedy Airport and we got lost. We finally found our way and I dashed into the terminal, slightly panicked, and looked up to see, among a group of arriving passengers, the one and only Milton Berle.

"Milton!" cried I.

"Jimmy!" cried he.

After a summer in upstate New York, I suddenly felt as if I was with my own folks again.

"Come and sit a minute," he said and I did, not caring if I missed my plane or not.

"Where are you going?" he asked.

"To L.A. for the Emmy Awards."

"So am I," he said, "but first I have to go to Buffalo. Fifty years ago I opened a theatre there and they're having an anniversary. I'll be back in L.A., though, in time for rehearsals for the Emmys on Saturday. I'm going to do a production number and make a presentation."

I felt like a slouch. Here was I making such a fuss about getting to L.A., and here was this seventy-eight-year-old man headed for Buffalo to do a show there before going back to Los Angeles for the Emmys. Perked me up. I always loved seeing Milton. I never left him without learning a little something more about show business.

Two years before, when she was nominated, I went with Charlotte Rae as her guest to the Emmys. So this time I took her as mine.

She laid on the limo and dressed to the nines, and we were driven through the hot southern California afternoon to Pasadena to the Civic Center. It's always so odd to be dressed in black tie in the middle of a sun-drenched day, as Show Folk do for this and the Oscars.

The crowds screamed when they saw Charlotte—she was then the star of *The Facts of Life*—and we played it to the hilt, waving and blowing kisses, at least I did. Charlotte was more restrained.

The television reporters kept calling Charlotte over and she kept pushing me into the limelight, saying, "*He's* the nominee," but they couldn't have cared less.

"Tell us about the dress, Charlotte," was the extent of their interest in me.

A bar was set up outside the building so we had drinks before going in, talking with John Lithgow and his wife. John was up for two awards. I said, "You'll win," and he said, "You'll win." He did win once, and made a charming speech.

We joined George Schaefer and Merrill and Suzy Karpf and went in. I must say there was an awfully nice feeling about it, as if we were all family, all workers in the same vineyard. Despite the fact that some of us were nervous, everybody chatted easily.

Harold Gould appeared, bearded, having flown down especially from

a stint in Canada in *I'm Not Rappaport.* I wanted him to win terribly because he'd been nominated so often and had never won and, I thought,
he deserved it for *Delafield.*

Well, he lost. And Kate lost. And we lost.

I wasn't surprised. As the evening went on, I saw that *Delafield* was
like a soufflé among the other meat-and-potato productions. I could
see that we weren't going to make it and so I began to relax and enjoy it
now that I wouldn't have to make an acceptance speech in front of millions of viewers.

And at the supper afterward, we danced and laughed and congratulated the winners. I was tired when I got home, but that night I loved
Show Business.

I telephoned Kate the next morning to commiserate, but she seemed
somewhat vague as to what I was talking about.

When I got back to New York, I had lunch with Kate and then took her
and Phyllis to a matinee of Shaw's *You Never Can Tell.*

The theatre was in the round and Kate, pointing to the ladies sitting
opposite us, said, "You see why I never wear dresses? You can see right
up their skirts."

And, indeed, you could.

The production was good. I get hungry for language and every so
often I need my fix of Shaw. And Kate adores his work.

At intermission I caught sight of Kate Wilkinson, a wonderful actress, and went over to talk with her. Her husband, Bruce, had died that
year and only a few months later her son, too, was dead of AIDS. My
heart sank when I thought of it. I asked her to let me introduce her to
Miss Hepburn, but she said, "Oh no, Jimmy, I couldn't!"

I wish she had. Never miss an opportunity to meet Katharine Hepburn. I went back and told Kate about her and she was sorry not to have
talked with her.

I told Kate I had a date with Raquel Welch the next afternoon at the
Russian Tea Room at 3:30, and hinted that maybe Hilly could drive me
home afterward to Stone Ridge, but she didn't pick up on it.

I had never met Raquel Welch. I'd heard rumors that she was difficult to work with, and I wasn't entirely sure of her talent (although I'd
heard her nightclub act was a wow), but I was certainly interested in the
Libby Holman story.

At 3:30 on the dot (I had learned from Miss Hepburn), I arrived at the Russian Tea Room and announced to the maître d' that I was meeting Miss Welch. He led me to a table and a few minutes later I saw someone come in whom I would never have taken for Raquel Welch, which was probably the idea: peasanty clothes completely disguised the body and a babushka covered the head.

I watched as the maître d' handed her a note. She unfolded it, read it, looked nonplussed, read it again, and came to the table.

"I think this is for you," she said.

I looked at it and immediately recognized Kate's handwriting.

On the outside it said, "Jim Prideaux Raquel Welch same table 3:30." Inside was, "Dear Jim, Call Kate about Hilly. K."

"Oh," I said, "it's from Katharine Hepburn."

Her eyebrows flew up and I could see my stock rising in the east like the sun.

"Would you excuse me if I make a quick call?" I asked.

"That's all right," she said. "I have to go to the ladies."

As fate would have it, the public telephone at the Russian Tea Room is on the wall of a hallway that leads to the restrooms.

I called Kate and she said, "Listen, when you leave there go and pack your suitcase and get a cab and come here. Hilly can drive you home. He can stay the night and come back in the morning. I've got an old friend coming for dinner, but you can have a drink before you go."

I told her that was great.

It was then I realized that the sleeve of my jacket was being tugged.

There stood Raquel. "Tell her I'm her biggest fan!" she insisted.

"Uh, Kate," I said, "Raquel Welch is here and she says to tell you she's your biggest fan."

"That's nice," said Kate. "Now, listen, be here by . . ."

But Raquel was tugging at my sleeve again.

"Tell her I love her!" she said.

"Uh, Kate, Raquel says she loves you."

"By *six*," said Kate and she hung up.

"She says thank you," I told Raquel.

We went to the table and, when Raquel ordered a glass of water, I decided against having a martini. I asked instead for club soda. When the glass of water came, she sent it back. It had ice in it and she didn't want ice in it.

Then she started talking. And she talked solidly for almost an hour. I began to sweat. Generally when you meet new people there is a moment of rapport and you think, gee, I'm going to like this person. With Raquel there was nothing. She was there to sell me on this project, which she was going to produce as well as star in—warning signals went up!—and, boy, did she sell. I didn't have to say anything and, if I attempted to speak, she talked right through me.

I kept staring at her, wondering if she could really play Libby, that legendary performer. I asked her who was going to sing the songs? She said she was. She had optioned a book, which she would get to me.

Anyway, I ended up telling her I was interested. Who knew?

My glass of club soda came to five-fifty, which I paid.

"They'll never get rich off us," I said as we got up.

"Never mind," she said, "we decorate the place."

"Well, you do," I said.

We parted on the street and, desperately trying to dredge up some sort of affection for her, I kissed her lightly on the cheek. I knew instantly that it was a mistake, but she wanted me so badly for the project she only frowned slightly. Oh, well.

I hurried off to Chuckles's, packed up and got a cab to Kate's house. She was waiting for me.

"What a time I had at the Russian Tea Room!" she said as I bounded up the stairs to the living room. I thought I'd misunderstood her.

"What?"

"What a time I had at the Russian Tea Room!" she said again.

"You mean *you* went to the Russian Tea Room?"

"Oh, yes," she said. "I had to get the note to you so I said, 'Okay, Hilly, let's go,' and we went to the Russian Tea Room. Hilly parked at the curb and I went in and right up to the hatcheck girl and said, 'My friend, Jim Prideaux, is meeting Raquel Welch here at three-thirty. Would you please give him this note?' Well, she took one look at me and went 'Aaaaaahhh!' I could see that she was upset so I gave her a hug and she went 'Aaaaaahhh!' again! And then I looked around and, do you know, there were people actually *eating* at tables so I thought, 'Crikey, I'd better get out of here,' and I started across the sidewalk to the car, but a little crowd had gathered and a man grabbed me by the arm and he said, 'Miss Hepburn, I must tell you . . . I have to tell you . . . it would be wrong if I didn't tell you . . . you're *wonderful!*'"

She sighed.

"It made the whole trip worthwhile," she said.

I was in stitches. Kate, who hadn't been in a restaurant in years. What a pal! And all so that Hilly could drive me home.

The hot news, in late September, was that *Me and Phyllis* had fallen apart.

Kate claimed that she had time and again said to Joe Levine, "Joe, are you sure you want to go ahead with this? You don't want out?"

And Levine had assured her that he didn't want out.

He did, however, want a big star opposite Kate as Phyllis, and he'd been turned down by every star it'd been submitted to.

So he came to her house for dinner one evening and, as Kate handed him a drink and he sat down, he suddenly said, "Kate, I'm not going through with it."

Kate remained standing, reached down, took his drink back, and said, "Then I think we have nothing further to say to each other, Joe."

"Don't you want to know why?" he asked.

"No," said Kate coldly, standing, staring at him.

Poor Levine shifted uneasily and then finally stood up.

"Good-bye, Joe," she said.

Well, she reported that she then couldn't be impolite, so she walked him downstairs and out to the curb.

Unfortunately, his car had gone to wherever cars go while their owners eat dinner, and they had to wait and wait and wait until it was brought back. They stood in silence at the curb.

"Don't you really want to know why?" asked Levine again.

"No," said Kate firmly, concentrating on the cross-town bus as it went by. After an agonizing time, she said, his car finally arrived.

As he got in, she held the door and said, "I'm glad you've done this to me, Joe, because if I'd done it to you my conscience would have destroyed me!" And she slammed the door.

So that's that. A faint whiff of hope wafted past my nostrils. Would she now turn to *Guest Appearance*?

I was soon to find out.

Merrill and Suzy Karpf arrived in Stone Ridge for the weekend. Suzy had one shoeless and bandaged foot due to a broken toe, but she offset the handicapped look by wearing a fabulous mink coat. (This was before we started stoning people for wearing animal skins.)

Merrill reported that both Goldie Hawn and Sally Field had "passed" on *Guest Appearance* (did they use the same readers?). Kate, however, was beginning to show a renewed interest. Merrill was hopeful, as always, and thought that we would get it on.

I looked around at the spectacular autumn colors bursting everywhere and decided that God was good. Whether He was good enough to get *Guest Appearance* on was another matter.

When he was back in New York, Merrill again talked with Kate. The upshot was that Kate appeared once more at my door, and this time she and Hilly were prepared to stay the night (Phyllis stayed away for fear of not having her own bathroom—in that three-bathroom house). We were getting serious.

Hilly immediately spread lunch out on the front porch. After lunch, he sunned himself in the backyard as Kate and I huddled over the treatment in dead earnest, going over page after page.

She began to speak of herself in the third person.

"She wouldn't do *this*," she'd say, meaning Katharine Hepburn, not the character. But I knew that they were one and indivisible.

We eliminated the old man entirely, which didn't bother me a bit. What did bother us was the ending. Kate felt it wasn't about her.

"I'm over, I'm dead," she said, not meaning it literally, "but the movie still has ten minutes to go." That wouldn't do. Many other reservations, but at least we were working.

We were in the middle of this discussion when the most horrendous sound burst over the countryside. Buzz saws!

"God Almighty!" shouted Kate, the great noise-hater.

I rushed to the telephone and got my neighbor, Merrilee Pope, who had chosen that afternoon to have her trees trimmed.

"Listen," I said, "Katharine Hepburn's here and we're trying to work."

"Oh, my God!" said quick-witted Merrilee, and the buzz saws stopped instantly.

In the late afternoon, the working session behind us (and I was greatly heartened), we went out to look at antique shops in Stone Ridge, causing something of a stir in the shops we visited. Kate liked the stir, and I'd even see her purposely touch an admirer, knowing what that touch might mean. Kate bought Christmas presents, among them a green fabric frog that enchanted her.

"Will you take my check?" she asked them at the Nutcracker.

They would and did, though I doubt if they cashed it.

She also bought a big, floppy, funny hat that she immediately popped on her head for comic effect. We laughed a lot.

We came home and had drinks on the porch as the sun cast long shadows over the sweeping lawn, now being blanketed by the falling leaves. Feeling mellow, Kate had a second scotch, which I'd never seen her do, and she got just a teeny bit tipsy, which I'd also never seen before.

I built a fire in the fireplace as night came on, and we ate dinner in front of it. I was nervous, though, because Kate refuses to have a screen in front of the fire and it was crackling and popping and sending out sparks. Kate thought that was great.

By 9:00 she was ready for bed, but not before she oversaw Hilly going through the ritual of preparing her breakfast tray. That breakfast tray. I will never understand it—the three cups, one for lemon and hot water, one for coffee, and the third for God-knows-what—but it must be absolutely at the ready when Miss Hepburn goes to bed or she doesn't go to bed.

We thought she had gone to bed, and Hilly and I were talking in the kitchen when suddenly the door to the guest wing flew open and there stood Kate, all fresh and scrubbed and looking cute as a button in her white silk pajamas.

You may wonder how I can describe distinguished and octogenarian Katharine Hepburn as "cute as a button," but she was. And I realized that while she ostensibly came out to check the breakfast tray, actually she had come out so I could see that, in her white silk pajamas, she looked cute as a button.

It's an odd feeling, I must say, to lie in bed and know you have Katharine Hepburn sleeping in your back room. A feeling given to very few.

At some mysterious signal, I guess, Hilly took the breakfast tray in to Kate and she breakfasted alone, meditating on the day. That's her private hour. She was not to be disturbed until she burst upon you, dressed and ready to face the world.

We worked again the next morning, hunched over the treatment on the front porch.

"You've got to get that ending," she declared. "Laura's kept alive only artificially."

And then, after a splendid lunch, they departed—honking thirteen times and waving as usual—and I was, as usual, left limp as a rag. But we did seem to be making progress.

Kate in Spencer's chair at the St. Ives house.

George explains to Mrs. Delafield how her wedding is going to be. She's certainly dressed for the occasion.

Kate in her favorite get-up as the wealthy Mrs. Delafield. She loved it. The funkier the better.

*Kate studies Script-girl Pattie Robertson's script
for* Laura Lansing *as Karen Austin looks on.*

Opening night on Broadway of Mixed Couples. *George Schaefer,
Geraldine Page, Rip Torn, Julie Harris, and Michael Higgins.
This was before the reviews came out, hence the happy expressions.*

Obviously a riotous evening at Anne Seymour's with Jean Stapleton and husband, Bill Putch, and Melvin and Helen Gahagan Douglas. Mel said Garbo couldn't act her way out of a paper bag.

In Return Engagement, *I opened the film with Elizabeth Taylor's long walk across campus to acquaint the audience with the way she was looking.*

NBC

Joe Hardy directs Elizabeth Taylor and Joseph Bottoms on the first day of filming Return Engagement. *Elizabeth may well be wondering what she's gotten into.*

The first scene in Laura Lansing Slept Here. *We were scared to death that Kate's voice wouldn't hold up, but it got better and better.*

Laura Lansing attempts to interest Malcolm Gompers, not very successfully.

George: *"What are we going to do about this script, Kate?"*
Kate: *"I'm afraid it's hopeless."*

I'm explaining something to Kate on the Laura Lansing *set,
but I'm not sure she's listening.*

Hilly and Phyllis, both devoted to Kate, although Hilly occasionally had "fits."

Julie Harris and Patrick Duffy in the television version of The Last of Mrs. Lincoln. *Patrick had never acted on camera before and could he do it?*

Kate at her most exuberant at the end of Laura Lansing Slept Here.

Two of my favorite people, Patrick and Carlyn Duffy.
They've come a long way from that roach-infested flat in downtown Hollywood.

Ice cream and champagne with Kate and John Dayton
after the final shot of The Man Upstairs. *Kate had done it again.*

Could this be anybody but Kate?
George Schaefer snapped this on my lawn in Stone Ridge, New York.

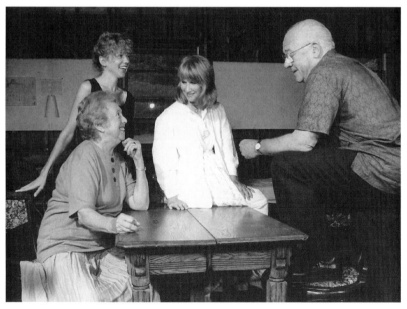

George Schaefer directs three of my favorite actresses, Brenda
Forbes, Linda Purl, and Julie Harris, in my Tusitala. *While*
he appears to be asleep, George is actually deep in thought.

With Ryan O'Neal. We had our happy moments.

Speakers at a tribute to Dame Judith Anderson in Santa Barbara,
including Jimmy Stewart, Mary Martin, Zoe Caldwell, Robert Whitehead, and me.
I was slow getting into my tux.

*In their garden at Beaconsfield with Dame Wendy Hiller
and her husband, the playwright, Ronald Gow.*

*With George Schaefer and Burt Reynolds in Palm Beach
after Burt's terrific one-man show.*

The cast and crew of Mrs. Delafield Wants To Marry. *On Kate's right is Walter Lassally, the brilliant cinematographer who photographs Kate better than anyone.*

Cast and crew of Laura Lansing Slept Here *gather for the group shot, including dogs. At the top, under the tree, is Kate's niece, the delectable Schuyler Grant.*

My favorite shot of Kate, taken by the late Len Tavares.

There was a problem, that year, about my car. Normally it was driven back to the West Coast by a friend who thought driving my car across the country twice a year, coast to coast, was actually fun. But he couldn't do it this time. I lamented this to Kate who, unfortunately, came up with a solution.

"Hilly can drive you," she said. "You can go together. It'll be an adventure. And you can call me every night and tell me where you are."

She was quite looking forward to it. I wasn't keen on that long drive—I'd done it before—but it seemed to be the only way I could contrive to get the car back to Los Angeles. And Hilly was dying to get back to the coast. (He had formerly worked for Eartha Kitt on La Colina Drive in Beverly Hills, and somehow equated that with fun and games.)

I thought I was crazy even to consider it, and suggested he take Raquel Welch, but, in the end, I went.

We were hardly down the driveway before I realized that Hilly didn't want me along at all. He would have been delighted to go it alone and live it up en route. I was stuck, however. I refused to call Kate that first night, spent in a crummy motel in Youngstown, Ohio. Let her wonder!

We arrived in Los Angeles six days later, after two major fights, one threat on Hilly's part to drop me at the nearest airport, and many miles of sullen silence. He was to have stayed with me in Los Angeles, but neither of us could face that, so he went off to stay with friends.

I picked up the tattered shreds of my life and went on. I was looking around for other projects because, if I was to be realistic, *Guest Appearance* might never get on.

Raquel Welch surfaced.

I spent an hour with her and her manager at the Beverly Wilshire. We greeted and kissed and were quite friendly. I began to like her. She was tough, but she was intelligent and articulate and damned ambitious. Impossible not to be fascinated. The body was simply superb, but I looked at the face and found her not in the least beautiful. And yet she managed to give the impression of beauty. Quite extraordinary. She'd bought the rights to a book on Libby Holman, which she gave me to read. I kept not saying no. Her manager called my agent later to say that he'd never seen Raquel have such rapport with a writer before.

Life went on.

Noel Taylor and Adnan Karabay gave Julie Harris a birthday dinner at Le Dome. Julie looked radiant, as always, and nowhere near whatever her real age was. I loved her and wondered if we'd ever work together again. It seemed wrong that she got into her little car and drove home alone.

I went to Barry Manilow's Bel-Air house and talked with him about a Christmas special he wanted to do. Nothing came of it.

I went back to work on *The Hollywood Girls*—writing it, I might add, on spec. Something to do, at least. Nothing came of that.

On New Year's Eve, Kate called from New York to wish me a Happy New Year. She and her pal, Cynthia McFadden, were having a celebratory drink or two alone at Kate's house. Phyllis, she joked, had made her way home from lamppost to lamppost. We laughed, and she rang off.

Ten minutes later she called again and said, "Did I wish you a Happy New Year?"

1987

To keep my brain from atrophying, I began to rewrite my play about Robert Louis Stevenson on Samoa called *Tusitala*. A couple of years before I'd had a terrific reading of it at Theatre West with Julie Harris, Robert Foxworth, Patrick Duffy, Linda Purl, and Anne Seymour. All it needed, it seemed, was a bit of polishing.

Merrill, meanwhile, said there wasn't much hope at the networks for *Guest Appearance* without a firm commitment from Kate, and that we didn't have.

My career appeared to be over, on the whole. I wondered if it was too late for me to go into poodle clipping.

Meanwhile, I flew to Illinois and spent a weekend at the University of Southern Illinois lecturing and talking with bright, energetic students. I couldn't have enjoyed it more. One does occasionally feel as if there's some hope for the human race. Very decent kids. I was treated very much like a celebrity, which embarrassed me a little, but if they wanted to treat me as a celebrity why kill it by telling them that I was just a struggling writer who hoped it wasn't too late to go into poodle clipping?

And then one day Merrill met with George and me to tell us that he had "taken a shot in the dark" and sent my treatment of *Guest Appearance* to Ken Raskoff at NBC. He informed him that I had written it for Katharine Hepburn, that she had "significant problems" with it, but he felt that our relationship with her was strong enough that she would view favorably any screenplay we sent to her.

This moved us along. Either they'd want her badly enough to take a chance on her liking it or they wouldn't. If they didn't, I, for one, was ready to forget the damn thing forever.

The very next day Merrill took me by the hand to NBC to meet with Ken Raskoff. I liked him right off, although he scared me because he was so young and energetic and astute. This kid really knew his beans where drama was concerned. He made some perfectly valid suggestions about rewrites. But he didn't say, "Let's go to screenplay." Perhaps he wasn't in a position to.

Then came a shock, and it had nothing to do with *Guest Appearance.*

Bill Luce called to congratulate me on my *Lyndon.* He'd seen a screening of it in New York and said it was great.

I didn't know what he was talking about.

Lyndon was the play I had written based on Merle Miller's book about Lyndon B. Johnson. Jack Klugman had played it at the Kennedy Center and in Los Angeles, and wonderfully, too.

The night of the opening in Washington, David Susskind had gone around shouting, "Jim Prideaux's written a masterpiece! Jim Prideaux's written a masterpiece!" It was most gratifying and showed, I thought, great perceptivity on David's part.

And now, without my knowledge, he had filmed it for television.

I called Laurence Luckinbill, an old friend, who starred in this skulduggery. He said they were told during production that I wasn't interested in being there and, indeed, implied that I might even be dead!

Well, David Susskind was dead at this point.

And when I got a video and actually saw what they had done on the screen, I thought it was sensational, beautifully directed, brilliantly acted. (And Larry has gone on to do it on the stage, so why grouse?)

One morning Raquel Welch telephoned from New York. She had gone ahead and written her own treatment for the Libby Holman project. Could she send it to me? Would I read it and give her my reaction?

I said I couldn't wait.

When it came, I had to force myself to sit down and read it. And guess what? It was the best treatment I'd ever read. The world was full of surprises.

We all got dressed up and went to the ballroom of one of those new hotels above Universal Studios for the annual Directors Guild of America awards. George Schaefer was nominated as best director of a television film for *Delafield.*

I'd called Kate to tell her and she was happy for George, but naturally vague about it all. She didn't know there were hotels above Universal Studios.

So there I sat with the Schaefers and the Karpfs waiting for George to lose, which he did. I was getting tired of our gang losing.

At our table, however, was the luscious Elizabeth McGovern. I couldn't take my eyes off her, and she couldn't keep her eyes off her date, Rob Reiner. I wanted desperately to ask her to dance, but she went waltzing off with Rob.

It was a very long evening that included Red Buttons doing a hilarious routine and Carl Reiner knocking out the jokes and Diane Schuur belting out the songs, and even an alarming power failure in the middle of it that almost cleared the hall. By the time George lost, we were groggy.

We slipped out early, not because we were peevish, but because getting your car can take as long as the ceremonies.

This was followed by three days of periodontal work and a case of food poisoning and a memorial service for Richard Levinson, who dropped dead while shaving one morning. It wasn't a great time.

But then, on April 1—April Fools' Day—Merrill called to say that NBC had come through. They were ready to take a chance on Kate's liking it, and I was "ordered" to go to screenplay on *Guest Appearance*.

It had taken me from September of 1985 to get to this point. If you're not patient in this business, you're dead. And if you're not persistent—as Merrill was—you don't stand a chance.

I called Kate and told her I was going to screenplay.

"Really!" she said in that noncommittal tone of hers that could mean anything, but I think she was pleased. I think she was ready to go back to work and more than ready to get to Vancouver.

I started work immediately and had twenty-five pages done by April 6.

But then Van Johnson came to town.

I'd never met Van Johnson, but we had the same New York agent, who knew that I'd written a part into *The Hollywood Girls* specifically for Van. (What he didn't know was that *The Hollywood Girls* was, for all practical purposes, dead, but agents sometimes remain hopeful.) He thought Van and I should meet. And so his manager, Alan Foshko, called and invited me to lunch with them at the Terrace Room in the Century Tower.

Van Johnson was a glamorous name from my young moviegoing days—a real movie star to me—and I certainly wanted to meet him.

The Century Tower was a new addition to the Century Plaza Hotel, and I wasn't sure how dressy it would be, but nothing was dressy in L.A., right? We went to the Polo Lounge in our open collars, right?

So I put on a white shirt with the collar open and white trousers and threw a sweater over my shoulders and went off to the Century Tower. The lobby was surprisingly gussy for L.A., and I was relieved to see a sign advertising their three restaurants with the Terrace Room at the bottom—hardly more than a coffee shop. Fine.

As I approached the reservation desk, I saw the hulking figure of Van Johnson leaning over it, dressed in a natty blazer with a red tie. He was deep in conversation and didn't notice me as I came up.

I tapped his shoulder. "You wanna have lunch?" I said.

He looked at me in great surprise. "You James Prideaux?" he said. I allowed as how I was.

"You came to have lunch with me dressed like that?"

"What?" I said, startled.

"Kiddo, you've been living in Los Angeles too long! You don't go to lunch dressed like that!"

I couldn't believe my ears.

"Well," I said, "it's the Terrace Room and—"

"You think I'd take James Prideaux to lunch at the Terrace Room? We're going upstairs! And you've got to have a jacket and a tie."

I was about to turn around and go home, but by this time I was catching on. This was his manner and his sense of humor. Big, blustery, funny and, in the end, affectionate.

"Well," I said, "this is it. What you see is what you get."

"No, it isn't," he said, as Mr. Foshko appeared. "Alan must have something you can wear. Let's go up to his room." I looked Mr. Foshko over and figured it was hopeless, but we went up to his room and I tried on jackets that were too tight in the waist and too long in the arms until finally we came upon a corduroy job that wasn't too bad, except that Van had to turn up the sleeves and pin them.

"I don't even want to have lunch now," I said, petulantly, looking at the pins.

"Yes, you do," said Van. "Come on."

"I'll walk behind you," I said, "so they won't know we're together."

"Good," said Van.

So we went up to a gussy restaurant and had a lovely lunch and a grand time.

Van was very open and responded generously to my many questions about MGM and the old days. He was in great awe of Hepburn, who lived only a couple of blocks from him in Manhattan. He said at Halloween he made a jack-o'-lantern and rang her doorbell, then ran and hid behind a tree as she came out and took it in.

"Why did you hide?" I asked. "Why didn't you just give it to her?"

"Oh, I couldn't," he said. "I'd be too shy."

It seemed odd considering that they'd worked together and been stars together on the same lot.

After lunch, I called Kate in New York.

"Your ears must be burning," I said.

"Why?"

"Because we talked about you so much today. I had lunch with Van Johnson."

"Oh, Lord, did he smile a lot?"

"Not especially. He *adores* you."

But she had already changed the subject.

I closed up the L.A. pad and flew to New York. It was jarring to make a move midway in a script, as I did with *Guest Appearance*, but I knew I could easily resume it once I was settled into the house in Stone Ridge.

I spent a couple of days in Manhattan, but didn't see Kate because it was the weekend and she was at Fenwick, her house in Old Saybrook, Connecticut. I called her, though, and she seemed eager to know how the work was coming.

After Los Angeles, New York was like a shot of adrenaline. Dirty it might be, and ugly now, and scary, but it was as electrifying as ever.

On May 15, happily settled in the country and working away, I duly noted that I was on page seventy-five of *Guest Appearance*, and took the laundry to the laundromat and had a haircut at Mickey's in Kingston, and then the piano tuner arrived. Rich, full days.

Sada Thompson came to visit for three days and was a joy, not disturbing my work at all, but always there for lively cocktail hours. I hated to see her leave.

By May 22 the screenplay was finished, and I poured the customary champagne.

But did I like the script? I couldn't tell. I was too immersed in it at that moment.

The next day, however, I reread it, polished it, had it Xeroxed in Kingston, and mailed it off to Merrill in Los Angeles. I didn't feel about it as I did about *Delafield*, which seemed so cohesive and elegant. This really *was* a device for Kate, and her character was shamefully based on what I knew of the real person. I worried that she wouldn't be likable — not that Kate wasn't likable — but the character was bossy and self-centered, and that might seem unattractive.

Anyway, it was out and I felt a marvelous sense of freedom.

My ex-neighbor, Jill Clayburgh, drove up in her car one morning to say hello with her darling daughter, Lilly, and her new son, Michael, in the back seat. She said David (Rabe, her husband) was writing a novel, and she wanted to do just one television film a year now. I immediately saw her as Melody Gomphers in *Guest Appearance* and almost mentioned it, but thought it was premature. I missed the Rabes. We had fun when they lived down the road.

Kate liked the screenplay better than the treatment, but she still wouldn't commit. Merrill flew in to New York in, I suspected, sheer frustration to talk with her.

She suggested they come up to Stone Ridge and discuss the script problems with me. So they arrived. With lunch, of course.

After Hilly had fed us (we were friends again, our trip behind us and forgotten; Hilly was too much fun to stay mad at), Kate and Merrill and I conferred on the front porch.

Interestingly enough, it was Kate who ticked off the problems, one by one, and then proceeded to provide what she felt were the solutions. (I wasn't sure they were *the* solutions, but they were certainly possibilities.) After a full afternoon of discussion, and wanting to get back into the city, she suddenly rose and asked when we would be starting the picture.

What a sense of drama the lady had!

Merrill was in a state of ecstasy.

I was in shock.

And now I was beginning to have real misgivings. Why tempt fate? I wasn't at all sure this was something Kate should do. We'd had such a success with *Delafield* (despite the dearth of awards), why not leave well enough alone?

To get away from it for a couple of days and gain a certain perspective, I busily reworked *The Hollywood Girls*. This was a script so slight it made *Guest Appearance* look like *War and Peace*. But it was fun. Was it not time, though, for something a little heavier? Was I not the author of *The Last of Mrs. Lincoln* and *Lyndon*?

I flattered myself, over a martini, that my difficulty lay in the fact that

I could do both, comedy and drama, with equal facility. Over a second martini, it came clear to me that I did them not only with facility, but with brilliance.

I had a conference call with Merrill and Ken Raskoff. Ken was delighted at the possibility of actually meeting Miss Hepburn, and made some good suggestions (nothing major) about the script.

I went right to work and did rewrites, incorporating Kate's suggestions and Ken's and adding some changes of my own. I mailed it off to L.A. again and was suddenly limp with fatigue. I wanted to do something that showed instant results.

Results came, all right, and almost instantly.

It was arranged that we would have a three-day summit meeting at my home in Stone Ridge.

Merrill couldn't make it, but George Schaefer drove in, having flown from Los Angeles to Newark and driven a rented car up, almost to the minute that Kate and Hilly arrived.

It was 8:30 P.M. on a Tuesday evening and I immediately assigned them their rooms in the guest wing. Kate knew hers, of course, the master guest bedroom, and wouldn't have settled for less. They slept by rank while they were there, George in the second-best bedroom, and poor Hilly in a smaller room. Kate commandeered the bathroom, naturally, so George and Hilly shared one off the kitchen.

Hilly gave us his usual splendid dinner on the front porch—it was deep into July and balmy—during which the talk was mostly about Kate's book, *The Making of the African Queen*, or, *How I Went to Africa with Bogie, Bacall and Huston and Nearly Lost My Mind*. Very much a Hepburn-type title.

She had brought a set of galley proofs, which I read in bed before dozing off. Kate very cleverly wrote exactly as she speaks, which gave one a sense of "listening in" on even her most intimate conversations. The book was very light and gossipy and told a great deal about her reactions to Africa and John Huston, but practically nothing about the making of *The African Queen*.

I predicted it would sell like hotcakes, which was music to Kate's ears. She had always fancied herself a writer. I really didn't think she was, but who was I to dispute it if she had a best-seller?

(Do you want to hear more about stars who think they can write? The worst are stars of sitcoms, who think only in terms of rewrites. I heard of one who was so conditioned by her sitcom she wouldn't consider playing Shaw in summer stock without "sufficient rewrites." Maddening.)

Anyway, everybody was tired that night and went off to their beds, and I took the galley proofs and went to mine.

In the morning I peeked into George's room and couldn't help laughing at the sloppy way his bed was made. I told Kate about it.

"I made that," she said indignantly.

We started working on the porch a little after 9:00 A.M., going over the script, line by line. We cut lines and added lines and, on the whole, strengthened it, I think.

Working with Kate, who was so strong and so powerful professionally, the thing was to stand up to her. I had decided nearly twenty years ago to do that. It was less easy to do now—the ego was bigger, hers not mine—but it was still the policy to follow. And she respected it. If George or I responded negatively to a suggestion, she generally backed right off with, "Okay . . . okay."

After lunch we all took naps. George went to bed, I went to bed, Hilly sunned in the backyard, and Kate lay out flat on her back on the hard floor of the porch.

It was hot and hazy, and I woke up and looked out on the porch to see Katharine Hepburn, spread-eagled and sound asleep, her gray hair coming loose and flowing over the floor.

We resumed work at 2:00, but we didn't get through the whole script so Kate (who really wanted to get home) said, "I think we'd better stay another night."

I thought, what the hell? Kate provided all the food and Hilly cooked all the meals, so why not? Also, we had to get through the whole script.

Kate had never seen our pond and wanted to, so I walked her down to it. It was really quite beautiful, nestling in a valley with a green sward of lawn and lovely trees around it. There was a kind of pier and a little wooden raft tied to the shore that Lord Margesson stepped onto and sank down into the mire before swimming away into the muck. I use the words *mire* and *muck* because, although Frank had spent hundreds—and maybe thousands—of dollars trying to keep the damn pond clean, it still looked to me like one of the La Brea tar pits.

I called it the Black Lagoon and wouldn't dream of going into it. Kate took one look and couldn't wait.

"Go away," she said, and I ran off as she stripped down to her undies and went swimming.

She returned to the house glowing and saying, "Paradise! Paradise!"
So then Lord Margesson started calling it Paradise Pond.

The Margessons joined us for cocktails on the porch, and then Hilly
served dinner. After dinner, George wanted to read Kate's book and
Kate wanted to go to bed, and Hilly got into the car and drove off to
find some nightlife in the area. (Good luck, Hilly.)

Kate made one of her surprise appearances in her white jammies,
but that was it.

The next morning we went right back to work and got to the end of
the damn thing, which still troubled everybody. No real resolution
there. But the commitment was made and I had ten thousand changes
to do, and it looked as if I would see Vancouver again come fall.

We had lunch and then they departed to drive George to Kennedy
Airport. They weren't gone five minutes before I discovered Kate's
reading glasses on a coffee table. So I got into my car and flew after
them, catching them halfway up Mohonk Mountain. I honked, stopped
them, and thrust the glasses in the window at Kate, who said casually,
"Oh, I have another pair."

I then went home and did what I always did after Kate left. Collapsed.

Kate called a few nights later, Kate at her worst. She'd obviously had a
rough day and a drink. I attempted to take notes as fast as the famous
voice talked:

> From the time she meets him something in your eyes says "see me
> again." He's sophisticated, she's not. Howard's waiting to take you home.
> Says good night to children but nothing to Laura and Walter. Melody
> drives him to station. (By the way, go to periodontist.) Back home says
> same thing to Laura. Now it's a reality. "Take care of Malcolm." Drives
> around block. Laura calls Walter. Walter goes. Conway opens door ex-
> pecting to find Melody, finds . . . Walter and Laura go back to house . . .
> big scene at home . . . so glad to see each other. Walter's job earlier. I'm
> *dead* for the last ten minutes!

She was still harping on being dead for the last ten minutes.

Ten minutes later I got a call saying I had to fly to Los Angeles immediately to confer further (rewrites) with George and Merrill and
probably Ken Raskoff.

The next morning was Sunday, and while all good Christians were on their knees in church, I was in George Schaefer's study in Beverly Hills. Once more we went over the script. Once more we tried to make it more cohesive. The basic idea was just not as clean, the story line not as straight as was *Delafield*. This came as no surprise to me. I still wondered why anyone wanted to do it. Perhaps they saw something in it I didn't see.

In the afternoon, we broke and I went with Merrill and Ken Raskoff to see George's production of *Leave It to Jane* at the Doolittle Theatre, a lovely production of one of my favorite musicals. Ken was really very keen on *Guest Appearance*. The mere thought of meeting Katharine Hepburn set him salivating.

I hadn't been back in Stone Ridge a week before Kate came up with Hilly and Phyllis because she thought *Guest Appearance* needed more attention.

Would I survive this?

Anyway, we worked again on the front porch while Hilly and Phyllis fussed over food in the kitchen.

And I should say here that while I could bellyache from time to time about Kate and her bossiness, I should also record that she had some damn good ideas:

"*Laura* sees Walter's prospectus, shows it to Mr. Baumgartner."

Good. Keeps *her* alive, too.

"Her first telephone call in French."

Lovely.

"Cut reference to book *Little Women*."

(I had forgotten that Kate was associated with the film *Little Women*, but she hadn't. I made it *Valley of the Dolls*.)

"When she is arranging furniture, Laura is seen disappearing into a room with a chair over her head."

Great!

"Melody and Walter oversleep at end while Laura makes breakfast."

Yes.

"In grocery store, food piling up as she shops, series of scenes. Child disappears under groceries."

Splendid.

"Cut all *bathroom jokes!*"

Do I have a vulgar streak?

"Get rid of driver at luncheon scene."

Sensible.

"Next morning, Laura's cooking and Melody comes in and says, 'You've lost the bet.' 'But I've won something better,' says Laura."

Might play.

"Laura's eyes opened at end, sees life staring her in the face."

Of course.

"Return to an interviewer at the end, giving structure."

Neat!

"Needs scene with Walter, Jr."

It certainly did.

"Melody at end, 'I've learned how to live.' Laura, 'I've learned how to love.'"

I do not include here all the lousy ideas thrown in by both of us, and discarded. But the lady knew what she was talking about.

But, boy, was I exhausted when night came.

She decided to stay over, and didn't leave until noon the next day. However, we both felt we'd accomplished a great deal.

On August 29 I had seventy-five people for cocktails to celebrate my birthday. That was a lot of people. But you're only young once. I didn't even mention it to Kate, knowing how she felt about birthdays.

George and I had gotten into a discussion of our ages while Kate was there.

"You'll notice there's not a peep coming from this corner," she laughed. We changed the subject.

After the last of the guests had left, I laid in bed in a semidrunken stupor, staring into the dark, consumed by doubts.

Would the script of *Guest Appearance* ever be good enough?

Would Kate be able physically to do it?

(Crossing the lawn, she had said to me, "Remember, you've got a star who can't walk," as I struggled to keep up with her.)

And should she do it?

But then the usual memories of the happy experience of making *Delafield* swept over me and I couldn't wait.

In Los Angeles, George and Merrill had pretty much completed casting. *Guest Appearance* wasn't like *Delafield* in that there was no romantic lead to cast opposite Kate. Consequently, Miss Hepburn and Mr. Prideaux were fairly content to let others do the casting.

Karen Austin was cast in the important part of Melody. We didn't know her, but George and Merrill were pleased. She'd created the leading character in *Nuts* on the stage, the part Streisand was to play in the movie.

Her husband, Walter, was to be played by Joel Higgins, former star of a series called *Silver Spoons*. We'd never heard of him or the series, either, but it didn't matter. Kate now had complete confidence in George and Merrill, and so long as she could have Noel Taylor to do her clothes she was satisfied. Any difficulties that arose, I'm sure she felt she could deal with in Vancouver.

Four days before we were to leave, I sent off what I foolishly considered the last of the rewrites, then faced the business of shutting the house up for the winter, getting the car back to the West Coast, whipping my wardrobe into shape and, in short, getting my affairs in order. I wasn't good at any of those things, but I struggled on.

We'd decided that Kate and Phyllis and Hilly and Brenda Forbes and I would fly to Vancouver together.

"Won't that be more fun?" I asked Kate.

She agreed that it would. I was charged with getting her the seat she had to have on the plane in the first row of seats so that she could put her feet up.

We were ready to go.

The night before we were to leave, I got a frantic call from Kate.

"Hilly's had a fit," she said. "He walked out and so, as far as I'm concerned, he's fired!"

This was shattering news. Kate counted on Hilly for almost everything, now that Phyllis was growing senile. The thought of Kate in Vancouver without Hilly was very disturbing, not just because of Kate's peace of mind, but because the entire production depended on Kate's peace of mind.

PART THREE

1987

(Continued)

I checked in at Kennedy Airport and went straight to the VIP lounge.

Kate and Phyllis were already there, having some difficulty at the desk about their tickets.

Phyllis, now eighty-five and vague, was saying, "But I always carry the tickets!"

Kate was trying to be kind and firm at the same time, but she was refusing to hand the tickets over to Phyllis.

"Are you bright enough to take care of the tickets?" she asked me as I came up.

"I doubt it," I said, but she thrust them at me. I looked at them in dismay. There seemed to be a mass of tickets and dozens of luggage tags. I wanted to tell her I was as vague as Phyllis and hand them back.

We moved on into the lounge, where Brenda Forbes sat, neat as a pin, calm, controlled—everything that Kate and Phyllis weren't. (Brenda was going to play Kate's secretary in this one—a part, alas, too small for her large talent, but it was work.)

There was only one other person in the lounge, a heavyset gentleman who merely smiled benignly when he recognized Kate.

We settled down. We were early, as always, due to Kate. She opened up the morning newspaper and was vastly amused by a burglar who, when caught in the act and asked who he was, replied "I'm a burglar."

It seemed odd without Hilly, though.

That made me the man of the expedition, and I rather preferred Kate ordering Hilly around than ordering me around. I braced myself for whatever might lie ahead.

We boarded first, thanks to her celebrity status, and the other passengers had to pass by us to get to their seats. They all ogled Kate.

"I liked your book," said a young man to Kate as he passed, referring to her *African Queen* book, which had just come out.

"Oh, did you read it?" beamed Kate. He nodded and moved on.

We were off to a good start.

As soon as we could, Brenda and I ordered drinks. It was still pretty early in the day and this gave Kate the opportunity to observe, "I didn't know I was with two *drunks!*" We laughed and ordered seconds.

Brenda asked about the casting. I told her about Karen Austin and Joel Higgins and mentioned that, for the daughter, they had found "a wonderful actress" in Vancouver named Christianne Hirt. Lee Richardson, now a character actor—I remembered him from my youth as the young romantic lead opposite Geraldine Page in *Summer and Smoke*—would play the agent.

We changed planes in Chicago with all the privilege and convenience due a Movie Star and a Legend, but there was a wait of almost two hours.

We left our plane and were immediately put into a large electric cart that transported us to the VIP lounge at O'Hare. Miss Hepburn, never one to fade into the background, didn't sit like the rest of us, but stood with one foot up on the front of the vehicle and stared ahead, rather like that painting of Washington crossing the Delaware, as we moved through the terminal.

Once in the empty lounge—we were in a special lounge within the VIP lounge—she lay on her back on the floor while a young attendant with prominent teeth fetched drinks for us.

"Where is Chicago?" I asked him when he returned, "I want to see the Chicago skyline." I hadn't been in Chicago since I was a kid.

He assured us that there was a splendid view of the Chicago skyline from the other side of the terminal, and he would be delighted to take us there.

"It's not far," he said.

"I want to go, too," said Kate.

Phyllis and Brenda sensibly declined so off we set, the three of us, Kate and I expecting we were only going down the hall a few steps. (The electric cart had gone off to fetch the next celebrity.)

Well, we walked the length of the terminal, up escalators, down escalators, through miles of corridors jammed with people who looked, gasped, turned to look again when they saw the small figure charging along (but even she was puffing) at the accelerated speed she always used to get through crowds. We thought we'd never get to the damn view of the skyline. When we finally got there, panting and peevish, we looked out the window and couldn't see a thing.

"Oh, dear, a little overcast today," said our guide.

Kate and I exchanged a look, then turned and started the torturous journey back.

Anyway, it killed the time in Chicago.

The plane to Vancouver was somewhat larger, and Kate was in her favorite seat again, but Brenda and I were a couple of rows back so we couldn't chat across the aisle.

At one point in the flight, Kate got up and motioned me up and we stood in the aisle, she with her hand on my shoulder, as she discussed some minor point in the script.

I knew why she was doing this: to give the passengers in the rear of the plane a chance to see her, just as she did that day in the Westwood movie house when she was ostensibly turning around to count the seats. She was fully aware that seeing her provided passengers with a small thrill; it was more an act of generosity than self-gratification.

A little later a girl came to me from the back of the plane and asked if I thought Miss Hepburn would sign an autograph for her. Knowing Miss Hepburn's ironclad rule about never signing anything for people she didn't know (though she'd sign anything for people she did), I softened it as best I could, but told her Miss Hepburn really wanted to rest and please not to bother her. She didn't.

Merrill slipped through customs to help us with the luggage, which took forever. Brenda appeared to have lost a little blue case, and Kate and Phyllis just had so much luggage, suitcase after suitcase.

"If she always wears the same clothes," Merrill whispered to me, "what's in all these suitcases?"

"Probably pots and pans," I whispered back.

At the customs desk, the girl said, "Oh, Miss Hepburn, what are you doing here?"

"I'm here to make a movie."

"Really? What's the name of it?"

"I don't know," said Kate, blithely.

She insisted on pulling her own luggage, all of it, on a cart to the curb, and shot right by a little girl, pushed forward by her mother, who wanted to hand her a wilted bouquet.

I took it and said, "Thanks, she'll love it."

Kate and Phyllis were ushered into a limousine with Merrill and, after we waved them off, Brenda and I got into the company van. But not before our unit production manager, Justis Greene, had introduced himself and handed me an envelope filled with hundreds of Canadian dollars: my week's per diem. Glory hallelujah!

Brenda and I were taken to the Denman Hotel, where George and Merrill were staying. It had a terrific swimming pool in the basement, among other attractions which included a complete shopping mall under it—handy when it rained. Originally it was built as an apartment complex, so every suite had a full kitchen and a terrace. I had a sweeping view of the city and the bay beyond.

Kate had gone back to the digs she'd had before, but this time she was in the penthouse on the top floor, which worried me a bit because it meant she had to walk one flight up after getting off the elevator, but I called her later and she was "mad about it."

She was getting settled in, although she groused a bit that the girl on the production who stocked it for her in advance was sloppy. I'd heard that the girl, scared to death, worked like a Trojan to satisfy Miss Hepburn, and I told Kate so. Kate didn't mind finding fault—rather enjoyed it really—and it was a good idea sometimes not to let her get away with it, especially if it was unjustified. Anyway, this was only momentary grousing and didn't mean anything. As poor, absent Hilly said, she couldn't hold a grudge.

She might yell at you one moment and have completely forgotten it the next. (The question was, had you?)

Merrill found someone named Pavlik, a hulking chap, who was to take over Hilly's chores, at least the driving and cooking. I couldn't wait to see how that turned out.

We had a lovely weekend ahead of us before we started work. Kate laid low and wasn't heard from, although I suspected she was reunited with Dr. Kievel. We had beautiful, sunny days, and Adie Luraschi and I wandered the streets of Vancouver, browsed in places like the Hudson Bay Company, and enjoyed looking at the attractive people of Vancouver. There was an awfully nice air of anticipation around us on Sunday.

Noel Taylor arrived with Adnan Karabay. So they were there. A festive air. The actors were flying in from all over, but I hadn't met any yet.

We all gathered that Monday afternoon at the Holy Rosary Cathedral for the first reading of the script.

When I arrived Kate was already there and fussing about the small triplets who had been hired to play Malcolm, the baby.

"They're too young," she told George and me. "They're just too young." She was right. I felt sorry for the young parents who had brought their three babies in to be stars.

I had a suspicion that Malcolm was going to be an older baby.

Kate seemed anxious, and quite upset that there were so many people present. George had invited every member of the cast, almost down to the extras, and it did seem like an army.

"I never heard of inviting everybody to the first read-through," Kate mumbled, apparently forgetting that we had done the same with *Delafield*. But that had been a smaller cast.

George suggested we go around the table and introduce ourselves. Kate, ever theatrical, leaped up first and said, "I'm Katharine Hepburn," thereby endearing herself to all there.

Kate didn't much take to the way Joel Higgins looked, although I thought he was perfect.

She was nuts about Nicolas Surovy, though, the talented son of Risë Stevens.

Karen Austin, who looked a little too attractive to me—I envisioned Melody as being a plainer woman—sat next to Kate and read beautifully. Everybody read beautifully, except that Kate complained of a sore throat.

I had one, too, and so did several others. Adie had a theory that airplanes were crammed with germs and I suspected she was right.

That's all that it was.

The first rehearsal took place the next morning at the Cathedral. Kate went through her big scene with the daughter, played by the Hirt girl, and I was delighted with it.

But Kate complained about her throat.

"I feel like I'm choking," she said, "and I can't act with that."

Merrill went off to find a doctor to look at it.

The cast and I—with the exception of Kate—walked down the street to the Four Seasons Hotel for our free lunch. The hotel laid it on and we were a happy bunch.

When we got back, Kate had been whisked off to the doctor. Merrill and I went to some dreary loft someplace to look at kids on video. We had to replace the lad who'd been hired to play Walter, Jr. I felt badly about it, but he, too, came off as simply too young. We settled on one named Sean Harmon, a bright boy who really listened when he was acting instead of the mugging that most of them did.

I got to my hotel expecting to hear that Kate merely needed some strong lozenges or some such, but there was no word until Merrill called me around sunset to come up to his suite. His voice sounded funny.

I went up, we made drinks, and he said he was waiting for a call from the doctor. It was all taking too long and he felt it was faintly ominous.

The telephone finally rang and I stood by, listening. I could tell there was something terribly wrong.

When he hung up and turned to me, he was ashen.

"Kate has cancer of the throat," he said, "and she needs six weeks of radiation."

I began to cry. I couldn't stop. For some time, we couldn't talk. There was a beautiful sunset over the bay, but the world suddenly seemed as bleak as it could ever be.

I wasn't crying because of the production—it was, after all, just a television movie—I was crying because it probably meant the end of that extraordinary voice, the end of the extraordinary legend.

I can hardly remember what happened next.

Merrill talked to Kate in the hospital, who was scared, but game. In the morning, she said, she would decide what to do.

George appeared, as did Stacy Williams, who was our executive producer, Ken Raskoff, who had come up to represent NBC (and meet Miss Hepburn) and Justis Green. We sat like zombies.

I continued to break down and cry from time to time, but the talk gradually drifted to, what do we do now?

There was talk of replacing Kate in the film, and Loretta Young's name came up. But this was and always had been a Hepburn vehicle, tailor-made, and it was ridiculous to think of anyone else playing in it.

I knew the production would be canceled. And I didn't really care, even after going through so much to get to this point.

I cared about Kate.

I awoke the next morning and lay in bed trying to make some meaning out of life. Poor Kate was in the hospital, her fears of cancer confirmed, and while I knew she was staunch and brave, I knew, too, that she had the normal feelings that anyone would have under the circumstances. We'd often talked of the terror that life holds.

It was a strange, eerie kind of day during which all the wheels of production came to a sudden, jolting stop.

Merrill was up in his suite desperately trying to salvage the production. He called to say that NBC was interested in doing *Guest Appearance* only with Katharine Hepburn. No fools, they.

And what was I going to do?

I'd shut up my house in the East and sublet my apartment in the West.

In the evening, Kate left the hospital and returned to her apartment. Merrill called to tell me that she wished to meet with the cast and crew tomorrow morning at 9:00 A.M. in the rehearsal hall at the church and make a speech of apology and explanation.

Oh, God! What a horror it was.

Kate swept into the rehearsal hall the next morning, head held high. We all applauded as she entered.

She made a very touching little speech, explaining that she had nodules on the throat (we in the know had been sworn to secrecy; the word *cancer* was never to be used), that she was sorry but she couldn't go on, that she had let everybody down.

"Jim," she said, looking at me, "has the most to lose."

Had it been *Delafield* I would have, but I didn't seem to mind much about this one.

The actors behaved splendidly, offered her their consolations, and declared that they would have other work and that just to know her had been thrilling.

As she was walking out, she whispered to me, "Come to dinner tonight."

I then walked through Vancouver alone, wondering when I would pack up and leave. And where I would go. And if I had other work to go to. And would I lose my mind?

Kate had quite a dinner party that night. There were George and Millie Schaefer, Noel, Adnan, Brenda, and me. It was remarkably merry, without any sense whatsoever of an underlying pang. Kate was in great form and, I might add, her voice sounded strong and fine. She told story after story of the Hollywood days and we laughed and hooted and asked questions and had a great time.

I thought wistfully of Hilly because Pavlik cooked and it was utterly tasteless. I glanced at Kate, as she ate, to see if she was going to register a complaint, but she didn't.

And the big news, which she broke to us at the right dramatic moment, was that Hilly was coming back to her. He'd called to apologize.

"I know when to swallow my pride," she told us. And she'd taken him back.

Did that account for the gaiety of the evening?

As we walked the three blocks to the hotel in the dark, we were in a state of shock. It was such an oddly festive evening.

What was going on?

The next morning Kate went to a doctor for the results of the biopsy, not, I might add, the doctor who told her she had cancer. There now appeared to be several doctors involved, including one who had flown up from Sacramento to represent the insurance company.

It was a very tense morning and I was walking the streets, as usual, when Kate's car pulled up beside me and she said, "Get in."

She was very grim and equally mum. She had met with the doctors and was on her way to our hotel to meet with George and Merrill. No indication to me of what the biopsy had disclosed.

She and I went into the hotel lobby and called George's room, only to be told that Merrill was delayed at the production office and would be back in thirty minutes.

So Pavlik drove us into Stanley Park and waited in the car while we walked briskly along the bay. Kate knows how to keep her mouth shut. We talked in the casual way of old friends, about the sea and the sky and how beautiful it was, but not a word about her condition or her plans.

We wandered into the children's area and swung for a few minutes on the swings.

Then back to the car and to the hotel.

She went up to George's room to meet with him and Merrill, promising that she would stop by my suite before she left.

I had food sent up and Brenda ate with me, a quick lunch because I wanted her out and she wanted out before Kate came.

After Brenda left, there was a knock at the door and in came Kate. I couldn't wait any longer. After all, wasn't I one of the producers, too, and didn't I have the right to know?

"Kate, what did the doctor say?"

"Oh, it isn't cancer."

I almost fainted. (And shouldn't that doctor who said it was be drawn and quartered?)

"Well, what is it?"

"Well, apparently it's basically nerves."

"Nerves, Kate?"

"Caused by nerves. The situation with Hilly and Phyllis's senility and all affected the throat."

My relief was simply staggering.

"What are you going to do?" I asked.

"Well, I've talked to George and Merrill and we've agreed that I'll go back to New York and rest for two or three weeks. Then I'll come back. You want to go to a movie this afternoon?"

And we went to the movies, Kate and Brenda and Phyllis and I.

But we were early, of course, by a couple of hours, so Pavlik drove us out to the Eskimo Museum, one of Kate's favorite places in Vancouver. She became the tour guide, pointing things out and leading us to her "special" totem poles.

I couldn't get my mind off what she had told me and concluded that it was nonsense for her to go back to New York "to rest." Better she should stay here and rest. She loved Vancouver and the apartment and she'd be away from all the New York pressures.

We went back into town and Pavlik left us to find our way through an underground mall to one of those dinky screening rooms that now serve as movie theatres. We saw *My Life as a Dog*, which we all agreed was overrated, but possibly our minds were on other things. We consumed tons of popcorn, though, and emerged just at the rush hour.

Pavlik wasn't there.

We stood on the sidewalk waiting for him, I, for one, thinking longingly of Hilly. He'd never keep the Legend waiting on the street; he'd be there.

It really got a little scary with people going by, doing double takes, coming back and saying, "Is it really you?" And then just standing there and staring while we pretended they weren't there. A crowd was actually collecting.

I was beginning to sweat when finally we saw Pavlik approaching and ran for the car. If it'd been Hilly, Kate would have chewed him out royally. She was fairly easy on Pavlik, although she did point out that this tardiness just wouldn't do. One really did have the sense of an escape. Thank God I'm not famous — I couldn't take it.

Kate called in the evening. She'd been thinking, and it really made more sense for her to rest in Vancouver than in New York, so that's what she would do.

She'd been to Dr. Kievel's house for a swim in his pool. And she was going to have her old Vancouver friend, Hugh Pickett, by for dinner. Quite a social life. I think she was enjoying her reprieve from the dreaded cancer.

The cast was sent back to their various homes, although kept "on hold," and the production office remained open with a reduced staff.

Kate's "rest" was pretty exhausting.

She called me the next morning and said they were going on an excursion up Grouse Mountain. Did I want to come? I thought I'd better. Somebody had to keep an eye on her, especially if she was going to go into mountain climbing.

She and Phyllis and Pavlik picked me up right after breakfast and we were halfway to the mountain when I foolishly mentioned that my throat was a little sore and Joel Higgins had recommended zinc lozenges. Had they ever heard of them?

"Heard of them," said Kate, "I've got some. Turn around, Pavlik."

I protested, but nothing would do but we go all the way back into Vancouver. We waited in the car while Pavlik, under Kate's orders, went up to her apartment and found the zinc lozenges and brought them to me. Then we started off again.

"You should have known better than to mention them," Phyllis whispered to me in the back seat. Grouse Mountain, where there was a tramway Kate had hoped to ride to the top, was crawling with tourists that Sunday morning, so we didn't get out of the car.

Instead, we drove down Capilano Canyon and stopped at the entrance to a famous suspension bridge. Kate had never seen it. This is a spectacular bridge that spans a deep canyon, weaving and swaying as you cross it single file, clinging to ropes on either side.

Kate was in her element.

"Don't look down," she said as she headed across it. "Just keep going." Good advice; looking down made the knees go limp.

Halfway across we encountered another couple coming toward us, a middle-aged man and woman. It was obvious that they recognized Kate. And she felt like talking to them.

"Do you know anything about trees?" she asked the man, pointing to a huge tree at the edge of the canyon. "Do you know what kind of tree that is?"

He didn't know what kind of tree that was, but they chatted for a moment, Kate comfortable with someone who knew who she was, but was clearly above asking her for an autograph.

On the way back, though, as we made our way gingerly across the bridge we came upon an older man with a camera aimed toward us. Kate covered her face.

"Don't bother," I said and we laughed as he frowned and tried to wave us out of the way—pesky tourists!—so he could take a picture of the bridge.

"Now let's hike through the woods," said Kate, once we were on firm ground. "Come on, Phyllis."

"No, Kate," said eighty-five-year-old Phyllis. "I'll wait here. I'd stumble and fall."

"Better to try and fall than not to try," declared Kate.

"I'll stay here," said Phyllis, firmly.

Poor Phyllis, I thought, what Kate puts her through. She demanded so much of herself and others. I sometimes had to bite my tongue to keep from saying, What are you trying to prove? You've already proved it. Relax!

Anyway, off she charged into the forest primeval. I huffed and puffed, trying to keep up, but Miss Hepburn—who was, remember, resting—raced ahead like a steam locomotive.

We came to a terrible sign.

It read: WILD BEES! DANGER! DO NOT ENTER!

"Look, Kate!" I cried. "Wild bees!"

"What about it?"

"Well, wild bees!"

"Oh, shoot, they're not going to bother us!" she said. "Come on, follow me!"

And I followed her into the World of the Wild Bees and, of course, we didn't even see any. What wild bee would take on Katharine Hepburn, anyway?

We were out for the day, so we then drove to Horseshoe Bay, a beautiful place where the big ferryboats come and go, a bustling community of travelers and tourists with a sprinkling of little fast-food restaurants.

Pavlik parked on a small rise so that we could stay in the car and watch the ferryboats coming and going.

"I want a hamburger," I said, overcome by the Great Outdoors and the Fresh Air and the Pacific Northwest. I never eat hamburgers.

"So do I," said Kate, also overcome. "We'll all have hamburgers with French fries."

Phyllis gave him the money and we sat snugly in the car while Pavlik, who was really very nice, went to fetch the hamburgers.

As we waited, I teased Kate about Dr. Kievel.

KATHARINE KIEVEL, I told her, would look great on the marquees—so much better than KATHARINE HEPBURN. The alliteration was fabulous. This could be the big breakthrough she was looking for. She could have a career.

She said she'd take it under consideration.

Pavlik returned with the hamburgers.

"Don't eat the top half of the bun," Kate instructed us, "just the bottom. It's better for you."

But that pure air was getting to me and I was ravenous so I ignored her instructions and ate both. But I made a mental note that Katharine Hepburn had learned not to eat the top of her hamburger bun.

After that, we drove aimlessly until we came to something called Lighthouse Point. But you couldn't see the lighthouse and you couldn't see the point, at least from the road.

"How far is it?" Kate asked Pavlik. "Could we walk?"

"Oh, yes," he said. "Not far."

So we left Phyllis to doze off in the car in a parking lot while Kate and Pavlik and I started down on a path through the woods. Very downhill, very steep, very long, very rugged. I'm sure we went a mile. Even Kate was winded. We grumbled and laughed and groaned and gasped as the path seemed never to end.

"Do you realize we have to go back up again?" I said to Kate. She let out a moan.

"Not far now," Pavlik kept saying. Kate and I would exchange a look.

When we finally got there it was a very small, very uninteresting lighthouse surrounded by tourists. We turned right around and started back up. We stopped several times and leaned against tree trunks, though, partly because we were exhausted and partly because we were laughing so much.

After that we hunted for and found the rustic little church where we had filmed the wedding of Kate and Hal Gould in *Delafield*. I was touched that Kate wanted to see it.

I was ready to go home and even Kate was wearing out, so they dropped me at the hotel, but not before I had been invited to dinner.

At 6:00 P.M., showered and shaved, I walked over to Kate's apartment — the weather was lovely still, a perfect day — and found her seated before the fire. She was radiant.

"Pour yourself a drink," she said.

I went to the bar and when I turned around, there stood Hilly holding a tray of hors d'oeuvres.

Much rejoicing, I can tell you.

"The family all together again!" exclaimed Kate. I had never seen her happier.

"And hear how strong my voice is!" she said.

We had a great dinner, just like old times. I came away with the feeling that she'd be working soon. Had it all just been the loss of Hilly?

He drove me home, except he didn't drive me straight home. We drove leisurely around Vancouver, talking. I told him how wonderful it was to have him back, how we had missed him, how Kate had missed him. But would he stay, I wondered?

My suitcases remained half unpacked. The fate of the production was still very much up in the air.

But the next day was calming.

I attended production meetings until noon, which meant that somebody thought this movie might actually get made.

I lunched at an Italian dive with Merrill, George, and Adie. They seemed hopeful, especially after my report of the evening before.

At 5:00 I took my masseur, Peter Roach, to give Kate a massage. He was very Canadian about it all, passive, hardly what one would expect from somebody who was about to lay hands on one of the most famous people in the world.

Kate appeared in the living room in her white silk pajamas, looking like a little girl.

"Our Miss Hepburn," I said to Peter, and they disappeared into her bedroom while Hilly and Phyllis and I had a drink. Then I went back to the hotel.

After Kate, Peter came by and gave me a massage.

"Well, how was it?" I asked him eagerly.

"All right," he said, shrugging. That was the most I could get out of him. Sometimes the Canadians were just too damn laid back!

George and Merrill flew to Seattle the next day to audition more boys for the part of Walter, Jr.

We were hanging in there.

But Adie was to leave at noon to fly back to Los Angeles. We spent the early morning walking along the bay, picking our way through the greenish poop of the Canadian geese, speculating as to what was to become of us. Would she come back?

I spent the afternoon shopping at the Bay Company—more sweaters because of the burning per diem in my pocket—and then was invited to Kate's again for dinner.

As I entered the apartment, an excited Hilly came rushing up to me.

"She's had an accident!" he whispered.

"Accident?"

Kate appeared, dramatically framed in the doorway.

"I crashed *twice* on my bicycle in Stanley Park this afternoon," she announced.

My God, I thought, what was she doing cycling through Stanley Park when she was supposed to be resting?

Kate suddenly unbuttoned and dropped her slacks, standing before me only in her underpants.

"Look at this!"

There, on her upper thigh, was the ugliest black-and-blue mark I have ever seen in my life. It was the size of a billiard ball.

"For God's sake, cover yourself, woman!" I cried. "Am I to be spared nothing on this production?"

She laughed and pulled up her pants.

"Went right over the handlebars," she said happily.

I made myself a stiff drink.

And we had a wonderful evening. Her thigh might have been a mess, but her face was luminous and, in the best of moods, she embarked once again on our favorite pastime: reminiscing about the past, Hollywood, Spencer, the making of movies, happy and relaxed before the fire.

It was the calm before the storm.

She was in the hospital again the next day.

The night before she had never looked or sounded better, but today it was decided that she would have to have an operation on her throat to remove a carotosis, a minor operation, but an operation nonetheless.

I felt as though we were on a roller coaster.

It would mean a long recuperative period for Kate, and before the day was out George Schaefer had returned to Los Angeles. We had lost our director, for the time being.

Now only Merrill and Kate and I remained.

She came through the operation with flying colors, but she was warned that for a week she must not use her voice and then for a second week use it only minimally. I wasn't sure Kate knew what "minimally" meant. At the end of that time, we would know whether she could do the film or not.

Kate returned to her apartment, but I didn't talk to her right away because, of course, she couldn't over the telephone.

On her second day of recuperation, the silent Miss Hepburn indicated via a note that she wished to see a movie, so Merrill and I met her and Phyllis at the little movie house in the mall under our hotel. The movie was a British film called *Wish You Were Here*. Hilly had already seen it—and whispered to me that he wasn't sure it was Kate's "kind of movie"—so he went off somewhere in the car.

We got our popcorn and settled into our seats. Kate with her little pad and pencil dashed off notes to us every second until the picture began.

Then I started to get uneasy because it was so sexual. Halfway through the film, a man dropped his trousers, eased himself onto the heroine, and provided us with a full view of his bare behind as he entered her.

Kate sprang to her feet and in a loud voice said, "*Let's go!*"

The audience was then treated to the spectacle of Katharine Hepburn storming up the aisle, followed by meek Phyllis, easygoing Merrill, and timid Jim. It was the only time I'd ever known her to walk out on anything. And I can't say I blamed her. Hadn't the movies gone too far?

Hilly was off with the car, so we walked her to her apartment building, Merrill chatting at her side, Phyllis and I following behind.

Then we went up and had tea with her while she bombarded us with notes like, "How can they make films like that?" And "Do you need something stronger to drink?"

Merrill and I did have something stronger to drink afterward at a restaurant called Humphrey's atop our hotel, where one sat facing windows overlooking the entire city. We sipped martinis and watched the sun setting behind the mountains and toyed with the question that was ever foremost in our minds.

Could she or couldn't she do it?

I happened upon a theatre memorabilia shop during one of my walks and bought a charming still of Kate and Spencer Tracy, young and holding hands, in *State of the Union*. Couldn't resist it, but wasn't sure I should show it to Kate.

I had lunch with Merrill in a window of the English Bay Cafe, and it was pretty difficult not to dwell on the weather, which was spectacular. Halfway through October and not a drop of rain. And all those people lying on the beach, half-naked in the sun. My heart sank when I thought that we weren't out there cranking the cameras.

We were going to try another movie with Kate so we met her and Phyllis at the Stanley Theatre for the 2:00 showing of *The Untouchables*, hoping not to be dragged out before it was over.

She was still in her silent period so, just for fun, I had prepared a little questionnaire for her to answer in writing as we waited for the picture to begin.

Kate laughed and studied it carefully. I had provided three possible answers for each question:

> 1) How have you been since last we met?
>   a) Fascinated by my surroundings
>   b) Bored to distraction
>   c) Meekly silent, but staunch
>
> 2) How does your throat feel?
>   a) Lousy
>   b) A little sore
>   c) Recuperative
>
> 3) How have you been spending your time?
>   a) In meditation
>   b) With strenuous exercise
>   c) With Dr. Kievel
>
> 4) Is your household in order?
>   a) Yes
>   b) No
>   c) Don't ask *me*

5) How do you like the script?
   a) Wonderful
   b) Marvelous
   c) The best ever

6) When would you like to start work?
   a) Later
   b) A year from now
   c) Don't bother me; I'm writing

Kate sort of played the game, but pretty much ignored my answers, supplying her own.

Beside #1 she wrote "Victim."

By #2 she simply drew a big "0."

She checked answers "a" and "b" of #3, but opposite "With Dr. Kievel" wrote "Big fight!" And then got so carried away with that she skipped the following questions and went right to the bottom of the page, where she wrote: "We were going to take ferry to Victoria — got up at 5:30 — at 7:00 A.M. he called (his niece) — said he'd decided to fly so I told Phyllis to say forget it. His niece said Monday, I said forget it."

At that point, the lights went down and the picture began. We were all delighted not only by the film, which was great, but also to be seeing it in a real theatre with a huge screen and glorious sound. We came out in a glow.

Merrill had to go off somewhere so I rode back to the hotel with Kate.

"Sean Connery and Robert DeNiro are real stars!" she wrote happily on her pad. No mention of Kevin Costner.

She invited me to dinner so I had a quick nap and a swim and walked over to her place through the warm, balmy evening.

I did take the photograph of her and Spencer and showed it to her, which set off a stream of recollections, all by notes that filled the living room. I threatened to publish them.

Something came out in the course of the dinner that upset me.

Kate was pushing her niece, Schuyler Grant, for the part of Annette, the daughter, which had already been cast, and very well cast, with Christianne Hirt. I'd heard rumors of this, but this was the first confirmation of it and I decided on the spot that I wouldn't have it. Christianne had won the part, fair and square, and I had seen what she could do on that first morning of rehearsal.

Well, she was let go and Kate's niece was hired the next day. I'd rarely been so angry. There were times when I wasn't proud of the people in my profession. If that wasn't dirty pool I didn't know what was. Kate — and George and Merrill, too — claimed that Christianne was hired only because Schuyler wasn't available at that time. That's the way they rationalized it. I didn't believe it.

George had read Schuyler in Los Angeles and found her "perfect for the role." Merrill said that Christianne was a star in Canada, and so losing this "fairly minor role" wouldn't harm her career. I wondered about her psyche.

It might all be beside the point, considering that we didn't have a production, anyway, but I was livid.

Young actors, beware. When the niece of the star wants your part, she gets it. You'd better learn that early.

I might add that I was the only one connected with the production who thought it was awful.

Well, I tried to stay calm and even have a little warmth in my heart for poor Schuyler Grant, who would come into the production as Miss Hepburn's niece and would have to overcome that. On the other hand, she'd better be damn good.

That night I had a pizza sent up to my room. Didn't want to see people.

I met Hilly early the next morning for a brisk walk, during which I let off steam. He knew and liked Schuyler very much.

Nobody called me that morning, and I wondered if I was being ostracized. I decided to forget it all and go to the Aquarium, which turned out to be a great idea. I've never had much feeling for fish, but this was sensational. Especially those brilliant whales who put on such a show and could, I was convinced, write plays if they ever set their minds to it.

I walked back to the hotel — the weather was beautiful — just in time to get a call from Merrill, who was about to take Kate to the doctor for her checkup. He was a bit anxious about what I had said to her regarding the Schuyler business. (I had sworn that I would confront her with it.)

"Nothing," I said, coward that I was. What good would it have done? Whatever Kate wanted, Kate got. That was the name of the game.

Relieved, he took her to the doctor and called later to report that she was coming along fine. Filming was now scheduled to begin on October 26.

That would be almost one month to the day since we first arrived in Vancouver. It would also be one week short of the day when we would have finished the picture.

We went out to scout locations, Merrill and Justis and a location gang and I, looking for a suite that would serve as Laura's Manhattan penthouse. We found one at last at the Western Bay Shore Hotel, a tremendous suite that Prince Philip (he and the Queen were visiting) had vacated only thirty minutes before, having attended a reception of some sort there.

It was a great boost, actually scouting locations. We seemed to be on the track again.

But then I went to Kate's for dinner and, walking home in the dark with Hilly, we agreed that she would never be able to do this film. She seemed more feeble and rambling that night than I had ever known her.

Alarmed and depressed, I put in a call to Merrill. And then I stuck a video of *The Philadelphia Story* into my VCR to remind myself of what she had been and, hopefully, still was.

Merrill took me to breakfast at the Brasserie the next morning to calm my troubled nerves.

Whether Kate could do it or not, he said, we had to go on for insurance reasons. We had already spent over a million dollars, but the loss to Gaylord Productions, who were underwriting the production (as they had *Delafield*), was no more than a paltry $125,000 or so. Not to worry. And there would be no cost to his company, Schaefer/Karpf/Eckstein, through this delay.

I went back up to my suite and finished watching *The Philadelphia Story*. When it was over, I called Kate to say how wonderful it was and was astounded by the sound of her voice. The night before it had been hopeless; today it sounded strong and firm.

I really did think I was going mad.

Merrill said we were now slated to start production on October 28.

I walked along the bay in the afternoon, but then came home to a frantic call from Kate.

"Hilly's gone bonkers," she said, her voice loud and clear now. "He yelled at me and ran out."

I could see the scene. All-consuming Kate expecting utter devotion day and night, Hilly resenting the dominating female, exploding finally, running away. Neither of them really meaning to be impossible, but unable to stop themselves.

"You'd better come for drinks," said Kate. "No dinner, though. God knows if we'll even have a dinner with Hilly gone. Bring Merrill."

As fate would have it, I went walking and ran smack into Hilly having a cup of coffee at a sidewalk cafe.

"Oh, hello, Hilly," I said, casually. "What's this I hear? I hear you yelled at Katharine Hepburn and ran out?"

We both laughed, couldn't help it. It was funny, these fusses, once they were over.

"They're driving me crazy," Hilly said, "she and Phyllis."

I knew what he meant. Phyllis was dotty at her age and even Kate, joking though she was, said, "I'm as dotty as Phyllis." I felt sorry for Hilly. I knew he was devoted to Kate and Phyllis, and they to him, but Kate had the strongest personality (and, under normal circumstances, the strongest voice) in the world. I recalled how drained I was after a mere weekend of her as a houseguest. Poor Hilly got it every minute of his waking life.

I made a mental note to delicately discuss with Kate the importance of Hilly having some time off. Even the slaves had days off, didn't they?

I left him sitting there. He was wondering what to do next. Hilly loved Vancouver as much as the rest of us. I suspected he'd think twice before chucking all this.

Merrill and I went to Kate's that evening rather dreading it. Would she be in despair? Wringing her hands? Facing the prospect of Pavlik again?

Not at all. She couldn't have been jollier.

"Terribly funny," she said. "Hilly called me a dreadful name and stumbled as he ran out the door. Have another drink."

We were into our second drink when the front door suddenly opened and Hilly came grimly in, said not a word, slipped past us as if we weren't there, and went into the kitchen.

Phyllis came out to report that he was cooking dinner, and normality appeared to have returned.

We then got on the subject of the goodness of man, a topic that frequently occupied us. Kate and Phyllis and Merrill argued that it exists and is a powerful force, though I claimed to be unable to find much of it. (I wasn't the one who kicked out the Hirt girl in order to put my niece in.)

I then went home and opened a can of soup, but only after I had stared at my face solemnly for a good minute or two in the mirror to see if I was aging.

I was.

I love Vincent van Gogh. It's my personal theory that he was not only not mad, but had one of the great minds of the time. Read his letters.

So I was excited to discover that the Vancouver Film Festival was showing an Australian-made documentary on him in a suburban movie theatre.

I talked Kate into going. She loved paintings and painters and considered herself one of them in a, for her, fairly humble way.

Phyllis and Hilly came, too, and we found ourselves in a packed house of film buffs. Luckily, few of them were aware of Kate's presence. (Indeed, there had been very little press about her being in Vancouver and nobody expected to see her there.) They all seemed to be very young and very ardent and very bohemian. I was a bit put off by it, probably because I was none of those things.

Unfortunately, a girl with a great head of wild hair sat down right in front of Kate.

"Oh, dear," said Kate, attempting to peer around it and giving up.

She suddenly reached forward and started rearranging it. Very startled, the girl whirled around and was about to attack when she realized she was staring into the face of Katharine Hepburn.

"*I . . . just . . . can't . . . see*," said Kate.

"Be my guest," said the thrilled girl. So Kate sort of pulled the hair back and tied it up. It was the kind of thing you would have to be Katharine Hepburn to get away with. I suspected the girl would always wear her hair that way now and dine out on the story.

The film, alas, was long and not very good. John Hurt was not the man to narrate. Even some of Vincent's words, which I cherish, fell flat and seemed cold. Furthermore, they "dramatized" some scenes, which meant we saw happy peasants (actually amateurish extras) dancing away in Arles. I felt guilty that I had dragged Kate out for this (at night, too!), but she was a good sport about it.

But that night my heart sank again because she seemed especially shaky and aged.

Maybe that's why I sank into a depression the next morning. Couldn't get out of it. I felt adrift and going nowhere.

By October 23 the weather was beginning to get a little cooler, a little cloudy. Surely that meant the rains would soon follow and we would start filming.

Karen Austin returned briefly—I wasn't sure why—and I lunched with her and her friend Larry Gilman at the English Bay Cafe. Karen was very attractive, but also kind of raucous and earthy. She was fun. She had been to South Carolina and had brought back a garnet-and-aquamarine necklace that she said had magical powers. I was to give it to Kate for her throat.

I hesitated, knowing that Kate didn't really like to get gifts, and finally asked Karen to write a note to go with it explaining the necklace and its powers, which she did. I promised to pass it along.

Phyllis and Kate returned from a visit to Victoria happy and rested. With some trepidation, I took them to see the film *Maurice*, at a matinee.

It was to be on me, my little treat.

They stood near me as I went to the box office to purchase the tickets.

"Three, please." I made the mistake of saying, "One adult and two senior citizens."

Kate screamed like a stuck pig.

"Don't you *ever* do that!" she howled. "Three adults! *Three adults!*"

It didn't bode well for the afternoon.

We settled into our seats, but I wasn't sure for how long. I suspected the homosexual theme wasn't going to sit well. And I had heard, furthermore, that the film included frontal nudity. I could be back at the hotel in a matter of minutes.

She stayed, though, although there was a bit of moaning and squirming. None of us liked the ending of the film, which didn't seem to be an ending at all.

I rushed home afterward because Merrill and I were giving a party, believe it or not.

I'd suggested it to Merrill because I felt the production people at the office, left hanging in midair while we waited for Kate, needed a little morale booster. We had the hotel cater it in Merrill's penthouse and had a blast. Kate didn't show, but we must have had twenty-five people, counting spouses and lovers. Lots of drinks and plenty of laughs, and the mission was accomplished. At the end of it, I think we all felt we were part of an ongoing project, whether we were or not.

On the twenty-fifth, the rains came at last and I noted on my calendar that we had now been in Vancouver a month and there was not one inch of footage in the can.

I talked to Howard and Annie Koch in Woodstock, who said they had telephoned Kate to congratulate her on her *African Queen* book, and she told them that, so far, this production had been "much anguish."

Never had a star been so cosseted or provided such comfort—not to mention her $2,500 weekly living expenses plus $765 for Hilly and car—but I knew what she meant. She was referring to the weight, the responsibility of it all on her shoulders. If she couldn't deliver now, would she ever be able to deliver again? It was too heartbreaking to think about. Just as she had been frightened, all those years ago, of her first directing job, now she was frightened, I was certain, of not even being able to do what she was famous for. And what was expected of her. And she kept saying that she mustn't "let everybody down." Great stars didn't let people down.

The next day I actually did a little rewriting—I hadn't had the heart before—just in the event we actually started shooting in a couple of days.

I went to Kate's for dinner that night, however, and threw in the towel. She sounded terrible and repeated exactly the line that had first plunged us into the abyss: "I feel like I'm choking and I can't act with that." We were right back at square one.

And yet the doctor had said she was totally recovered.

Noel Taylor telephoned while I was there to tell Kate he was about to return to Vancouver to start work, but she told him not to be so ready to do that.

It was the ball game.

She looked so pathetic, I was touched.

"It's not your fault," I said, "it's just damn fate. Don't take it all on your shoulders."

"Well, it *is* on my shoulders," she said.

My timing was awful, but I remembered Karen's necklace and took that moment to present it to her.

"Why would anybody give me *this*?" she said.

But when she read the note, which was all about a witch woman who had given it especially to Karen "for Miss Hepburn" and about its presumed magical powers, she put it right on. Kate believed in magic. And, at that point, so did I—if it worked.

And it did.

I piddled with rewrites the following morning and I went through the charade of sending them to the production office, but I stopped after talking with Merrill.

He told me Kate was to see her doctor at noon. We agreed that we had never seen her so anxious before.

"Two valiums," said Merrill, "could save us a million-and-a-half dollars."

And what happened with the insurance if she said she couldn't do it and the doctor said she could?

It was crazy. I spent the rest of the morning planning my return to Los Angeles at the same time I talked to Adie in Los Angeles who said she and George Schaefer were planning to return to Vancouver in two days.

I leaped into the car and drove to the Capilano suspension bridge, where I swung for a symbolical ten minutes.

In my madness, I got stopped by a cop for speeding on the way back, but pleaded foreign ignorance of kilometers, and he let me off with a warning.

I ran into Merrill and he said, "Come and have lunch." He had something to tell me.

And when he told me, I couldn't believe it.

After her meeting with the doctor, he had arranged for Kate, should she agree to it, to meet with a shrink.

I gasped.

Kate didn't believe in that sort of thing. She was strictly New England and you didn't have mental problems in New England. Work and exercise took care of that.

I'd been trying to get her to get Hilly to a shrink for years, but she would only say, "Hilly's no crazier than anybody else. He just has fits."

And who would believe that the strong, vital Kate, revered by the world, could possibly need a shrink? Well, it was all damn tough to have been a great beauty and now, at her age, to have to present herself not only to the public, but to that terrible eye, the camera. Why not a little anxiety?

She'd never do it, of course.

The afternoon was spent in aimless walking—avoiding the Hudson Bay Company and the lure of more sweaters—and I found a message from Merrill when I got home. He'd had dinner with Kate (his night in the barrel), and I was to call him at whatever hour.

I did and he was bursting with news.

The doctor told Kate that her throat was completely healed and any problem she had was in her head. She had then gone straight to the psychiatrist and spent an hour with him. At dinner she was radiant—a revelation!—and all systems were go!

I had an excited breakfast with Merrill and, among other things, we discussed a new ending. How different it was to discuss a new ending when you were not just going through the motions, as I'd been doing for the past month, but you knew the film would really be made.

I didn't see Kate all day, but got a report that our darling fusspot was running around checking the sets, decor, and furnishings. The commitment was made and now she had to see that things were right.

I rewrote her little speech to Malcolm, the baby, in the afternoon. It still wasn't good.

The cast began flying in again.

The following morning, October 29, I had a swim and a sauna at dawn, then tackled the damn ending again. It still defeated me. Nevertheless, I drove the new pages to the production office where everything was now buzzing.

Kate spent the day in costume fittings with Noel and poking about her "penthouse" at the Western Bay Shore Hotel. The set people complained to me that she was ruining their beautifully dressed set with clutter—Kate adored clutter—whereas they saw it, as I did, as all light and air and modern. I told them they didn't have to do everything she said, but maybe they did. Kate was very pleased with her penthouse, though, and that was a blessing.

I ran into Karen Austin in the hotel lobby. She had just taken Sean Harmon, who would play her son, to the Aquarium. She'd also been playing with the new little twins who replaced the triplets as her baby. Her theory was that by the time we got into filming she'd really be like a mother to them.

And Schuyler Grant arrived, although I hadn't met her yet. I trusted Kate was taking care of her.

Adie and Merrill came to my suite for drinks, but I was too tired to join them and George for dinner. As the Big Day approached, I found myself careening from a souped-up elation to utter fatigue.

Just for the record, October 30, 1987, was a drizzly day in Vancouver, British Columbia—it would rain from now on—but for one screenwriter the walk of a few blocks from his hotel to St. John's Church for the first rehearsal (although *second* try) of *Guest Appearance* was very pleasant, indeed.

No Miss Hepburn, who was still busy with fittings, but we rehearsed the entire Gomphers family and it was all very encouraging.

And, after all my screaming, Schuyler Grant was delectable and one of the nicest people I'd ever met. No pretensions there. Actually, I felt a little sorry for her. She'd been very happy in the large one-bedroom apartment the hotel gave her, but Kate had moved her into a dinky studio because "you must have the early morning sun."

George, Merrill, Adie and I convened at 11:00 A.M. for a story conference the following morning. The night before, George and Merrill had dined with Kate, and she had come up with a new idea for the ending. She was pushing it like mad.

They told it to me and it was really awful. Terrible. I yelled a bit, but they said, "Well, you'd better talk it over with Kate." And at 4:00 I was booked to go over to Kate's apartment.

I was angry with her and prepared to do battle. The entire afternoon was spent building my case, firming up my arguments, rehearsing my lines. I would stick to my guns, no matter what.

She was sitting before the fire, as I walked in.

"Well, what do you think of my idea for the ending?" she said immediately.

"Kate," I said, gulping, "I think it's lousy."

"Okay," she said, "that's that."

And we had a very pleasant drink.

There's a handsome office building at 401 West Georgia Street in Vancouver and it was here, on the twelfth floor, that we started filming *Guest Appearance*. The first two scenes we shot with Lee Richardson, and then Kate came in and did an unfilmed telephone call with him, sitting on the sidelines out of camera range.

The voice was not good. I think it scared her — God knows it scared me — and she went off to do a makeup test in a state of nerves.

I went home after lunch to grapple with the ending again. If I blasted Kate's ending, I knew I'd better come up with a damn good one of my own. Why was it so difficult? Kate was right, of course, that the dratted thing was over once Melody and Walter were together again, but I didn't agree that the audience wouldn't care about her bet, slight and silly as it was. Would we not all be waiting, glued to our television sets, to see whether she won it or lost it? If they didn't care, then I'd failed.

It was cloudy and rainy outside the next morning, but inside on the twelfth floor it was cozy, and there was an air of excitement as the crew, many of them for the first time, prepared to work with Katharine Hepburn. George and I were both a little breathless, I think, and Merrill went around looking like a Cheshire cat, as well he might. Had it not been for his perseverance, we'd never have come to this moment.

I might put in a word for Kate here, too, who was going before the camera and laying everything on the line: her looks, her talent, her reputation. And I swear there wasn't a one of us that day unaware that we were looking upon what was still one of the great faces of our time.

We were filming in sequence as much as possible, so this was her first scene in the movie, where she was being interviewed on television by a Johnny Carson type. She was nervous, but even in that brief scene I began to see her getting into character, to see what Laura Lansing would be. And I knew she was going to be fun. By the time we finished that day, Kate was "making a movie."

The voice was only okay. A bit croaky. I hoped it would get better as we went along.

It was gray, wet, and foggy again the next day, so we couldn't shoot the exteriors we had planned. Instead, George spent the day shooting at Conway Reed's apartment, which meant that Kate had very little to do, as prearranged. George wanted her to continue to get her voice back before doing too much.

She did appear, however, and poke about the set and rearrange and suggest and generally put in her two cents' worth. She was mad for Nicolas Surovy, who'd be delightful as the tacky soap star.

Everybody was keeping one eye on the sky. We should have been doing exteriors before the Vancouver winter settled in, but we needed a clear day. We were prepared to move at a moment's notice if the sun came out.

"Cloudy with sunny periods," said the call sheet the next morning, so off we trooped to North Vancouver to shoot outside the Gomphers's house, which was as middle-class a little number as I ever hope to see.

I'm always amazed when people permit film companies to come in and turn their homes upside down, though I know they're well paid. And I was somewhat alarmed at how we seemed to be spilling over to the house next door, but it turned out we'd paid for that, too.

The extras stood around looking so much like locals (which they were), I didn't know whether they were a part of our movie or not. I started to ask an elderly couple, gawking away, to move on just as the assistant director came up and positioned them for the scene.

Moviemaking is and always will be a mystery to me, anyway. How directors do it, I don't know. I loathe the auteur theory, which regards the director as the author of a film, but at the same time I see there's some truth to the idea.

Without the word, however, there is nothing. I created the plot, the characters, and put the words in their mouths. So was it George Schaefer's movie? And yet, when I observe what George makes out of it, I do understand the confusion. It's all collaborative. It wasn't my movie and it wasn't his movie; it wasn't Merrill's movie and it wasn't Kate's movie. It was our movie.

I began to get a little concerned as filming went on because so many of the extras were Asian. This story took place in Hicksville, Long Island, and I found it difficult to believe that every other person in Hicksville, Long Island, would be Asian. I asked Merrill to speak to the lady who cast the extras. I hoped they wouldn't think I was being racist, but neither did I want Hicksville to look like downtown Hong Kong.

Kate did the scene outside the house where Laura meets the family for the first time and I, at least, thought it was funny. Karen Austin was just fine and so was Joel Higgins. And I was already in love with Schuyler Grant. The twins—who were interchangeable; if one couldn't hack the scene they'd go and get the other one—were obviously going to work out and Sean Harmon, despite a slight Canadian accent that hardly conjured up Long Island, was also fine.

Kate then wrapped a towel around her head and did the scene where she sees the kids off to school. She was really getting into it, and I saw that she was beginning to have a good time.

After a mere three days of shooting, we found ourselves on a Saturday morning with a three-day weekend. Strange scheduling. We wouldn't go back to work until Tuesday.

This was all to the good, I suppose, since it gave Kate's voice extra time to strengthen, but it seemed a shame to take a break just when the momentum was going.

Kate didn't surface at all during those three days. Good for her. Resting, I trusted, although resting for Kate might mean a quick trip to the Klondike.

On Tuesday morning we resumed filming at a discount department store in North Vancouver, where we shot Melody's looking at television sets with Kate being interviewed on them. Fun to see Kate up there. Just as if it were real, folks.

That was easily and pleasantly accomplished, and then we moved a few blocks to a supermarket, where the staff was outside handing out leaflets that read: IMPORTANT NOTICE—We're Gonna Be In The Movies—SuperValu, Edgemont Village, will be CLOSED Tuesday, November 10, 1987, for the Filming of the T.V. Movie *"Guest Appearance"* starring KATHARINE HEPBURN—Sorry for any inconvenience—Tom Belich, Store Manager.

As a result of this subtle announcement, a crowd was gathering outside in the hope of glimpsing the star.

So was I. It had been a while.

And there she was suddenly, made up and ready to rehearse and waving to the crowd through the window. I pushed my way into the store.

"Isn't this great?" Kate was saying. "We ought to get a shot of this, them waving like that. Perfect for Laura."

But George had his shots set up, and another of Kate's ideas, good as it was, got shot down.

It was fun having the run of the supermarket and dreaming up things for Kate and Karen to do as they wheeled the baby around in the shopping cart.

Unfortunately, due to the ironclad rule that I watch the dailies with Phyllis, I had to leave before they got to an important scene at the checkout counter. I had a quick lunch and joined Phyllis and Merrill in his suite.

As always, I knew that Kate would ask Phyllis how she was doing. And, I suppose, how she was looking. In Phyllis's case, it was rather like asking a born-again Christian what she thought of Jesus.

"She's looking younger than ever," said Phyllis as the dailies ended.

I was pleased to see that Kate, on her second day of filming, was settling in and becoming less mannered, more firm.

I offered to walk Phyllis home, but she assured me she could get home perfectly well on her own and, being British, didn't mind the rain.

The energy, the powerful personality, the demanding ego, the voice—all of the things in Kate that could destroy Hilly—seemed to have affected Phyllis hardly at all.

Maybe that's love.

Armistice Day was called Remembrance Day in Canada, and at 11:00 A.M. at the studio we all stopped work and stood for a moment of silent meditation. I meditated on Kate, whom I could have killed at that moment.

She was at her worst that day—the "cranky old broad" Nick Nolte talked of—changing things and always, always carping about the pressure.

"It's so fast!" she kept saying. This was a common complaint of stars who were accustomed to the more casual pace of the old days of feature films made in major studios. This was television, though, and we had only twenty-two days to make this movie. She knew that, but she did like to harp on it.

We filmed the scene where she and Brenda enter the Gomphers's house for the first time. I had written this scene very carefully (several times) and it was a favorite of mine. At the last minute, however, Kate had a couple of brilliant ideas and changed it so that it didn't work at all.

George said he could work around it in the editing (if he did, it didn't help), but it was maddening for me to see a lovely little moment like that destroyed. I got frustrated and angry and avoided her until I got back to the hotel for the dailies at 4:00 P.M.

I wasn't at all happy with the checkout-counter scene, the point of which, to me, seemed garbled on the screen.

I didn't voice my dismay to Phyllis, of course, who rose and said, "Isn't she looking young!"

I then saw her down to the street and again offered to see her home, but she said, "Oh, no. I have my umbrella and I know my way." So I kissed her and off she went.

Ten minutes later I had to go back down to the lobby and, glancing out the front door, saw Phyllis walking past the hotel and going up the hill in the opposite direction of her apartment building. I ran out and grabbed her.

"Phyllis, where are you going?"

"Oh, dear," she said. "I seem to have lost my way."

So I walked her to the corner of the street. I wanted to take her home, of course, but she wouldn't allow that, so I carefully aimed her toward her building.

"I know my way now," she said. Very worrying.

It was pouring rain, so I stayed in and had dinner sent up. Kate called, quite cheerful after having had a perfectly fine day at the studio, and I told her about Phyllis.

"You must walk her home," she said firmly. "All the way home." And she was right.

I spent most of the following day watching them film Kate's first sweep through the house and the scene where she turned off Annette's radio. Very well done. Schuyler wasn't the way I saw Annette physically, but she was a good actress. She was also absolutely open and friendly and going out of her way not to be "Katharine Hepburn's niece." (She was there, though, I was sure, because of the publicity value in that very fact.)

I went off, as usual, with Phyllis and Merrill to see the dailies. Maybe I was tired, but I was very depressed after that, despite the fact that Phyllis thought Kate looked younger than ever. I thought Kate was overacting and George should have curbed her. I was wrong, as it turned out. In the final cut it was simply the old Hepburn "magic" at work.

What was new, though, was that Kate messed up her lines. When we did *Delafield* she was line-perfect. Two years later she was having trouble and she was the first to admit it.

"What's *wrong* with me?" she'd say. "I can't remember a *thing*!"

I reminded myself that miracles could be performed in the editing room. Once again, however, I couldn't help wondering what I had gotten us into. Had I done Kate a disservice? Should we have left it with *Delafield*?

I did walk Phyllis home, despite her protests, and she was charming, chatting away about Miss Collier as if all the years in between hadn't happened. She would even have a momentary lapse occasionally and refer to Kate as Miss Collier.

"I must get home," she would say. "Miss Collier will want her dinner."

It didn't matter.

On the morning of Friday the thirteenth I awoke and looked into the bathroom mirror—and screamed!

One of my eyes was simply a mass of blood. Somehow in the night I had apparently broken a blood vessel. It was a ghastly sight and it scared the bejesus out of me.

As soon as the pharmacy was open in the mall below the hotel, I went down and consulted the pharmacist, a pale and mousy man, who listened to my story, looked at my eye, and then, without a trace of humor, said, "Well, I don't know what it is, but I'd certainly keep an eye on it."

He offered no medication, so I prowled about until I found something on the shelves, which I bought but was then afraid to use.

I wondered how to find an eye doctor and then remembered that Kate was always having eye problems, ever since she plunged into the canal in Venice during the filming of *Summertime*. She would know what to do, and probably even had medication.

I put on sunglasses—making the bleak day even bleaker—and drove out to the apartment building where they were filming, the one where Conway Reed supposedly lived in Manhattan. (But, in spite of the sign they put on it that read EAST RIVER TOWER, it still looked pure Vancouver.)

It was drizzly and cold. They were shooting the scene where Laura follows Walter out of the building and then Walter has a scene with Melody and they all get into the car and drive away. This was the scene where Melody, in the original script, was to come to Laura and say, sadly, "You lost your bet!"

But Kate fought that from the very first—"Nobody cares about the silly bet!"—and it was out. (I finally got it into a later scene.)

As I now approached the cast and crew, Pattie Robertson, the script supervisor, came up to me and said, "Jimmy, she's going to cut this," and pointed to several key lines in the scene.

And I just didn't feel up to battle that morning.

Kate didn't always say "okay" and let it go, not when she was on the set and getting into it or when she'd rehearsed it her way at home, with the cuts, and couldn't get back to the original.

At that moment I saw Kate go into the lobby of the building for a break. I foolishly followed her in. My timing was terrible.

She was obviously having a rough day out there in the rain and she was obviously in a bad mood.

I went right up to her and said, "Say, what do you do for your eyes?"

"Why?" she snapped.

"Well, *look*," I said and I took off my glasses, lifted up the lid, and flashed my bloody eye.

"I don't see a damn thing," she said. (Later it occurred to me that she probably didn't, given her eyesight.)

"It's all bloody," I said, "and I—"

Then she yelled at me, right in front of the crew and the extras and everybody.

"I'm glad I'm not as neurotic about my health as *you* are!" she shouted. "Why don't you stop this and go and sit somewhere and do some work!"

Everybody froze. I'm sure I turned ashen.

I was shaken and hurt and terribly embarrassed. I turned and went out the door and got in my car and drove back to the hotel.

Every kind of mean thought went through my head. George didn't back me up when she cut lines and the dailies weren't good and I even composed a note in my head which read: "Dear Kate. You seem to think because of who you are you can say anything you want to anyone without regard for their feelings or intelligence. Love, Jim." It was somewhat unjust, but it calmed me as I sat in my room with my bloody eye that nobody seemed to care about. I would be blind soon and then, in all probability, dead and nobody would care.

I wondered if they'd dedicate the picture to me, posthumously.

Fortunately, my old pal, Trevor Pickering, escaped from Cannon Films the next day and came to visit. He looked at my eye—which was worse; the red was spreading—and announced with authority that I had a broken capillary. Not a serious matter and, oddly enough, no pain at all. He led me back to the pharmacy and found me the proper medication.

Hilly was sitting across the street, having his morning coffee outside the coffee shop.

He said that in the car going home, Kate was very concerned about my eye. I couldn't have been more surprised. But I did try to remember that she was not young, she was working very hard, she was cold and wet, she felt responsible for every inch of footage. And perhaps it hadn't been a good idea to go up to a star in the middle of a hectic and difficult day of shooting and say, "What do you do for your eyes?"

Later in the morning, Kate called to see how I was. She said she hadn't realized it was the eye, thought it was the lid, and while she didn't say she was sorry I knew that this was her way of apologizing. So that was behind us.

The weekend came and with it sunny days, naturally.

I took Trevor with me to the Western Bay Shore Hotel, where we were filming in Laura's penthouse. Kate may have meddled, but her meddling paid off. The place was dressed with the most exotic artifacts and had exactly the right look for the home of a famous woman who had traveled the globe.

Merrill announced that the dressing cost $450,000, but that might have just been for the press.

Kate was very happy with her penthouse and was in good humor. I introduced Trevor to her and she said, "Sit down, Mr. Pickering, and tell me about yourself."

Thrilled, Trevor sat down, whereupon she got up and walked away. Something else suddenly on her mind, I guess. Trevor was startled, but stoic. It had been, he said, too good to be true.

We picked up our lunches outside at the honey wagon and took them into a large dining room cordoned off for us in the hotel.

Merrill appeared carrying a large cake, blazing with candles, and sneaked up behind Adie Luraschi with it. This was the second birthday we'd shared with Adie in Vancouver.

George gave her a dinner that night at a little restaurant we all liked called 891. Adie is a dear, warm person and a loyal friend and we, the guests, toasted her handsomely with rounds of drinks. She'd been George's right hand for decades, literally, dating since the early days of the Hallmark Hall of Fame, and I couldn't imagine George without her at his side.

Having said that, I should add that as we went on all our nerves were getting a little on edge and Adie and I had a small squabble the very next day over the very important matter of giving a forgetful bit player her line.

"Give her the line," I said.

"Don't you tell me to give her the line!" said Adie.

"Well, why don't you give her the line?"

"Don't you order me around!"

That sort of thing. People getting tired and edgy.

I was in a curious position, anyway. I was the writer and these people who made television—or any other kind of movies—were unaccustomed to having the writer, of all people, on the set. They found it annoying, I think, and they resented it. Also, I suppose I didn't act like a producer, but I was and, while a writer might be considered the lowest form of life, a producer gets a little respect. I wanted that.

Okay, so that same afternoon we were in a small room that was serving as Laura's bedroom, and Kate was rehearsing the scene with Brenda. I was standing just behind the camera, watching, and it was tight and it was crowded and the assistant director, who was The Toughest Broad in Show Business, suddenly turned to me and said, "Jim, get out."

She didn't know, being busy being The Toughest Broad in Show Business, that Kate turned to me for confirmation after every rehearsal and every shot.

"Okay?" she'd say, or simply question me with her eyes. I'd generally nod happy approval.

So, having been told to by The Toughest Broad in Show Business— who would dare argue with her?—I slunk out of the room, stunned, and said to no one in particular in the hall, "She ordered me out!"

Kate just happened to come into the hall at that moment and said, assuming that only she gave orders around there, "*I* didn't order you out. You should have stayed."

Then Kate called me into her dressing room and handed me a slip of paper on which she had completely rewritten, ten minutes before we were going to shoot it, her final speech to the interviewer that came at the end of the picture.

I protested meekly, scratched some of it out, shrugged, handed it back to her, thought what the hell!

I went home and spent the remainder of that delightful day rewriting for the millionth time Laura's scene with Annette, which we kept working and reworking. When I say "we," I mean me and my collaborator, Katharine Hepburn.

The only uplifting aspect of the day were the dailies, which Phyllis and I watched with glee. All the stuff shot the day before was very good and, as Phyllis happened to mention, Kate had never looked younger.

Our feet were cold and wet, but between raindrops we were shooting outside the Gomphers's house in North Vancouver the scene where Brenda and Lee Richardson enter the house. They were the only two people in the scene.

As they walked toward the door, however, it opened and out came Katharine Hepburn with no makeup and her hair in curlers to have a quiet word with Brenda.

"Cut!" yelled George. "What are you *doing*, Kate!" We all burst out laughing. Kate, too.

"How could you be shooting a scene if *I'm* not in it?" she said.

Kate had her quiet word with Brenda, then called me into her makeshift dressing room—I always knew that meant her pen had been at work—and showed me some changes she had made in the famous scene with Annette, which I'd rewritten until I was cockeyed.

She wanted Schuyler to have more of a scene—"if she's to make her name"—and I did, too, but if she had too much, the scene would be wrenched out of shape. The scene had to do with Annette having put out to her boyfriend who, once he got what he wanted, dropped her, thereby causing her great adolescent disillusionment.

One of my lines had Kate saying to her—Annette thought she'd be unpopular if she didn't "do it"—that her behavior wouldn't make her popular, but "it makes you easy." Kate suggested we change that to "it makes you an easy lay."

I was somewhat shocked. "I think not," I said and explained that the network would never permit it. She didn't see why. I suggested "it makes you a pushover," which seemed acceptable for the moment, but I knew I hadn't heard the last of it. Fortunately, the scene was scheduled to be shot on almost the last day so we had some time to kick it around further.

As we were rehearsing the scene where Laura gives the bathroom schedule to the Gompherses, it occurred to me that I wasn't documenting the filming properly, so I took a flash photo.

Kate frowned and mouthed, "Don't do that."

I had thought it would be all right, since she had her makeup on. Without her "face" on she will never permit photographs, star that she is, and I'd always been very careful about that. George Schaefer took one of my favorite photos of her sitting on the grass on my lawn in Stone Ridge, legs out in front of her, but her head hidden by an umbrella. Hidden face or not, you couldn't mistake who it is.

Driving back to the hotel, I had a thought about her scene with Annette. What if she hadn't slept with the boy yet, but was considering it and Laura talked her out of it? Wouldn't that be better? I was very pleased with myself.

I got home and worked on it immediately.

Then I viewed the dailies with Merrill and Phyllis—perfectly fine—and walked Phyllis every inch of the way home as she reminisced about Miss Collier. And then, suddenly, about Spencer Tracy.

It seems he and Kate were watching a baseball game on television—

or was it listening on the radio?—and Tracy got a yen for the popcorn they sold at the stadium. He said to Phyllis, "Go get some."

And she did, little Phyllis, all the way to the stadium and back. She reported this as if it were nothing but amusing and an indication of the good times they had, whereas I was appalled that anyone would ask that of anyone: the distance, fighting the traffic, finding a place to park, getting into the stadium, driving back. And all because Mr. Tracy had a yen for that popcorn.

I wondered if Phyllis had the story straight.

The next morning I rushed to the studio with my rewritten "Annette" scene and, seeing George first, handed it to him.

"Got it at last!" I chortled.

He read it, frowned, and said, "See what Kate thinks."

I found her in her dressing room.

"Rewrote the Annette scene," I said briskly and cheerfully, as if I had solved the riddle of the universe. She took it, read it, made a face, and handed it back. So I supposed the scene would have to be rewritten. Why was it so tough? (And when I view the film on video today, it's the only scene that makes me "fast-forward.")

They filmed the breakfast scene, which I did think was funny, but I still worried that Laura wasn't likable. However, I assumed she'd grow on you—especially with the Hepburn charm—as she converted into a caring human being.

Speaking of caring, Kate, who really was trying to be a little selfless, offered Hilly some time off, but then he wouldn't take it. He hated her domination, but he seemed lost without it. At any rate, she was happy to see him take off the minute he'd finished cooking dinner. He appeared to be reasonably satisfied for the moment, and I prayed we'd get through the production without further incident on his part.

On Sunday, Karen Austin invited me to brunch with her and Lee Richardson and an actor she was enamored of, Kevin Spacey, at the Teahouse in Stanley Park. I never turned down an offer to eat at the Teahouse, but first I spent the morning rewriting that scene.

Kate called to discuss once again the final scene in the film, the ending that had given us so much trouble. Her idea now was that Laura would repeat Melody's last line in the car as she was driven away.

I was less than enthralled, said I'd certainly take it under consideration, which meant I'd sweep it under the rug and hope she'd forget about it.

Karen was quite mad for Mr. Spacey, and I expected to see an Adonis walk in, but instead he was rather dark and dumpy and slightly Brooklynese. Karen hung on his every word, which actually wasn't that many words. We had a perfectly pleasant lunch, but then we went out to the parking lot to get into our cars.

Karen, who had arrived with Lee and me, was leaving with Kevin for, I assumed, an afternoon of passion or, at least, after having numerous Mimosas, revelry.

The cars were parked not bumper to bumper against a curb, but diagonally, side by side. I pulled out and backed up and started forward just as Kevin, without looking, backed up with a roar and rammed into the side of my car. The whole back of the car was smashed in. A moment earlier and he would have killed Lee, who sat beside me in the front seat.

I stopped, horrified, and sat there, stunned. Lee and I were both in a state of semishock.

Not Kevin and Karen. They got out of his car howling with laughter, bent double. Thought it was the funniest thing they'd ever seen.

I said something, I don't remember what, and drove off leaving them there, still laughing.

Quite shaken, I got us back to the hotel, dropped Lee, and immediately drove to the rental place.

The upshot was that I had to spend the next morning at the police station making a report, which I did without mentioning Mr. Spacey, pretending it was hit-and-run. I expected to encounter some gruff old sergeant, but behind the desk was a spinstery lady with graying hair and dressed in a frilly blouse. She gave me the form to fill out and when I handed it back to her, she said, "Oh, the Teahouse in Stanley Park! Don't you just love it? What did you have to eat?" Typically Vancouver.

(Two days later a lovely bottle of champagne arrived from Kevin Spacey with an apology. He hadn't realized how serious a matter it was. I sipped and forgave.)

Meanwhile, George was filming in the lobby of a snazzy hotel. Kate and I went into a jewelry store that had a display window in the lobby, not that Kate had the slightest interest in jewelry, but it gave the employees a lift.

In the afternoon, we moved to the studio and filmed Laura's rearranging the furniture in the Gomphers's house. That moment with Kate disappearing into a bedroom with a chair over her head worked like a charm. Good for Kate! Nor did she hesitate to do it, despite her bum shoulder and her bum foot and God knows what other ailments.

I was very happy with the dailies, and I need not mention what Phyllis said about them. I really did wonder how much Kate depended on her opinion or if she was just humoring her.

"Oh, no, Phyllis must see the dailies," she said to me once. I think she meant because it had always been her job, like carrying the plane tickets, and she must be made to feel useful. I couldn't imagine that Kate took her word on the dailies as gospel, especially since it was always so positive. On the other hand, stars feed on good things being said about them. Maybe Kate didn't wish to know if it was really true; she just wanted to hear it.

I had drinks with Noel Taylor and discussed his dressing of Karen Austin. She was a terrific actress and perfect for the part, but she had a slight tendency to show her flesh. Always one button unbuttoned on her blouse or, as with a skirt the day before that buttoned up the front, one more button unbuttoned at the bottom. I suggested clothes for her without buttons. If I protested, she countered that she had good legs, and why not show them? I argued that it wasn't in character.

It was an uphill battle. I saw Melody as plain and Karen just wasn't plain and, I think, was rather frightened of plain. I urged Noel to be firm with her, but Noel Taylor is the sweetest man on earth — has never worked with a star he didn't like, with the glaring exception of Zsa Zsa Gabor — and wouldn't dream of being firm with anyone. I took him to dinner anyway.

Kate's book, *The Making of the African Queen*, was now on the bestseller list, which gave her great pleasure and added to her estimation of herself as a writer, although I don't think it did much for her estimation of me.

Everybody was buying copies, so I called the biggest local bookstore, Duthie's, and ordered ten copies, thinking that if she'd sign them for me they'd make splendid Christmas presents.

A memo was circulated saying that we would complete principal photography on *Guest Appearance* on December 2. That was only eight days away. It seemed to take forever to start, of course, and then once started it seemed interminably slow, but somewhere in the middle the pace accelerated and before we knew it, it would be done.

The mere sight of that memo gave me a pang. I'd lived with this production so long, life without it seemed impossible. Empty. I'd be glad to get home to Los Angeles, certainly, and yet there was that curious pang.

I drove Noel out to the studio in my new, replacement rental car, and we filmed the scene where Melody says she has to watch the soap opera, which was called *The Storm Within*. Laura then responds with, "What the hell is *The Storm Within*? A laxative commercial?"

George and I had fought over that "laxative commercial" line since the very first time he saw the script. He hated that line. I loved the line. Kate was ambiguous about it (unusual for her), could take it or leave it. But I fought for it, calling it the funniest line in the script, and I lost. What Laura ended up saying was, "What the dickens is *The Storm Within*?"

The Canadians had had their Thanksgiving, but on November 26 we celebrated ours and a festive air pervaded the set.

I told Kate about my ten copies of her book.

"Bring them to the studio," she had said, "and I'll sign them between shots." She was really very good about signing them for various of the cast and crew.

She was full of fun that day and joking with everyone. There wasn't a member of the crew who wouldn't die for her—or for George either, for that matter.

I liked the dailies and walked Phyllis home, arm in arm, talking about Miss Collier. She and Kate were having a quiet dinner at home, but the rest of us Americans went over to North Vancouver to a charming restaurant in the Park Royale Hotel where they served "a traditional American Thanksgiving dinner." I'm not sure the Indians would have recognized it, but there was the usual sweetness and easiness among the waiters and a splendid meal at two round tables with many toasts to each of us who were lucky enough to be a part of that special evening.

And we were all aware, I think, that in all probability we'd never be together like this again.

"Money, sex, and toilet flushing" was how one of the scenes was described on the call sheet the next day, and that's what it was.

Laura attacked Walter on the subject of money and sex, following him into the bathroom. Real steam was blown in; the sound of flushing would be looped in when she flushed the toilet, which she did so that Melody couldn't hear what they were saying.

And this was the day we were to have our formal group photograph taken. We did it at the lunch break, everybody assembling on the sound stage—cast, crew, secretaries, and drivers—and waited for our star to make her appearance, which she did at exactly the right moment.

We broke into cheers.

We placed her in the center of us all, with George on one side and Merrill on the other and me right behind her. And, as the photographer focused, somebody suddenly started it and we all burst into the "Hallelujah Chorus," all of our voices raised. Great laugh. Wonderful moment.

I got all choked up. Proud of Kate, George, Merrill, and everybody there.

In the afternoon my agent, Michael Peretzian, appeared at the studio, having just flown in from Los Angeles. One of the pleasures of filming on location is that people come and visit, and when you've got Katharine Hepburn they come and visit faster than usual.

Michael had never met Kate, despite her years with the William Morris Agency, so when we'd finished a scene I waited a moment to catch Kate on the way to her dressing room.

"Kate," I said, stopping her, "I'd like you to meet my agent, Michael Peretzian."

She shook his hand.

"You're James Prideaux's agent?" she said.

"Yes, I am," said Michael.

"Well, you have my heartfelt sympathy," said Kate and with a chuckle she went off to change. Michael was enchanted. It's amazing how people treasure one moment with her.

Kate said, "I don't know *why* I'm so venerated. Why is it?"

I've suggested it's because we have no heroes anymore and she's just that. Maybe the last of them. People look up to her as a woman who has known her own mind and lived by her own rules, but with intelligence and dignity and taste.

When I first met her all those years ago, she was, she felt, washed up, but then she came back and with a vengeance. She was a survivor and, more than that, late in life she came through looking like a million bucks. She had the biggest ego of anyone I'd ever known and yet there was that astonishing empathy with other people, looking outside herself, caring about things.

A crate arrived at my suite in which were 150 copies of Kate's book. Kate had signed them all, George had signed them all, Merrill had signed them all, and now I was to sign them all so they could be given out as gifts to everyone—and I mean everyone, including lawyers in the San Fernando Valley I'd never heard of—at the wrap party.

It was a nice idea and marvelous of Kate to have done, especially since she'd written a little personal note to all those she knew. They'd be prized possessions.

I thought it would be fun to sign them, but I put it off as long as I could, which wasn't very long.

"Countdown—four days to go!" was written across the top of the call sheet.

It was a cold, stormy day with high winds and I had a bit of a run-in with Kate.

She was rehearsing—she had taken to rehearsing like a duck takes to water—the scene where Melody asks her not to bug Walter about making more money.

Kate's line was, "Is that all you ask?"

She kept saying, "Is that all you care about?"

I broke in and corrected her.

"Shoot," she said, "what's the difference? There's no difference."

"Kate," I said patiently, "There is a difference. We know what she cares about, she cares about her home and her kids and Walter. She's said it over and over. Now you're saying, is that all you ask? Two very different things. See?"

And she got mad.

Her wit was sharp enough to make me look a complete fool, if she wanted to. She patronized me in front of the crew, said I was so silly. I was fully aware that she always had to be right, especially in front of them, and could not admit to being wrong. It was an important mistake, however, and I felt it had to be corrected.

George must have silently agreed with me—he would never speak up against Kate—because he shot the scene several times and at last she said it right. So we weathered that little storm.

In the afternoon, that behind us, she called me into her dressing room and we went over that damn scene again, the one she had with Annette. She'd cut it to the bone.

"Now that's better, don't you think?" she said.

Weakened, I shrugged. "I'm not sure."

So we shot all afternoon and after work she came to me and said, "You're right. It's *not* better." And we put it back.

"Countdown—two days to party time!"

Kate did the scene where she tells a story to the baby. The point was to get the child to listen and fall asleep as he listened. Not easy, and I was curious to see how Miss Hepburn, the great baby lover, would handle it.

I finally had to leave, so I called her later to hear how it went.

She was positively bubbling.

"Forty-five minutes," she said. "Forty-five minutes of sitting there. I just stroked his chin for forty-five minutes. He'd start to go to sleep and then he'd wake up again and I'd stroke and stroke and finally he'd start to go to sleep again. It was *fascinating!*"

She couldn't have been happier. Hard work, well done, that's what she thrived on. The challenge met and conquered.

I went home and signed more of Kate's books.

We added an extra day of shooting.

And finally we shot the scene between Laura and Annette, as George called it, "the most rewritten scene in film history."

And I was furious with Kate.

After going over the scene a thousand times and it was set—absolutely set—when we came to the moment when Kate said, "Well, in my day . . ." and Annette was to reply scoffingly, "*Your* day!", Schuyler skipped right over it. Didn't say it.

"Where's '*your day*'?" I asked.

"That's *cut*," said Kate, flatly and firmly.

"By whom?" I said, but nobody listened and nobody cared. The star had said it was cut and it was cut.

Why? Did Kate feel it reflected badly on her character? Aged her? It was exactly what a kid would say and was badly needed, I felt, if Annette was the tartar I wanted her to be. Otherwise her gradual change wouldn't mean anything. But it was cut.

I don't think Kate wanted her niece to be a tartar.

Well, I got over it, and after lunch I returned just in time for another incident.

They were now rehearsing the scene where Laura dresses up Melody for her lunch with the soap star. Kate got the bright idea that their hair would be in curlers. Lovely. But Karen balked. Said she wouldn't do it.

We all pleaded, said if Katharine Hepburn was willing to appear with her hair in curlers, why wouldn't she? We continued to plead, where-upon Karen blew her stack and she walked off the set, out of the studio, and disappeared down the street.

(In fairness to Karen, she had been on the set since dawn and waiting to work. She sometimes rightly felt that she was neglected as we all rushed off to cater to Kate. I'd worried about it and made a point of telling her how wonderful she was in the role, which she was. But by the time we got to the curler incident that afternoon, she'd had it.)

I went to Kate's dressing room and knocked on the door.

"Karen's walked out," I told her.

Kate didn't seem very perturbed. "Well, when she comes back, send her to me."

If she comes back, I thought gloomily. Countdown in two days and now one of our stars walked out.

George had a cup of coffee.

Everybody waited.

Karen finally reappeared and went into Kate's dressing room. There were raised voices. Not loud, but raised.

Ten minutes later, Karen came out and said, "Okay, get the curlers."

Kate emerged shortly thereafter and, as she passed me on the way to the set, she smiled slyly.

"I do enjoy a good fight!" she said.

On December 4 at 1:30 P.M. the last scene of *Guest Appearance* was shot, a memorable and especially moving event because all of us on the set felt, I think, that we might be seeing Katharine Hepburn play her last scene before the camera. Ever.

I think maybe Kate thought so, too.

It was the scene where she lay in bed her first night as the Gomphers's guest and says a prayer, lying in the dark. Artificial moonlight came through the window and her hair hung loose over the pillow.

> Now I lay me down to sleep,
> I pray the Lord my soul to keep;
> If I should die before I wake,
> It might be just as well.

She did it a couple of times while we watched, breathless.

And then George said, "It's a wrap!"

She had come through, she had done it!

She was flushed with pleasure. George gave her a hug, I gave her a hug. I couldn't keep back the tears.

The crew was shouting and cheering her.

Kate pulled herself together and walked through them to her dressing room, laughing and joking, an elderly woman who had delivered the goods with energy and style and even a dash of glamour.

I walked out of the studio and, I swear, the sun had broken through just like at the end of an old Joan Crawford movie. A glorious sunset.

I drove to the hotel and and poured myself a glass of champagne. I sat alone, thinking back over it all, how it happened, what it meant, where I was going next.

Then I got dressed up—even put on a tie—and went off to the wrap party.

I didn't expect to see Kate, who avoids parties as she would a visitation of the plague, but there she and Phyllis were as I walked in, already there, sitting, chatting, having a drink. I joined them.

It was an enormous room on the second floor, all glass and colored lights, with a bar at one end and long tables of food set up around it.

I'm always shocked at the cost of these things, but then I remind myself, "it's all in the budget, Prideaux." Merrill had done us proud. Wonderful food and drinks flowing as fast as the bartenders could make them flow. And everybody was there, from Kate to the lowest extras, from the office staff to the seamstresses. And what an air of relief and jubilation. I think we were all pretty tired, but this was the night to celebrate and we did.

The crew had presented Kate with a little silver flask, inscribed lovingly, which touched her and which she showed to everyone. George had been presented with a small plaque at the studio.

(And isn't it curious—I merely ask—that nothing is ever given to the person who *created* the story, without whom none of it would have happened, none of us would have been there? As I say, I merely ask. And I thought Merrill deserved something, Merrill who weathered those weeks, appeasing the network, jockeying with the insurance company, keeping the office open, finding doctors, making Kate happy, swearing that it would happen. I thought he deserved a gold medal.)

Not that I was counting, but I think Kate had three drinks and then, to my astonishment, she said she wished to make a speech. The books had been passed out and a microphone was set up near the bar so she got up and walked over to it. I watched in amazement. I had never known her to do anything like this.

There had been loud music and dancing, but now a hush fell over the room.

"When I started making movies," Kate said, "I noticed that I was being helped. The cameramen, the lighting people, the grips—all of the crew on the set were helping me. We all worked together and I was grateful to them and it was fun. Making motion pictures is fun. I thank you all and I hope you never lose that sense of fun."

Well, we cheered her enthusiastically, and Kate, knowing when to make an exit, disappeared out the door with Phyllis and Hilly.

Somebody came at me with a bottle of champagne and I decided to get very drunk and I vaguely recall dancing the night away with the delectable Schuyler.

I took a taxi home and somehow got to bed and lay there in the dark thinking, "Well, it's over."

I called Kate the following morning to say a final good-bye.

I had barely spoken a word before she exploded.

"Oh, Christ, you're *fired!*" she said, and hung up on me.

I sat by the telephone for a matter of minutes, stunned, hardly able to believe what I had heard. Kate could be brusque and very abrupt when her mind was on something else, but this was so ugly. I felt deeply hurt. With those words, she utterly shattered the sense of accomplishment, the happiness, everything I had felt the night before.

Why?

I went around in a state of shock all day. Packed. Saw Brenda off, looking chic and well organized, except that when she got to the airport she had forgotten her ticket.

At 5:15 P.M. a limousine picked me up and took me to the airport and I flew away from Vancouver, I thought, for the last time.

As the plane gradually descended into the Los Angeles basin, I should have had a feeling of homecoming, but I couldn't get those awful words out of my mind.

Why, Kate?

1988

After the experience with *Delafield*, I expected the rough cut of *Guest Appearance* to be a disaster. And it was. Interesting how editors, with no sense of the comedy or drama, do that first rough cut of a picture. Everything wrong.

George was at the screening to calm me, however.

"We will fix it," he said, and he then settled into the (to me) tedious business of editing it, frame by frame, second by second. Grueling work, but vital and surprisingly creative.

An editor can make you or break you, no matter what you've got in the can. I was glad George was overseeing it.

My life went on.

I had taken Roderick Cook to Jean Stapleton's annual Christmas party in Bel-Air. Her old gang, all of them wanting to hear Hepburn stories. I didn't tell them how we parted. It hurt too much.

Adie had given her Christmas party, too, the one I looked forward to most of all and the one that really meant Christmas to me. And George was there, assuring me that I would be delighted with the newly edited version of *Guest Appearance*.

I saw it on the last day of 1987. It was greatly improved, but I knew it'd never be another *Delafield*. George seemed happy enough with it, however.

I stayed cozily at home on New Year's Eve, although I did crack open a bottle of champagne with Andy and Patti Langer, who appeared in splendid attire on their way to the Polo Lounge. I was thrilled not to dress up and go to the Polo Lounge. They asked eagerly about *Guest Appearance*. I hedged a bit. Who knew what we really had?

Kate didn't call.

We were well into January when Hilly finally telephoned from Old

Saybrook. I think he made his long-distance calls surreptitiously downstairs when Kate was upstairs, upstairs when she was downstairs.

He said "we" didn't want to see you for a while, but now "we" miss you. Meaning Kate. He had no explanation for her last words to me. "We" were tired. "We" wanted to just to get away for a while. He said that she spoke fondly of me, as always.

I said I was glad to hear it, but I was grumpy.

A week later a terrible storm raged through Los Angeles and, in the middle of it, I got an uncontrollable urge to talk to Kate. So I called her in Connecticut.

She answered the telephone herself. I started the conversation just as she would have done.

"We're having a terrible storm in Los Angeles. Are you?"

"Oh, no," she said, "no terrible storm here. As a matter of fact, I'm going out to hang my sheets on the line."

"In January?" And we went on from there. It was just as warm and friendly a conversation as we had always had. I think that either she had forgotten what she'd said to me, or that it hadn't mattered to her, much as it may have hurt me.

It never came up again and I never mentioned it.

I'll go to my grave not knowing why she said it or what it meant.

An incredible call came from Merrill one morning saying that NBC wanted a title change. I couldn't believe it! Now? After two years? After tons of publicity had gone out about *Guest Appearance* and it was slated to air on March 7?

Yes. Merrill said they tested these things (probably on laboratory animals) and *Guest Appearance* tested a disaster. People would think Kate was just doing a cameo.

He suggested, as a new title, *A Week to Remember.* I suggested he think further.

But I was an absolute blank. I'd had trouble enough coming up with *Guest Appearance* (and I didn't; Bradley Slaight did) and I'd thought of the damn thing as *Guest Appearance* for so long I could think of nothing else.

I hung up and went off to lie down with a wet cloth on my forehead.

I decided to leave show business.

A few days later, Merrill called to say that Kate was enraged over *A Week to Remember.* (By that time, I had sort of come to accept it.) She wanted to call it *It's Only a Week, Dear.* I went limp. I suggested a compromise and we call it *It's Only a Week to Remember, Dear.*

Hilly then got into the act, sending me his list of possible titles:

> Guestry Rides Again
> Guestzilla
> The Valley of the Guests
> Beyond the Valley of the Guests
> The Guesting Game
> Guest Again
> Guest of Endearment
> The Princess and the Peons

Why wasn't Hilly famous?

NBC, alas, in the meantime had tested some titles and had come up with one they were really enthusiastic about: *Guess Who's Coming to Breakfast, Lunch and Dinner?*

I didn't dare tell Kate about that one. I spent the day trying to think of a way to commit suicide with a minimum of pain and maximum of dignity.

My friend Chuckles arrived from New York and I threw him a party. Charlotte Rae came with Ken Raskoff, my NBC pal, who went around with a little pad asking for title suggestions of the guests. I thought that was a bit tacky, but it was also rather fun. My buddy, Lee Brandon, a singer, who was sitting at my bar, turned on his stool and without a moment's hesitation said, "Why not call it *Laura Lansing Slept Here?*"

It was the best suggestion I'd heard so far.

I went to Paramount to watch Peter Matz score the picture, one of his lovely scores, as always. I loved sitting in the control booth and watching Peter conduct the orchestra and seeing the scenes come to life, but would it save us?

Merrill called to say reluctantly that NBC loved *Laura Lansing Slept Here,* and was surprised to hear that I rather liked it. He said George hated it, screamed when he heard it. He supposed Kate would loathe it. I told him to tell her the alternative was *Guess Who's Coming to Breakfast, Lunch and Dinner?*

He called later to say that Kate wasn't mad about it, but she was resigned. So he called George and then Ken, and then he called me to say it was official.

I didn't seem to care anymore, one way or the other.

We started mixing *Laura Lansing Slept Here*, working with editors and engineers and George, Merrill, and Adie in a studio in Burbank. It was a slow process of several days, but it was marvelous to see what a difference it makes when you put the sound of a barking dog into the distance or add the mournful wail of a train whistle.

I made the mistake of calling Kate to appease her about the title, but she wasn't about to be appeased.

"That title is cheap and moronic," she said, "and it's the last for me." Meaning the end of her career. Hung up on me. I didn't bother to take it personally.

I was interested to hear from Ken Raskoff, however, that she had put a call through to Brandon Tartikoff, the president of NBC, to protest the title. He was out, but his awed secretary had alerted Ken.

When I got to the mix that day, Merrill was in high dudgeon. NBC had decided to change our air date from March 7, when we would have been up against nothing much, to March 2, when we'd be opposite the Grammy Awards! They'd wipe us out. Merrill was furious and in despair. You could get this far and still lose the battle!

He asked me to draft a letter to Tartikoff, so I went into the next room and wrote this:

Dear Brandon:

This letter is being written on behalf of Katharine Hepburn, George Schaefer, James Prideaux, Gaylord Productions and the creative people who have worked so hard to bring you *Laura Lansing Slept Here*.

I have just learned that NBC is intending to telecast the picture opposite the Grammy awards on March 2, 1988. We understand the reason for such programming is that NBC deems *Laura Lansing Slept Here* to be a strong picture. It should rate well against the Grammys. We are, of course, pleased that you have such faith in the film. This film may well be Kate's final appearance before her great public, however, and it seems that to schedule it against the Grammys is not only insulting, but destructive to the entire project. Miss Hepburn deserves better, as do we. This picture is a "major" event and should not be used as counter-programming.

This is a respectful appeal to NBC to reconsider the March 2 air date. I would very much appreciate the opportunity of meeting with you as soon as possible to discuss this matter further.

Sincerely,

Merrill H. Karpf

And we won. Brandon Tartikoff was a reasonable and a smart man, anyway, and it seemed unlikely that he'd throw Kate away. We were moved back to March 7. They weren't especially happy about our letter, according to Merrill, but they backed off.

I then sat down and checked it out and discovered we were still up against a formidable adversary: a Barry Manilow special. Was life not a series of strange and interesting events? How would we do against Barry? I tried not to think about the ratings—art was all—but I'd been in lotus land too long.

When the film was ready, I stopped by Merrill's office and picked up a videocassette and watched it alone at home.

I didn't think the color was quite right, nor was the sound, but on the whole I was heartened. I could see a couple of things I would have changed if I could have gone back, but I wasn't ashamed of it. Not proud especially, but not blushing, either. The actors were very good and the script was decent, if not great. And I thought there was a lot of fun in it.

Kate was . . . well, I still had reservations. I think it would have been nicer if she had gone out with *Delafield*. I still wasn't sure I had done her a favor.

On what used to be Lincoln's birthday, but wasn't anymore, Merrill and Suzy Karpf celebrated by giving a dinner at their house in Hidden Hills to show *Laura Lansing* to whatever members of the cast they could gather together.

That included Karen Austin and her manager; Nicolas Surovy and his wife; Joel Higgins and his fiancée, Stacey; Noel Taylor and Adnan Karabay and me; and the ebullient Schuyler Grant, who had flown down especially from her home in upstate California. George and Adie were there, too, of course, and Peter Matz and his terrific wife, Marilyn Lovell.

Only Kate was absent. And we missed her.

People magazine came out with a so-so review of *Laura Lansing*, although they gave it a B+. I was prepared for anything. I knew that criticism, however, didn't matter in that industry. It was all ratings.

Still it was pleasant to receive the best review I ever got in *Variety*.

"The sparkling combination of Katharine Hepburn and writer James Prideaux . . ." and on and on. Undeserved, but there it was. And the

Hollywood Reporter wasn't far behind. These were the trades, and very important in those parts.

The *Los Angeles Times* review wasn't as good, but it wasn't chopped liver.

On the evening of March 7, I went out to Joel Higgins's house and watched "our movie" on the telly with him and Stacey. It was riddled with commercials, of course, and so we switched over from time to time to see what the competition was like. Barry Manilow's show looked like fun.

I came home to find numberless calls on my answering machine from across the country, all congratulatory.

The ratings came in, and while we didn't do quite as well as *Delafield*, which was in the top ten for the week, we were no. 12. Barry Manilow's special was no. 48.

It was Kate's brother, Richard, who offered me the ultimate accolade, though, as reported by Hilly. He had liked *Delafield*, but he was crazy about *Laura Lansing*.

"He's really captured her this time," he said. "That's her. That's Kate!"

In late April, I went east to open up the house in Stone Ridge and called Kate somewhat tentatively as I passed through New York. She couldn't have been warmer.

"You must come to lunch," she said.

And so I went to lunch and we had a wonderful time, chatting and laughing. We reminisced a lot about *Laura Lansing*.

And what fun it was to make.

I spent a part of the summer at the Berkshire Theatre Festival in Stockbridge, Massachusetts, trying out a new play of mine, *Tusitala*, about Robert Louis Stevenson and his wife, Fanny, and his final days in Samoa. The delectable Julie Harris played Fanny and in neighboring Williamstown we found a terrific actor, Tom Tammi, to play Stevenson. I snagged Linda Purl, to my mind one of the finest young actresses of her generation, to play the daughter and Brenda Forbes was with me again as Stevenson's mother. Furthermore, George Schaefer was on board to steer us safely into port.

Or fairly safely. The local critics hardly enthused. It was "fragmented," they said, and suggested it should be a movie, a suggestion I couldn't entirely disagree with.

I was curious to get Kate's reaction. She said she'd come up for a Saturday matinee with Phyllis and Cindy McFadden. Cindy's fiancé, Michael Davies, would drive them, and they'd bring a picnic lunch.

I was backstage well before the performance when an excited apprentice rushed up to me and said, "Jim! Jim! Your guest is at the box office!" I hurried out and there was Kate, early of course, picking up their tickets.

The immediate problem was where to have the picnic. The theatre was mostly surrounded by parking areas, and soon the audience would begin to gather. There was no place pastoral or secluded.

Kate, naturally, solved the problem. There was a kind of outdoor booth from which the apprentices sold T-shirts and memorabilia.

"We'll eat behind that," said Kate.

It wasn't very attractive—there was nothing but some underbrush and a trash can—but they opened the wicker baskets and I provided champagne and we had a wonderful time. The audience arrived and milled all about, never suspecting that Katharine Hepburn was hiding nearby.

Cindy was the perfect foil for Kate, teasing and joking without a trace of the awed fan that would have bored Kate to death. They thoroughly enjoyed one another, and Michael, publisher of a Hartford newspaper and later the *Baltimore Sun*, seemed to fit right in. Phyllis was Phyllis, aging but dear. She had taken care of Kate for forty years and now Kate would have to take care of Phyllis. She bemoaned the fact—it was a devastating reversal of roles—but there was no question of her doing it.

We finally emerged from our hiding place just before the curtain went up, and headed in to the theatre. I had thought they could make a quiet entrance, but an usherette led them down the wrong aisle, so they had to turn around and go all the way back up the aisle and down the other one. I could have kicked that usherette. Every person in the theatre now knew Katharine Hepburn was there. A buzz went over the house. Would they watch the play, I wondered, or would they watch Kate?

At the end, I quickly whisked Kate downstairs to the cast dressing rooms. I didn't ask her point-blank what she'd thought of the play. I didn't have to.

"That's a fascinating story," she said.

So I knew. Not a word about the play.

She visited with Julie, who would never refer to Kate as anything but Miss Hepburn, much as one would have done with the regal Ethel Barrymore. She visited with Brenda, too, of course, and gave a nod to the other actors. It was the usual post-performance appearance by Katharine Hepburn, and it was electrifying.

I saw them off, but not before I had taken Kate up to the picture gallery on the second floor and showed her a photo of herself as a young actress appearing in this very theatre all those years ago.

We both stared at it and were silent for a moment.

1990

A producer came up with an idea for a movie of the week, something about a single lady in the north woods who gave kayaking lessons to a young boy. There was a whiff of the old lady and the wimp about it—Kate would have hated it—but he'd gotten to Angela Lansbury and she was interested.

He wanted me to write it. I wasn't mad for the story, but I was mad to work with Angela Lansbury. Even Kate respected and, I think, looked up to her.

My agent called to say that Miss Lansbury would like to meet with me. Fine, I said. Where? When? I'd be there.

He called back. "She'll come to you. Is next Saturday morning at ten all right?"

I almost dropped the telephone. Angela Lansbury wanted to come to my apartment? She was the biggest star in television. Big stars did not go to the homes of lowly writers to have meetings; the lowly writers went to them, of course. Furthermore, it was the morning of December 31, 1989—just hours before New Year's Eve. Did big stars take meetings with lowly writers on holiday weekends? I thought not.

But Michael insisted that she would appear at my door on Saturday morning at 10:00. This was especially surprising in view of the fact that we had never met.

On the following Saturday, we had a torrential storm. A driving rain was beating at the windows. I waited for the inevitable telephone call. Miss Lansbury might be democratic enough to visit the writer in his home, but even a duck wouldn't go out in this.

And I waited. The telephone call didn't come, but at precisely 10:00 I looked out the window and saw the most famous lady in television getting out of her car and dashing through the rain to my gate. She had two men with her. Bodyguards?

I rushed out and got them through the gate. She couldn't have been cheerier, and by the time I'd ushered them all in to my dry flat, we were laughing away like old friends. The two men turned out to be her son, David Shaw, and one of her brothers, Bruce Lansbury.

They wanted coffee, of course, which I'd anticipated, but it was Miss Lansbury who took over in the kitchen and served us. She was as comfortable as an old shoe. I considered her a great star with a career that was remarkable in its longevity, but I saw nothing of the star attitude. This was a real person and a delightful one.

I'd been at Jean Stapleton's house one Sunday, just after *All in the Family* had closed shop, and Jean pointed to a pile of scripts that had been offered her. "Awful!" she said. I was later to recall that moment because the script on top was the pilot for *Murder, She Wrote.*

We sat cozily and discussed the kayaking lady. Miss Lansbury was eager to do "something physical" while she still could. Looking at her, I saw no reason why she shouldn't do "something physical" for some time to come, and, indeed, she currently had an aerobics video on the stands.

I don't remember how long we talked, but two cups of coffee later it was time for them to leave. We parted feeling, I think, almost like old friends. Nothing was to come of the kayaking idea, but I knew the meeting was anything but a dead loss. I had encountered a remarkable lady, a star whose ego hadn't taken over. Possibly the dues she had paid in her profession over the long years had kept her humble. Humble, though, isn't the right word. Nobody ever attained her heights being humble. On the other hand, very few had attained those heights being what she was: nice.

I hadn't seen Kate at all in 1989.

We did talk on the telephone, however, and at my request she sent, signed, one of her glossy "programs," a kind of retrospective of her career published during one of her stage performances, to be auctioned off at the Stone Ridge Library Fair.

When I called to tell her it fetched $100, she was delighted.

"I feel so proud," she said.

I discovered London and spent six weeks there in the spring. So enchanted was I, I determined to give up the Stone Ridge house and spend those six months the following year in London.

Kate had embarked on a new project.

She'd accepted a figure in the millions as an advance for her "auto-

biography." Her earlier book on *The African Queen* had been a comparative
snap to do, and I don't think she quite realized that this one wouldn't be.

"Oooh," she moaned over the telephone, "I'm going through a very
difficult patch. About my parents."

"Have you thought of a title for it yet?"

Pause. "Yes."

"Oh, good, what is it?"

Another pause. "*Me.*"

"Oh, my God!" I cried. "How did you ever think of it?"

In May I was in New York en route to London and had drinks with
Kate at her house before going on to dinner at Brenda's. Noel Taylor
and Adnan Karabay were there, too, and we had a marvelous cocktail
hour. Kate was in rare form, although she confessed to being worn out
from writing the book.

I lorded it over her because I had just been given an honorary doc-
torate at Lincoln College in Springfield, Illinois. I explained my superi-
ority to her, but she didn't appear to be impressed. She knew she took a
back seat to nobody.

As Noel and Adnan and I walked up Second Avenue to Brenda's, we
agreed that Kate looked great and seemed to be in fine shape.

"Why don't you write something else for her?" Noel asked.

I had sworn, after *Laura Lansing*, that I wouldn't, but the prospect of
presenting Katharine Hepburn in a work of mine was eternally allur-
ing. I couldn't resist.

Consequently, I worked out an idea for her: an elderly actress (still
glamorous!), living in London (I wanted to work in London), who met
the director who'd first made her a star. He was now on his uppers, she
was rich, and it was about their relationship. It could go either way: a
thriller and he was dangerous and threatening, or a comedy and they
fell in love.

I also worked out a sequel to *Delafield* in which we picked up Mrs.
Delafield and her doctor five years later. (*Mrs. Delafield Wants a Divorce?*)

Both of these ideas I sent along to Merrill Karpf, who forwarded
them to Kate.

Her response was, as usual, instant:

Dear Merrill: I read the two suggestions sent to you by Jim Prideaux —
and I have to say to you quite honestly I have not the vaguest idea at this
point whether I'm going to be interested in doing something in the

fall—I don't want you people to feel sort of tied to me—I'm so busy now with this book—and it's so difficult to do—that I'm really just stuck on it at the moment—To go back to Jim's suggestions—I don't think it's too good an idea to do a second version of *Delafield*—Sorry to be so black. Kate.

So that was that. Probably just as well.

I lived in my flat in London, commuting from time to time to Copenhagen to work at the Nordisk Film studio (the oldest film studio in the world) on a film version of Ingrid Bergman's life and career, which was to come to naught. But I met Liv Ullmann in the course of my research, a charming plus, although Liv was so adoring of Ingrid, she could only gush in a muted, Norwegian way.

Seeing Derek Jacobi in *Kean* at the Old Vic was a revelation. I went back for a second look a week later and luckily ran into Tim Pigott-Smith in the lobby during the interval.

"Well, of course, you know him," Tim said, after I'd extolled Jacobi's extraordinary talent. I admitted I didn't, so Tim took me up to his dressing room at the play's end and we chatted. Oh, to work with Derek Jacobi.

Alec McGowen performed in an adaptation of Isherwood's *A Single Man* in Greenwich and, while his portrayal wasn't Christopher as I knew him, he was first-rate. David Bulasky was with me and knew McCowen, so I met him and was able to congratulate him, although without the fervor—splendid as he was—that I saved only for Jacobi.

And then I met the best of all.

Julie Harris had paved the way, saying that I must meet her dear friends the Gows. Ronald Gow had written *Love on the Dole*, a famous English play of the 1930s that had actually affected reform in industrial England. Few plays have any effect on anything, which is why Tony Kushner's work is so important. Mr. Gow was in his nineties, had had a recent operation ("a slice clean across my middle"), and had been married for fifty-three years to an enchantress, Dame Wendy Hiller.

I had seen Dame Wendy on the London stage in *Driving Miss Daisy*. Originally, I had caught the play in New York and thought it was all right—static, short scenes, fairly shallow and sentimental—but when I saw Dame Wendy do it in London, it became a play of real depth.

But I hadn't met her, although we'd spoken on the telephone several times, arranging a date when I could go out to Beaconsfield and lunch with them. When the day finally came, I hired a car and driver, and carried along a tin of sweets from Fortnum and Mason. It would have been a bottle of liquor, but who knew? They were older people, although Dame Wendy was "only" in her late seventies, and perhaps they didn't drink. Sweets were safer.

It was a small village, but even that had a "better section" and that's where their house, Spindles, was. Typically English, typically cozy, and with a typically English garden in the rear.

She came right out to meet me. Her figure, as the British press had noted when she got down to a slip in *Daisy*, was that of a young girl, but her bearing—not to mention the exquisite voice—was right out of the ballroom scene of *Pygmalion*. Or would have been if the manner hadn't been so warm.

I fell in love with them on sight, partly because they loved each other so much. After those fifty-three years, their consideration and concern for one another was almost thrilling to see. One remembered that it can happen. Like my own parents, who never exchanged a cross word in fifty years, there is a lasting love that doesn't diminish, turn sour, rankle, or die.

They accepted the tin of sweets graciously, but I think I'd made a mistake. Before lunching, they wanted to know wouldn't I like a nip? They would. And since lunch was composed, as Dame Wendy confessed, "of starters," one suspected that they kept their figures by eschewing sweets.

Later, we sat in the garden and Fred, my driver, photographed the three of us so beautifully that Dame Wendy, when she saw the photos, claimed that "we can all have new careers."

I wouldn't have missed that afternoon for anything in the world.

As we drove away, Dame Wendy came running across the lawn to wave us off, moving like a young gazelle.

I had made two lasting friends. Letters flew back and forth. I was greatly honored that Mr. Gow signed and sent me copies of his wonderful plays. And when Dame Wendy came to Los Angeles to attend the American Cinema Awards at the Beverly Hilton, she asked me to be her escort.

It was quite an evening, a gathering of two hundred stars of the present and past, that began with a cocktail reception we avoided because she didn't want to stand for an hour making small talk. So we had a drink in her suite and I said, "Tell me about the making of *Pygmalion*." And she did.

She was the unknown, and so she was the only member of the cast required to work on weekends. Her pay, too, was minimal, something like five hundred pounds for the whole film. Both Anthony Asquith and Leslie Howard appeared to be directing and, in confusion as to her character, she ran from the set to her dressing room in tears one day. A knock came at the door. It was an old character actor who had a minor part. He was all sympathy.

"I can't do it *their* way," she had sobbed.

"Oh, love," he said gently, "that's all right. Do it *your* way."

And she did and it was all right, more than all right.

We went downstairs to join Joseph Cotten and Patricia Medina at their table for the dinner. It broke Dame Wendy's heart to see her beloved Joseph Cotten as he was, cancer of the throat having destroyed his voice, but he had Patricia, that wonderful wife, to look after him. Robert and Dorothy Mitchum were also at our table and on either side of him, Mr. Cotten had Teresa Wright and Maureen O'Sullivan. And also we had the biographer Donald Spoto and a strange lady who turned out to be Alida Valli.

I might also add that Burt Reynolds and Loni Anderson were at a table behind us. I'd never met him, but that was to be rectified later.

The only person whom Dame Wendy wanted to find and say hello to was Sidney Poitier, and gentlemanly Bob Mitchum silently got up, found him, and brought him to her. I remember, too, Lauren Bacall leaning over me to talk to Dame Wendy, her right breast tucked neatly into my left ear.

Ronald Gow was soon to die. His death was not unexpected, and he was hardly nipped in the bud, but it was a terrible loss for Dame Wendy.

She did work, though, which must be a part of the answer to grief, and I'm delighted to say she worked on a play of mine. It was a one-act called *Laughter in the Shadow of the Trees,* and she apparently loved it the moment she read it. She wanted very much to do it on the stage and tried to get it on.

First she sent it to Paul Scofield, who was initially interested, I think, but then he wandered off. She then told me to take it to Cyril Cusack, who was appearing in a production of *The Three Sisters* at the Royal Court. I dropped it off and "old Cyril," as Dame Wendy called him, liked it, but then he, too, died. A couple of years passed and, ever determined, she now got it to the best of all, her dear friend Sir John Gielgud. At ninety, that greatest of all English actors was, perhaps, not up to learning lines, but why not do it on radio? And that is why *Laughter*, under the masterful direction of John Theocharis, and with a third member of the cast every bit as fine as Dame Wendy and Sir John, the untitled Elizabeth Bell, was performed on BBC radio and aired around the world.

One night the telephone rang and it was Kate. It was very unlike her just to ring up.

"What are you *doing* in London?" she asked. That seemed to be the only reason for her call. A friend, Liam Kelly, was visiting me and he practically went into cardiac arrest when he realized that I was talking to Katharine Hepburn. I motioned him to relax, but he continued breathing heavily.

"How's the book?" I asked.

Another of her pauses, and then she said, "Short." She sounded very weary of it all. I began to wonder if she could really deliver it. So, I suspected, had she.

In late October I was again going through New York on my way to Los Angeles, London behind me, and spent a Sunday afternoon at a rehearsal of a one-woman show that Maxene Andrews, of the Andrews Sisters, was planning. Directed by Cash Baxter, it was sensational.

I then went on to Katharine Hepburn's for drinks and from there to dinner with an ex-vice president of the Foreign Policy Association. I decided that my life was varied and amusing and I had made the right decision by going into show business. Otherwise, my Sundays would have been dull.

Kate was excited by the new picture book John Bryson had just brought out called *The Private World of Katharine Hepburn*. I said I hadn't seen it and Phyllis brought me a copy.

It was a cool evening and Kate got up to bend over and poke the fire in the fireplace just as I came across a photograph of her in the book, bending over and poking the fire.

"Oh, look," I said. "Here's the same pose of you in the book. Except in the book your pants aren't falling down."

She hiked up her slacks, which were falling down her behind. It was a beautiful book and, the next day, I searched out several copies—they were sold out almost everywhere—and the William Morris office delivered them to Kate, who signed them for me as gifts.

Hilly was long gone and I missed him, as I'm sure Kate did too. (He'd stormed into her bedroom one day, told her off in no uncertain terms, and headed for the bus station and his sister's house in Long Island, but ended up in Santa Fe, New Mexico. That was Hilly. And then he died too soon.)

She was left now with the bustling, cheerful Norah and poor Phyllis, who seemed more vague and confused with every passing moment. A new man named Jim drove her, and he was perfectly pleasant. His only trouble was that he wasn't Hilly.

And did she want to work again? Act again?

We talked about it. The book still weighed her down, but presumably someday it would be done and out—the publishers were apparently snapping at her heels like bloodhounds—and then what would she do? She was too exhausted at that point, I suspect, even to think about what would come after. And yet she loved acting, loved being a star, and she loved playing the legend. Whereas at one point in her life she was very private and averse to any kind of publicity, now it seemed to me you could hardly open a magazine without finding an interview with her or turn on the telly without seeing her chatting away with Barbara Walters or Melvyn Bragg or somebody. There were times when I wanted to say, "Enough already! Shut up!"

But you couldn't blame her. Katharine Hepburn loved Katharine Hepburn—or, rather, loved *being* Katharine Hepburn, strange as it might be. She was in little danger of losing that, but great stars had great trepidations. Worse than being recognized, far worse was not being recognized.

And so one continued the career. She might turn them down, but she couldn't resist asking me one question when I brought up the possibility of her acting again.

"Have you got an idea?"

She'd turned down the American Film Institute Life Achievement Award, and she wasn't even very good about picking up her Oscars, but when, at last, her government offered her the Kennedy Honors, it was impossible to refuse.

I say "at last" because while the Reagan Administration was in power she was apparently purposely overlooked.

She'd known Nancy Reagan warily since Nancy's early days at Metro. Kitty Kelley suggests in her biography of Nancy Reagan that there might have been something between Spencer Tracy and Nancy Davis and perhaps that had something to do with it. Anyway, for whatever reason, Kate was wary of Nancy.

And Kate was an insider in Hollywood. She was smart and she knew the people in the industry and what they were like, the good and the bad, unlike much of the general public. She knew what Nancy Davis was like and she knew what Ronald Reagan was like.

And so, when Nancy called Kate and asked her to campaign for Reagan when he was running for the presidency, Kate was ready with her reply.

"Nancy," she said, "I'm against everything Browny stands for."

That was the end of the Kennedy Honors for her. And, once more, the political Hepburn surprised me. At one point she would seem an archconservative and at another a flaming liberal. I suspect, however, that she is comprised of both, and she simply believes what she believes in.

Anyway, the Bush Administration was in and Kate packed her best sneakers (for her bum foot) and went off to Washington with Cindy McFadden.

When it was aired, I watched the show on television and was disappointed in Kate's segment. How one managed to make Kate or her career seem boring was beyond me, but they managed it. She deserved better. But there she was, smiling away, apparently enjoying it all.

She wasn't easy on President Bush. Her mother before her had championed Planned Parenthood, and Kate was still carrying the torch.

When she was introduced to President Bush, she told me, she looked him right in the eye and said, "You're wrong about abortion! Why is that?"

He must have been taken aback, but he replied, "It's what I believe in."

"Well, you're wrong!" she said again and turned to Mrs. Bush.

"Why do you put up with that?" she asked her.

"Because I love him," Mrs. Bush replied.

"I don't see how you could," said Kate, thereby, in one fell swoop, endearing herself to both Bushes.

"You didn't say that to the President of the United States!" I exclaimed, when she told me.

"I did." She was quite happy about it, having gotten her licks in.

1 9 9 1

When Laurence Luckinbill performed my *Lyndon* on television, it opened a new door for him as an actor. He was, in a word, brilliant, and the performance was unlike anything Larry had ever done. Consequently, he did it on the stage (as Jack Klugman had done before him), touring around the countryside. And he finally opened it in mid-January of 1991 at the little John Houseman Theatre in Manhattan.

I flew in and invited Kate to see it with me. She agreed and, of course, asked me to dinner at her house before going to the theatre.

It was a miserable evening, pouring rain, and I arrived soaked.

The moment I saw Kate I knew she wasn't going to the theatre with me. She had a wretched cold and looked terrible. I had rarely known her to admit to any kind of illness—meeting physical ailments like broken ankles and faulty throats, yes, but not illness. She was, however, admitting this night.

Cindy was there and Kathy Houghton, and we all watched Kate sneezing and sniffling and behaving, well, ill. A strange sight.

"I can't go out," she said.

"No, you certainly can't," I said.

I was dying to have Miss Hepburn at my show for two reasons: I thought she'd be impressed with the work I'd done in whittling Merle Miller's nearly seven-hundred-page book into a coherent theatre piece, and I knew the publicity value of her appearance at the theatre. It would be in all the papers the next day and give a handsome boost to the box office. Not to be.

But Kathy would go with me. I told her she certainly didn't have to, but she insisted she really wanted to. She was so beautiful I loved the thought of having her on my arm. But she was more than that. She had a transistor radio in her hand and would, from time to time, plug tiny earphones into her ears. She would then explain to us what was going on because it was the night the Gulf War started.

Kate didn't understand it, I didn't understand it, and Cindy didn't understand it. Kathy, however, did. We plied her with questions and she had the answers. Katharine Houghton knew the situation in the Middle East like the palm of her hand. She studied things like that. She wasn't just beautiful.

We sat around before the fire in Kate's living room, all of us, I think, apprehensive and concerned. We would actually be at war. We still had the memory of Vietnam and that was enough to make anyone apprehensive.

The rain kept beating on the windows as we ate our hurried dinner on the inevitable trays. Kate was fading fast and probably should have been in bed. She saw Kathy and me to the door, though, just as she did everyone.

I kissed her on the cheek, despite the prospect of germs.

"I wish you were coming," I said. And I meant it.

It was a remarkable evening. Larry was great, as I knew he would be, but what was astonishing was to hear LBJ going on about the Vietnam War and then, at intermission, to hear Kathy repeat what Bush was saying on the radio, which was almost verbatim.

The audience knew and felt that.

"Goddamn war!" LBJ said, and the audience roared.

My mind wandered, however.

I was remembering the night of June 16, 1966, the night I first heard an audience react to lines I had written in my lonely room. I had become a member of the Albee-Barr-Wilder Playwrights Unit and Richard Barr himself was directing the first production of my first play, *Postcards*.

It was at the Cherry Lane Theatre, a tiny theatre in Greenwich Village, and I was terrified. When finally Richard forced me into the theatre, there were no seats left, and so we had to sit on the steps next to the exit. The lights came down. The curtain went up. And the audience began to laugh. And clap. And laugh. And clap some more.

Postcards was hardly more than thirty minutes long, but they were the greatest thirty minutes of my life. My heart soared, literally soared as I listened to the audience. At the end they wouldn't stop applauding and Richard pushed me to my feet, saying, "Jimmy, you'd better go up." So I ran up on stage and took a bow with my beaming actors. I suppose I went someplace after that. I assume I got home. But I have no recollection of it. I was in another world.

It was a revelation and an affirmation. I would go on writing plays. But that particular thrill never came again, even when audiences were packing the Opera House at the Kennedy Center for *The Last of Mrs. Lincoln.*

It was still raining slightly as Kathy and I left the theatre and walked east on Forty-second Street along Theater Row. We passed the darkened Judith Anderson Theater and I blew it a kiss.

Kate finished her book.

I called her up.

"Miss Hepburn," I said, "it's James Prideaux."

"Oh, God!"

"Kate," I said, "it's not very heartwarming when you call somebody up and they say, 'Oh, God!'"

She laughed.

"Well, if you'd been through what I've been through, you'd say 'Oh, God!' too."

But the book was done at last. I hoped it was wonderful, but I doubted if it was the sensational piece the publishers and the readers would be looking for. Still, it would sell like hotcakes and the legend would be carried on.

In all my life, I have never encountered a single person who didn't respect, and possibly adore, Katharine Hepburn. Not one. Perhaps she wasn't always at the top of the popularity list. There was that spell when she was known as "box-office poison" because, as she explained to me, "I did all those period pieces," and, worse, she and Turhan Bey were even Chinese in the forgettable *Dragon Seed.*

And I suddenly remember when she was being considered for the film version of *Driving Miss Daisy.* She called and we talked about it.

"But you can't play Miss Daisy!" I said.

"Why can't I play Miss Daisy?"

"Because Miss Daisy is Jewish and who's going to buy Katharine Hepburn as Jewish?"

"Oh, shoot," she said. "She doesn't *have* to be Jewish." Thereby throwing out the plot.

That's what they did with *Summertime,* which was based on a play called *The Time of the Cuckoo.*

"Why did the film work so well?" I once asked her.

"Because we threw out the plot," she said.

She hadn't always been at the top, but she had never been less than rock strong, never failed to fight her way back up again.

One evening we were having drinks in her living room in New York and dark was coming on. There was a fire in the fireplace, but she suddenly realized that the candles on the mantelpiece weren't lit. She got up and, moving across the room, found the matches and began lighting the candles.

Looking up, I caught the reflection of her face in the mirror over the mantelpiece, lit by the soft flickering of the candles.

My heart leaped. The moment was magical. Over eighty, yet I was gazing upon a face that was one of the wonders of the world. I wanted it to last forever. But, whatever was to come next, I knew I would keep this moment in my heart always.

Because the summers in Los Angeles are unbearable, I keep insisting, and because I'd given up the house in Stone Ridge, I spent those hot months of 1991 in Santa Barbara. It may not be the most exciting place on earth—Los Angeles is rapidly becoming that, what with six-thousand homicides a year—but Santa Barbara is beautiful and peaceful. It also has as near a perfect climate as I know, unless you resent a little fog rolling in from the ocean.

Furthermore, I resided in a charming poolhouse on the estate of John and Biky Alexander, high above the city in the Riviera section. I rapidly became accustomed to dancing fountains, formal gardens, and statuary. Not to mention John and Biky. Biky is an aristocratic Mexican lady, beautiful and kind. John is a Texas gentleman, elegant and kind. Except for the fact that they went to Paris in the middle of it, the summer was idyllic.

And our darling Judith Anderson was nearby in Montecito, at ninety-three, slowly dying, occasionally muttering "too long . . . too long . . ." but able to rouse herself for the inevitable cocktail hour and be witty and amusing, at least until the second vodka. John and I spent many late afternoons with her, cherishing every moment. When at last she died, our afternoons seemed bleak and colorless.

In her will, she left me the magnificent French mirror that hung over the fireplace in the living room of the Montecito house. She knew I coveted it and this was her surprise. It's far too grand for my small apartment, but here it stays, a lovely link with someone I loved.

On an October morning I got an unexpected telephone call from John Dayton. He was creative director for Burt Reynolds Productions.

He called to tell me that he had marched into Burt Reynolds's office and told him that he knew the best writer in Hollywood. The name of the best writer in Hollywood was James Prideaux. As a result of this bombshell, Burt suggested that they have me in to talk. Would I come by the office?

Who didn't love Burt Reynolds? I had never met him, but he seemed to be charm itself on talk shows. Witty, too. And, after a slump in his career, he now had a hot television series, *Evening Shade*. What writer in his right mind would turn down a meeting with Burt Reynolds?

My first meeting with Mr. Reynolds was fleeting. He was about to go across the street to a sound stage and tape one of his shows. John led me into his office as Reynolds stepped out of his private bathroom, a lady attendant putting the final touches on his makeup. (Burt Reynolds seemed always to be heavily made up.) He was wearing a colorful sweater and blue jeans.

"You look good," I said.

"You look good," he said.

That was about the extent of our conversation. He went off to tape the show. John and I followed, the idea being that I would watch the taping. My little treat. I hate watching tapings, though. I watched Burt and Marilu Henner do one scene and suggested to John that we leave. He was startled by the suggestion, but he saw me out into the street. Unfortunately, I had to go back to the Reynolds office for something and was greeted by raised eyebrows among his staff. Why was I leaving? I could see their little minds clicking away. I doubt that their first impression of me was particularly good, especially since I wasn't prepared to sit through the boss's taping. What kind of Burt Reynolds fan was I?

Well, I was fan enough to ask at one point for a Burt Reynolds mug. They had mugs with a picture of Burt on them and I thought it would be fun to have one. (I'm easily amused.) They saw that I got one.

John and I had originally discussed a Christmas show. Every television producer in Hollywood wanted to come up with a Christmas show, something that the network could trot out every December with accompanying payments and residuals. So I mapped out something called *That Crazy Christmas* about a middle-aged man (Burt) and his wife (Loni?) and their kids, all of whom had lost—or misplaced—their values. Easy to do in this Age of Sleaze. In the end they regained their values, of course, when they lost all their money and found out what Christmas was really about.

John didn't think my suggestion of Loni working with Burt was so hot. I didn't know why, but who cared? There were plenty of stars ready to work with Burt Reynolds.

And then I got an excited call from John.

Forget *That Crazy Christmas*, he told me. Burt had confessed that the great dream of his life was to work with Katharine Hepburn. We could still do a Christmas show, but couldn't it star Burt Reynolds and Katharine Hepburn? In that order?

I had sworn never to open that can of peas again, not after everything we went through with *Laura Lansing*. Besides, Kate was now admitting to her real age and had gone, in two years, from seventy-five to eighty-four. Wasn't she simply too old?

Once again, however, the star billing was enticing. Wouldn't everybody in the world watch a television movie starring Katharine Hepburn and Burt Reynolds? And wasn't it an interesting team, as far as acting went? They could be such opposites. The elegant older lady and the tough younger man. And, of course, at Christmas.

I went to my files and pulled out the roughly sketched short story I had done with Kate in mind, the one that took place in London—in those days we wanted to go back to London—and she was a retired star, well heeled and living alone in a large house in one of those handsome London squares. The director who had given her her first job (and first romance), now on his uppers, seeks her out. She lets him stay as a guest on an upper floor, hence the title: *The Man Upstairs*. He's out for money, but a relationship develops and they end up living happily together as companions.

I was summoned back to Burt's office, where I spent two hours in that room—every inch of wall covered with posters and photographs—listening to Burt talk about his life. Nothing wrong with that. Stars do talk about themselves. It's their favorite subject.

He repeated that working with Katharine Hepburn was the great dream of his life. I nodded. I said I thought it was a wonderful idea. And, really, I thought, why not?

Burt also said that he had always wanted to play a character with the name of Moony. That was because, as I knew, there had once been a play called *Moony's Kid Don't Cry* and the name had stuck in his mind. Mine, too. I looked at him and suddenly dreamed up Moony Pulaski, his rough background, the lifelong pain that had lured him into a life of crime, his charm as a con man, his need for love, real love, not the tawdry sex that he knew with cheap broads. Love, indeed, that a principled older lady like a Katharine Hepburn could give him. Yes, what a pair they could make.

I could see it all.

Burt was off to Florida to do his one-man show at the Royal Poinciana Playhouse in Palm Beach. He wanted me to see it. Furthermore, if George Schaefer was to direct this picture, as we hoped, then George must come to Florida and see it, too. Once we saw his show, we would understand him, Burt said.

Meanwhile, Burt (through John) had requested that I call Kate and feel her out on all this. I thought Burt should do it. It'd be too easy for her to say, "Oh, no, no," to me, but not to Burt Reynolds.

Burt, however, was shy—or scared—and couldn't muster the courage to call her. He telephoned me and I said there was nothing to it. Kate would answer the telephone herself, or Norah might, and he should simply state who he was and that, like Raquel Welch, he loved her and hoped to work together with her. That was all. She would be vague, of course, but the contact would be made, the ground broken.

Kate, who saw every movie, pretended never to know who anybody was, never to have heard of them. She enjoyed that. I think, viewing them as unknowns, made her seem all the more famous. "And who is Tom Cruise?" she might ask blankly, having seen all his films.

Anyway, Burt screwed up his courage and telephoned and got Kate. Except that he thought that bleat on the other end of the wire was Norah.

"Hello, Norah?" he said.

"Who is this?" said Kate, bluntly I'm sure.

"It's Burt Reynolds."

"Well, what do you want with Norah?"

That's Kate's version. Burt, who probably remembers it more clearly than Kate and loved telling the story on talk shows, said she told him to call back later. And he didn't know whether "later" was ten minutes or ten hours. Anyway, he finally got to talk with her.

The next day she called me to ask, of course, who he was.

I flew to Palm Beach, for some reason a day earlier than George did. It was an uneventful flight and fairly dull, except that Jay Leno was in the seat behind me and everybody was clamoring to congratulate him on his forthcoming career as Johnny Carson's replacement.

I was met at the West Palm Beach airport by Burt's driver, Bob Soli, and driven into Palm Beach to the Breakers. I still find the humidity that hangs over Florida oppressive, but if you have to be in Florida I recommend the Breakers. The view of the ocean is terrific.

It had been arranged that George and I would see Burt's show the following night, but I would meet John Dayton and Burt that very night after the show. There was to be a party. I dressed and taxied to the Royal Poinciana Playhouse at about 10:00 P.M., assuming that would be close to curtain time. But, when I peeked in, Burt was still doing his second act. I waved at John, who was running lights or film clips or slides—it all looked very multimedia to me—and slipped into the club next door where the party was to take place.

I was astonished at how dressy it was. A crowd was gathering, and it was hardly a bunch of tourists in resort togs. These were women in gorgeous evening gowns and wearing their best jewels. Dressier than London, New York, Santa Barbara, or anywhere, it seemed to me. Obviously one didn't spend the winter in Palm Beach in culottes, although they did during the day, I was to discover.

I found a table and a waiter brought me a drink, but I felt a little self-conscious sitting all alone trying to look casual. Everybody else appeared to be out to have a good time. It was really quite festive.

Two elderly women sitting near me, decked out, smiled and I smiled back and they asked me to join them. I laughingly told them I'd love it, but I couldn't because I was waiting for Mr. Reynolds. We joked back and forth a bit and I felt young, desirable, and somewhat like a gigolo. And if it hadn't been for Burt I would have joined them. They were fun.

It seemed to take forever—three drinks, I think—before John and Burt did appear, and when they did Burt made straight for me and gave me a big hug. Gee, I thought, this is a genuinely nice guy.

We picked up George Schaefer at the airport the next day, and at 7:30 in the evening we were at the Royal Poinciana to see Burt's show. It was pretty much his version of his life and career, amusingly and touchingly told with the aid of film clips. It was stupefyingly long—I think the second act alone was almost two hours—but I was fascinated to see that the audience stayed with it. He was very, very good.

As George and I were leaving the theatre, George said merely, "Worth the trip." I got excited all over again about Kate and Burt working together.

Burt gave a party afterward at the Brazilian Court Hotel. Before he made his entrance we all collected, drank champagne, and ate delicious ravioli. John Dayton was irked because he knew Burt was conferring with some businessmen about becoming a spokesman for the Florida orange juice industry, which he felt would overextend him. Burt was elated, however, when he appeared, having made the deal. He made straight for George and me and gave me another big hug. This guy was really full of love.

George had never met Burt, oddly enough, and so we sat down and talked. I can't imagine why, but somehow the conversation turned to Eugene O'Neill and his actress wife, Carlotta Monterey. I thought it was pretty terrific that Burt knew about Carlotta Monterey. This guy was not only nice and full of love, he was literate as well.

George and I flew back to Los Angeles the next afternoon. Just as everybody had gotten off the plane in Orlando on the trip east, they all got on the plane going west. No Jay Leno this time, but we were delighted to see Robby Benson, who got on with his little daughter and very pregnant wife. We had a great reunion. And, as I waited for my luggage in the Los Angeles airport, Robby introduced me to his daughter by saying, simply, "She's an angel." Lucky little girl to have parents like that.

I began immediately to write the treatment for *The Man Upstairs*. Within a week it was ready and sent to Kate. Normally she responded quickly, often overnight, but days passed. Finally George telephoned her and reported that she was vague, but interested. Did George think she could do it? She didn't want us "to go to screenplay" and then turn it down.

George assured her that going to screenplay didn't have to mean a commitment on her part, that many stars had screenplays written for them that, ultimately, they didn't do.

"Okay," she said. She'd like to see a full script. That was the word we needed. I was authorized to write the screenplay of *The Man Upstairs*.

I called Kate the following morning. She said she'd reread the treatment and "this could be good." I told her I was "going to screenplay." That got her quite enthused. "Great!" she said. "Great!"

A couple of meetings with Burt were scheduled for George and me, but he kept canceling. Couldn't find the time. I kept typing.

A couple of weeks later, I called Kate just to keep her interested and informed on my progress. She was vaguer than ever. I pushed Burt, singing his praises as actor and star, and also hit hard that this would be, in its way, a "romantic comedy." I knew those were two of her favorite words. But without sex, of course.

On December 27 I finished the first draft, but it was only eighty-eight pages and obviously too short. Nevertheless, I sent it off to be computerized—I was still using my trusty electric portable Smith-Corona—and celebrated New Year's Eve by being in bed at 10:30 with a good book.

To quote Queen Elizabeth, 1992 would be "annus horribilis." She was right on the money.

PART FOUR

1992

Elaine Hall, who worked for Burt, called to remind me that Burt Reynolds wanted to be Spencer Tracy. I had heard that before from both Burt and John, and I was tired of hearing it. I knew full well that Burt Reynolds would never be Spencer Tracy no matter how I created the character of Moony Pulaski. And what did it mean, anyway? I decided to ignore it.

On the same day copies of the script were delivered to the Reynolds office, I called Kate. She was more evasive than ever. She said she wasn't sure how much she wanted to work. I said, "Just say so." She didn't have to do this movie. I wasn't at all sure she should attempt it, actually, although I didn't tell her that. And if she didn't do it, it wasn't the end of the world. Life would go on.

John Dayton sent Kate a copy of the script the next day after talking to her on the telephone. That was the first, I assume, of the many pep talks Mr. Dayton would deliver to Miss Hepburn, pep talks that she needed and thrived on. His thinking was always of so positive a nature he made Norman Vincent Peale look like a slouch. In the end, it was what got the movie made.

As it turned out, Brenda Forbes had dinner with Kate the following evening. Kate said she'd gotten the script, but she hadn't read it. She had heard, however, that there was a good part in it for Brenda. And did Brenda think it would do for Kate's final film? Brenda assured her it would.

The meeting between Burt and George and me, with John Dayton in attendance, took place on a late Sunday afternoon at Burt's house on Mulholland Drive. This pad was strictly Movie Star Stuff, an enormous rambling modern house of vast rooms with huge windows providing a panoramic view of the San Fernando Valley. Real estate people told me

Burt rented it for $38,000 a month. Our host let us cool our heels for a bit while a very accommodating black man brought us drinks. Once Burt appeared, he gave us a full tour of the house. The paintings on the walls were mostly of a macho nature, cowboys and Indians. John Wayne would have been at home here.

Loni and his son were away so we didn't meet them, but we poked into every nook and cranny of the house, including Loni's bathroom, which was the pièce de résistance. It was the Movie Star Bathroom to end all Movie Star Bathrooms. Mae West couldn't have done it better.

I was also impressed by the fact that, although Mrs. Reynolds was off making a movie, there were two cats in her bedroom and the television set was on. I like people who see that their pets are entertained, but I do feel that some parental guidance might be required.

A terrific buffet had been set up so we piled up plates, sat around a table, and began our story conference. (I noticed that only one drink was offered, quite sensibly.) This was the kind of story conference I love, where everybody has really studied the script and everybody throws ideas into the hopper.

With Burt's permission, I audiotaped the session and, replaying it now, I'm impressed with how astute he was. For two hours we talked about any and all problems the script might have, what the solutions might be, and if we should possibly go in some other direction with it. Professionals can do this and gain a lot; amateurs take offense, generally. Burt really turned on the charm; he was, as John noted, at his best. Burt thought the ending was sensational. (Kate always harped about endings.) He wasn't entirely happy with the beginning, though, especially when he came off as any sort of wimp. Again, he brought up Spencer Tracy and how Kate didn't "blow him off the screen." He was obviously concerned that Kate might blow him off the screen.

His strongest statement to me, said quite gently, was "what I do best is taken away from me." He referred to the "dese, dem, and dose" aspect of Moony's character, as if Moony were a hood, which surprised me since Moony was carefully written as a charming, articulate con man. (Jon Voight later gave the same reading to it.) He also wanted to be sure the element of danger was there. Tom Selleck, he and his wife had concluded, wasn't sexy "because he wasn't dangerous." Macho, again, was what Burt was after. But with vulnerability underneath. Not a murderer, but with danger there. "We have to believe he's gotten along in prison because they know he could kill." The two sides to everything.

He told a couple of funny stories.

One was about one of the tabloids that showed him with a fat belly, sticking out over his belt. It had Loni saying something like, "You've got to do something about this!" He brought it home, incensed, and showed it to her.

"Isn't this awful?" he said, pointing to the picture.

"Yes," she said. "It makes me seem so cruel."

The other had to do with who's sexy and who's not.

He'd once worked with (or met) Jessica Tandy, who was then eighty-ish, and said to her, "I hope you don't take this the wrong way, but I find you sexy."

"I don't take it the wrong way at all," she said, obviously delighted.

Some time later, he was having a discussion with Warren Beatty and asked, "Who do you think is sexy?"

And, never having known of the former conversation, Beatty replied immediately, "Jessica Tandy."

When I asked him, Burt said he loved the poem Moony read in the last scene. He said he read poetry to his wife a lot, which surprised me. This man was full of surprises. (Kate would later try to get the poem away from the Moony character and read it herself, but I fought and won that one.)

As we ended this stimulating session, Burt said, "Thanks for being so open." We then discussed the possibility of alternate actresses if Kate wasn't up to it, such as Maggie Smith, Deborah Kerr. Just talk. There was, as always, only one Katharine Hepburn.

There was no reason to assume, as George and I drove along winding Mulholland Drive on the way home, that we faced any problems at all on this one. It was definitely a "go." We were elated and very much looking forward to it.

I had also, that day, asked Burt to sign my program from Palm Beach. He wrote, "Jimmy, you are such a wonderful talent and friend, love, Burt." Since I hardly knew him, I found this a little effusive, but I re-minded myself that stars are effusive. And they write what they think you want to read—and have your friends read. When Elizabeth Taylor wrote "Love always," I'm sure she was aware that in all likelihood she would never see me again and "always" was just for that moment, but what matter? The only one wary of this is Kate, who, to my knowledge, never goes beyond the word "affection," and rarely writes even that.

Nevertheless, I was touched by Burt's sentiment. On my second visit to his office, I had run into Charles Nelson Reilly in the outer office. Now, Charles Nelson Reilly is not only one of the most amusing people on earth, he's also one of the nicest. One might expect, due to his quick wit, that he'd be bitchy, but he isn't. Furthermore, he's not only a great acting teacher, he's also a great director. When Charles talks, I listen.

And Charles said to me that day, looking around the office, "These are nice people." I felt I had fallen into a pot of honey. And I wanted to give Burt something, something he'd really like, something special.

When I got home, I went over my bookshelves. He was literary, why not a volume of some sort? Not my first edition of *Ulysses* or my *Orlando* signed in her tiny hand by Virginia Woolf, but—aha! I came upon a treasure of mine, a beautifully bound copy of Gide's journals. Opening to the flyleaf, I remembered our conversation that night in Palm Beach because this particular book had belonged to Carlotta Monterey and she had written in it. What could be more appropriate? What she had written wasn't especially cheerful—"I feel as if all the devils of hell were after me, Carlotta Monterey"—but wasn't it fascinating? Wouldn't Burt be thrilled?

I hated giving it up, but I knew he'd cherish it so I gift-wrapped it and gave it to John to give to Burt. I attached a little note saying something to the effect that I hoped he'd love it as much as I did.

That was the last I ever heard of it.

Actually, I was to see Burt again only one more time, and that was ten months later when we screened the movie at the Directors Guild.

The morning following our story conference at Burt's house, Kate called me. She said she'd read the script twice and "it falls apart." Meaning the ending, of course. She said she "lost interest." She also said she would read it again and I said "take notes." Being specific, I had discovered, was the quickest way to eradicate her reservations. Once you pinned her down, she backed off or, indeed, forgot what she had objected to. Or wondered why you were objecting.

She said she'd screw her brain on. I said, well, I thought I should fly in to New York, along with John or George. She liked that idea. Kate always believed it meant something if you went to the trouble to confer with her. That's what you did for stars.

John telephoned to remind me that Burt (I was always being reminded of something about Burt) could never play a character who was a follower. He must be a leader. He must never appear weak, always strong. Unfortunately, in my first draft I had him following his fellow escapee out of a hole they'd created in the prison wall. No! Burt must come out first. I rewrote.

That same day there appeared in *TV Guide* a full-color, very prominent piece linking Burt Reynolds with Katharine Hepburn, photos and all, and announcing their upcoming film, *The Man Upstairs*. Marilyn Beck had written it and she and Burt were chums, I was told. I was sure Burt was pleased with it, although I would have worried about Kate's reaction if I thought for one moment she'd ever see it. At any rate, it was announced, and the Reynolds-Hepburn connection established. Mr. Reynolds's dream was coming true.

More astonishing, actually, was a piece in the Vancouver *West Ender*. This was Kate's pal, Hugh Pickett, quoting Kate in his column as if the movie was a sure thing. Since that could only have come from Kate, I began to think maybe it was a sure thing.

Stacy Williams was brought on board, a great comfort. She'd been executive producer on both of my Hepburn pictures. (John and I were trying to put together the family that would make Kate feel secure.) Stacy was the very best at her job: efficient, knowledgeable and, almost as important, warmhearted and fun. Burt Reynolds Productions hired her not only as a producer, but also as the unit production manager. She could do both, and they got two jobs for the price of one.

Stacy and John flew to Vancouver to scout locations. It was especially important that they locate "the Hepburn house," a house that looked like Kate would live in it—old, traditional, handsome—but also physically feasible so that George could have room for camera, lights, and other equipment. They located what they thought was the perfect house in Shaughnessy, an exclusive section of Vancouver where Dr. Kievel had lived. And they telephoned to say that George and I should fly up to check it out.

We did. Any excuse, as far as I was concerned, to go to Vancouver.

We spent the next couple of days searching further, interiors and exteriors, and also scouting about for a location that could serve as Kate's small hometown. It was tricky because we'd probably be filming in spring or summer, and this was a Christmas story. So I set it "somewhere in northern California, just south of the Oregon border," where, I assumed, one might have a Christmas without snow. This was further complicated by Burt's character going on about, "Why isn't there any snow?" Ultimately, there would have to be snow in the last scene, so Vancouver in the summer was a problem. We'd face that later, although George was carefully eyeing locations that were mostly in the midst of fir trees.

I called Kate Hepburn at the end of the second day, bubbling over about Vancouver.

"Oh, what a charming place!" I reminded her.

"Well, I'm just not sure I've got the stuff," said Kate.

I told her just because we were scouting locations, she didn't need to feel pressured. Actually, I wasn't sure she had the stuff, either.

"When would we do it?" she asked. This was late January. She was planning to rent a house in Boca Grande for February. That, I assured her, would be no problem. We couldn't possibly go before spring. I capped all this off by telling her we were trying to get her the same flat, the one at the Rosellen on the top floor. That pleased her. That perked her up. For a moment there, she sounded as if she had the stuff.

The next day we traveled from one end of Vancouver to the other. First we went north to a charming village on the water called Deep Cove, then to see a sheriff's station in Port Moody, then to the Naval Station in Stanley Park where the officer in charge showed us the art collection—paintings on the walls of a nautical nature. The officer advised us, "stretch your canvases once a year." We promised we would.

We didn't find all the locations we needed, but it was a full day, pouring rain, and I sank into bed that night exhausted.

Back in Los Angeles, John and Stacy and I met for lunch at the Farmers Market, then went up the block to meet with Trevor Walton, who was director of television movies for CBS. Trevor is English, literate, and has a great sense of humor. Nor is he frightened of people with gray hair. Many young people in this youth-oriented community of southern California are afraid to even say hello to anyone over forty for fear of catching "age." Trevor, who, like Ken Raskoff, knew his beans about comedy and drama, made some very sensible and helpful suggestions about the script.

We finished that day by lifting glasses of champagne at my place, John and Stacy and I. We felt good, really good, about what we could accomplish with this project. We knew we'd have to give Kate every support and it wouldn't be easy, but Stacy and I knew how to do it and I fig-

ured John could be helpful in that, too. We had put together a great little group which now included George Schaefer and Noel Taylor. And if
we could get Walter Lassally to photograph Kate — the only man in the
world, I felt, who could photograph Kate flatteringly at her age — we'd
be sitting pretty. And the combination of Katharine Hepburn and Burt
Reynolds (I refused to give him first billing) was box-office dynamite.

It was decided that now was the time for George and John and me
to fly to New York and talk with Kate, face to face, to show her we were
serious.

I telephoned to ask her if the following Wednesday would be a good
day for us to meet with her.

She was vague. "Where's my script?" she said, "I've lost my script."
Losing her script was a Hepburn habit. But Wednesday would be fine.
In the meantime, we'd send her another script, although hers was prob-
ably under the bed.

When we arrived in New York, awash with champagne, it was a jolt.
We had left hot, sunny Los Angeles; New York was cold, wet, dark, and
looked dirty.

I appeared at Kate Hepburn's door the next morning at 10:15, a few
minutes before John and George. Kate looked visibly older, a bit of a
shock. She was also anxious.

"What happens if I pass out?" she said, meaning in the middle of the
filming.

"Then we'll pass out," I laughed, making as much of a joke out of it
as I could.

George Schaefer was an old friend to Kate now, of course, and a
tower of strength. I knew that he'd calm her. I was a little more concerned about John Dayton. What if they didn't hit it off?

He was nervous, I suppose, but at that meeting I thought he was a little too ingratiating. I need not have worried. I'd forgotten that there is
no such thing as being too ingratiating to a star. Stars don't see through
the flattery; on the contrary, they eat it up. John was perfect for the part
he was about to play.

Norah served lunch and then George and John left. Kate wanted to
read the script with me, just the two of us. We read aloud to each other,
Kate stopping and making comments, until we got to page seventy. (It
was now the proper length of 120 pages.) Kate made some very good
suggestions, although she really wanted to read that poem herself. I
knew we'd have a conflict there. Burt wasn't about to give up his big mo-

ment, nor did it make sense for Kate's character to read it. I gently talked up the moment of his reading it and her wonderful reactions as he read. I described those thrilling shots of her eyes welling up as she was overcome with emotion. I think she bought it.

But at page seventy she said she was too tired to go on. So was I. We simply stopped.

As arranged, John reappeared to pick me up at 3:00. He brought with him a video of Burt Reynolds's movie *Best Friends*. John and I had discussed this over and over. Kate was still declaring that she didn't know who Burt Reynolds was. What this translated into was, why hasn't he come to see me? (I was later told that Burt thought she should come to see him.) We debated which of his films we should give her to show him at his best, or what she would consider his best. We certainly weren't going to offer her *Deliverance*.

We'd decided that *Best Friends* showed him being light and charming and romantic, qualities Kate would go for. We left it with her.

And then, being Kate, she insisted that we must go walking in Central Park. Jimmy brought the car around and Phyllis, John, and I sat in the back while Kate gave Jimmy, who'd driven this route a hundred times, directions as to how to go.

There was a set pattern. Jimmy stopped at a certain spot in the park and let us out, except for Phyllis, who remained in the car. Kate got the walking stick out of the trunk and led us into what I recalled as the most dangerous part of the park. Jimmy then drove on and met us at a designated point farther up.

Kate was dressed like a bag lady, and I don't think any of the questionable types who passed recognized her. I didn't think they'd mug her, but John and I were better dressed and made perfect marks. The hike wasn't long, however, although it was fairly physical. Kate had us going up and down over boulders. I was delighted to go around a little hill and find Jimmy and the car, though.

They dropped us at the Plaza, where John was staying. I dared Kate to come into the lobby in that getup, and she laughed and declined. We hugged and said, "See you in Vancouver!"

I telephoned Kate the next day, although I didn't see her. She was off to Fenwick for the weekend. She was neither enthusiastic nor unenthusiastic about the project. She said simply that she felt our reading of the script had been "fair." She hadn't watched Burt's movie yet.

I had been back in Los Angeles only a day when Kate telephoned me. She began by saying that we shouldn't count on her, that her arthritis was bad. But then she went on to say that she had looked at Burt's movie. And she wasn't happy about it. Or him.

I was stunned and I protested. I suggested that we had given her the wrong movie. She'd got the wrong idea.

There was no convincing her, however, and when she hung up I sat, staring at the walls, wondering what to do next. What I did next was to go to bed with a raging case of the flu. A storm struck, and for two days we were besieged by heavy rains. I moaned and groaned and avoided looking out the windows, where the palm trees were swaying in winds of almost hurricane force.

In the midst of this, John Dayton called. His voice was cheerfulness itself.

"Guess what?" he said, happily. "Good news! Burt isn't going to do the movie! We can get someone else!" His company would produce it, but he wouldn't act in it.

To this day, I don't know exactly why Burt Reynolds didn't do this movie. What happened to the big dream of his life, to work with Katharine Hepburn? To be fair to Burt, his schedule was tight. He was doing *Evening Shade* and would only be free during his hiatus, those summer weeks when sitcoms lay off. When *Cop and a Half* came along it would have to be filmed at almost the same time as *The Man Upstairs*. I suppose he had to make a decision. From now on, however, I wasn't crazy about the decisions.

First of all, one of the best members of our team got the axe.

But I'm getting ahead of myself.

Two days after John called with the news of Burt's withdrawal, I was leaving to lunch with him and Stacy when the telephone rang. It was Kate.

"I'm going to ruin your day," she said. "My leg is bad. I'm just on the way to the doctor. I can't do this picture. Who do I call to tell them this? I mean, officially?"

I told her I'd have John call her and she could tell him. I also said, "That's life." I said she wasn't to worry about it. I said it didn't matter. Burt was certainly never informed of her reaction to his performance in *Best Friends,* and I saw no reason to confess to Kate that he was no longer going to do the picture. When it came right down to it, neither seemed to want the other.

I walked up the hill to the Bel Age Hotel knowing only that we had lost both stars. Why not have a pleasant lunch? I did suggest, as I sat down, that they order stiff drinks. And then I told them about Kate's call.

John was undaunted.

We would go, he said, into Plan B. Plan B, it turned out, was Elizabeth Taylor and Burt. Burt suddenly seemed available again. And was there not always Jessica Tandy?

That night I confess I was talking with Army Archerd, the venerable columnist for *Variety*, and admitted that Kate was no longer a part of the project. I didn't get into Burt at all. Who knew what he was up to?

Army announced in his column the next day, of course, that Katharine Hepburn was no longer planning to appear in *The Man Upstairs*. When Army said it, the industry believed it. You could trust Army.

The next day John told me that Elizabeth Taylor wasn't a possibility. Burt had had some sort of falling out with her current husband, Mr. Fortensky, so forget Elizabeth. CBS, he went on, was still hot to trot and would even accept Katharine Hepburn in a wheelchair. I felt as if I were on some sort of mad carousel. One day we seemed to be trying to replace Burt, the next day we were trying to replace Kate, and then it switched around again.

The next day John Dayton called Kate and said, in effect, "Are you being honest?"

"Well," she replied, "Burt doesn't even call me."

The *next* day John, tenacious as always, called Kate again and had a long talk. Kate told him that she was not well, that we shouldn't take a chance, that we should get somebody younger.

The "somebody younger" was Jessica Tandy, we figured, although it was a matter of only a couple of years. I took in a matinee and saw *Fried Green Tomatoes*. I loved her, but Tandy did look awfully old. Nevertheless, it was decided that the script would go to Miss Tandy, but that I should do certain rewrites first. I said okay, send a check. They did, but I was told I had two weeks to do them. At the end of two weeks, I turned them in and went to the horse show with Carlyn and Patrick Duffy.

The revised script was turned into Burt Reynolds Productions, but I was peeved when I heard that Burt had gone off to Hawaii without even reading it.

John, who never says die, was still talking to Kate. He said she asked to see the revised version, which was sent to her. CBS was (to my mind) remarkably uninterested in Jessica Tandy. They wanted a Katharine

Hepburn movie. I don't think they cared who played opposite her (as was borne out later).

We began playing the casting game, assuming, just for fun, that we had Kate. She adored Judd Hirsch. Was he a possibility? John thought he had a winner when he came up with Michael Caine, until I screamed. A Brit to play an American convict? I pushed my friend, Patrick Duffy, who would be on hiatus from his hit sitcom, *Step by Step*. Patrick, I felt, could play anything. And get along with Kate.

The report came back that Kate liked the revised version. Our hearts lifted.

The next day she went into the hospital for, as she said, "eighty-five-year-old lady things." She was out in a couple of days, but it added to the drama.

And then Stacy Williams, our wonderful Stacy, was relieved of her responsibilities by Burt Reynolds Productions. It was pretty shocking. She'd put a lot of time and effort into the project, including the scouting of locations in Vancouver. She was given no reason, but was notified by Lamar Jackson, president of Burt Reynolds Productions, that she was not needed. John said it was Burt's decision. She was not only not needed, she was also not paid.

Stacy had a signed agreement that did nothing for her as producer, but as unit production manager she was covered by the Directors Guild and, consequently, was put into the humiliating position of going to them to help her seek retribution. They did, and a settlement was made.

But our happy little family was being destroyed. I began to wonder what I had gotten into.

After a meeting with Trevor Walton at CBS, John Dayton called to tell me that they were now unhappy with the character of Moony. He should be more dangerous, more violent. I was to fight this battle right through filming. I felt that the style of the film didn't lend itself to real violence—this wasn't *Rambo*—and if the guy was really violent Kate would have had him out of the house in two minutes. But you know television networks and violence. There's no stopping them.

And then John dropped his bombshell. The network wanted to put another writer on my movie.

Now, I know this is a common practice, but it had never happened to me. I was incensed. Who did they think they were dealing with here? I who had had three plays on Broadway and numerous off-Broadway and nine published plays and was a Doctor of Literary Arts! One simply didn't put another writer on a Prideaux script. I got very grand.

I called my current agent, Jeannine Edmunds at Curtis Brown, and told her to inform the network that I would take my star and my director and go. Miss Hepburn and Mr. Schaefer and Mr. Prideaux would walk. Jeannine said I was doing just the right thing.

Before this devastating information could be relayed, however, John telephoned to say that the network had reconsidered. Furthermore, the script had gone to Jon Voight and he was interested. My spirits rose. I'd never met Jon Voight, but I thought he was a wonderful actor and, I'd heard, an interesting and intelligent man. Even a refreshing lack of ego? No mood swings?

The phone rarely rang those days without riveting news, one way or the other. The call of them all came from John Dayton.

"I've been fired," he said simply.

He had lost his job at Burt Reynolds Productions, but he could stay on to be an executive producer on *The Man Upstairs*. "At half salary," he moaned. He would do this, but it was jolting to his morale. He felt crushed and, I think, betrayed.

I felt as if the production was falling apart. George Schaefer was getting impatient and cranky because he didn't have a contract.

Nevertheless, we met in the Reynolds office—sans Burt—the following day with Jon Voight. I liked him right off. He was a bit "on," but he was, as I'd hoped, interesting. He told lovely stories about Indians. There was a spiritual side to him that was attractive. He was huggable. (But then, so was Burt.) He read a bit for George and me and gave a different interpretation to the part of Moony. It was a shade too "dese, dem, and dose," but it was also touching. Here was a superb actor. Nor was he standoffish. He gave me his telephone number and I carefully tucked it away. I wanted to get to know him better and, as I told him, I hoped he'd play the part. I wanted to work with him.

The scuttlebutt the next day was that Voight might be offered a miniseries, but he called me that evening and we talked for a good half hour about all sorts of things. Jon was a man who thought about things. I couldn't have enjoyed it more.

This was repeated the following day when we talked for nearly an hour, this time delving deeper into things I was skeptical of, but curious about, like religion. His sprang from the American Indian, that sensible spirituality that included not only all creatures, but respected the earth and the air as well. "Show me a glimmer of truth and I will be loyal to it," he said. When I brought up the subject of death, which was surrounding us all due to AIDS, he said simply, "They're going to a miracle land—every beautiful dream magnified a thousand times." I liked hearing that, whether I could believe it or not. He also said, if I understood him correctly, that it was possible to communicate with the dead if you spoke the name of the deceased three times and relaxed and conversed. I found that comforting.

There was a sweetness to the man. I felt that by working with him and knowing him I could expand my horizons.

George Schaefer telephoned Kate. He was trying to get things moving. She complained that the part of Moony was better than hers, just as Burt had complained that her part was better than his. She said she would read the script again. How many times can a star read a script? The big breakthrough was that she admitted knowing who Jon Voight was, and she was impressed since he had presented one of her Oscars.

Early the next morning, I talked with Brenda Forbes in New York. She said she'd spoken with Kate, who never once mentioned the movie.

Later that same day, John Dayton called, his voice shaking with excitement. Kate had said yes. She was not, however, entirely happy with the script. John was obviously elated and told me they were going ahead and making a deal with Jon Voight.

I slept soundly that night. Kate was never entirely happy with a script, but that could be worked out later. I felt that the combination of Katharine Hepburn and Jon Voight, if not quite as commercially promising as Kate and Burt, was more artistically honest.

That was Thursday night. I had a very pleasant weekend, which included an Easter Sunday with a champagne brunch at the Bel Age. The Bel Age pulled out all the stops with their champagne brunches, especially on religious holidays. I took a deep breath and relaxed. Wasn't it great when it all worked out, especially after everything we'd been through?

On Monday morning I was informed that Jon Voight had been offered a feature film in New Zealand. He'd be leaving in a few days.

And I got my first telephone call from Renee Valente. I knew two things about Renee Valente: she was famous in the industry and she was tough. George Schaefer, who'd worked with her many times, also said,

"I'd trust Renee with my life." Sounded all right. I was sorry, though, that she'd been brought in to replace Stacy and John, although John would stay on in a reduced position. (He shared the title of executive producer with Lamar Jackson.)

Renee had one of those gravelly, Irma Diamond voices, the result, I suspected, of years of smoking.

Her first suggestion to me was that we cast Moony younger. (The network, I knew, would like that: capture the young audience as well as the older. Get a Luke Perry or a Jason Priestley.) I said no. I explained Kate's feelings about the older woman and the "boy." The bore and the wimp. I said she'd hate the idea. Renee accepted that. She'd never met Katharine Hepburn and knew nothing about her, really.

She next asked me what my per diem was. I thought this was a standard question and, although I was a bit startled to hear it right up front, why not ascertain it at the start? I told her I got, and had always gotten, $150 a day. There was no reaction from her so I assumed that was all right. (I mention this only because it was to become such a bone of contention between us later.)

She'd hardly hung up when Lamar Jackson called. He was merely reporting that Mary Tyler Moore had gotten a script and was dying to do it if Kate didn't. She had said she would age or anything. I was stunned. Who didn't love Mary Tyler Moore, but age? Play an eighty-year-old? Or, even if she played it younger, I couldn't imagine Mary Tyler Moore as Victoria Browne, much as I loved her. I preferred to watch her on those reruns.

Renee was now totally in charge. This hardly sat well with John, who claimed that she was getting three times the fee that he was. He had also been planning to go east to see Kate, but had been told not to. Only George, he said to me, was supposed to communicate with Kate now. That didn't stop John. He did talk to Kate and reported that she was very "up." But John always reported that Kate was very "up." It was a part of his philosophy of life: everything was wonderful. Except, possibly, his current position.

Lamar telephoned me again to say that John was going to New York—I just sat by the telephone and waited for these enlightening calls—and did I, knowing Kate as I did, think Renee should go with him? I said I didn't know.

The trouble was that Kate hadn't signed a contract. George didn't even have one. They wanted very much to get her signature on the dotted line. Renee could certainly help with that.

On the evening of Friday, April 24, 1992, Los Angeles had an earthquake. I went flying across the floor as my bedroom rolled about. I'd experienced earthquakes before, but this one was particularly scary. It put everything into perspective suddenly. I'd been losing sleep over a television movie when death could strike at any moment. Where was my sense of values? Who cared if Katharine Hepburn appeared in a movie for CBS?

Relax.

Have a drink before the next tremor.

John Dayton called me from the airport en route to New York. He had called Kate Hepburn, who said, "When you see me, you tell me if you think I can do it." So she was leaving it to him. He thought that was great. According to John, anybody could do anything.

That was a Monday. I also spoke with George Schaefer, who was really fed up. He said he'd laid down the law to the Reynolds people. Either a contract by Thursday or he was out.

Renee was in New York, and she did go with John to meet Kate. I can imagine that meeting. Later, Kate was only to comment on Renee's feet. She wore open-toed shoes over painted toenails and no hose. Kate was fascinated.

"Have you ever seen feet like those?" she kept saying. I had, but Kate hadn't. She was entering a world that was new to her.

Renee called me and said that Kate was questionable. She had a buzzing in the ears and was going to a doctor. I said I'd never thought Kate could, or should, do this movie. Renee said she wished she'd known that in the first place. And they were staying over another day.

The next day proved to be memorable.

I got the first inkling of what had transpired when Renee called and announced, triumphantly, "She signed her contract! I got her to sign her contract!"

I said, "Well done."

Later, I got the story as told by Kate and John. Kate said that Renee handed her the contract and pen and sat waiting. Kate imitated her, Renee tapping her fingers as she waited for Kate to sign . . . tap, tap, tap. Kate signed. It was really a historic moment.

Katharine Hepburn had met her match.

When I called her, Kate was actually eager to get started. "It'll be fun," she said. To some of the old stars, the making of movies was not only fun: it proved they were alive, needed, and could still deliver the goods. Not to mention the required attention it provided. Some older stars went on too long, just as Bette Davis had done and, according to some, Kate was now doing. But they just couldn't stop.

My eighty-five-year-old star now complained that Moony's part had energy and was more important than hers. I had carefully constructed this to make Kate's character fairly immobile — this side of keeping her in bed — so it wouldn't be too strenuous for her. Also, I knew we'd have a problem with her remembering lines so I tried to make her lines witty and Hepburnesque, but minimal. Now she wanted more to do and more lines.

I said I'd take it under consideration.

George Schaefer and I were called to a meeting in Trevor Walton's office at CBS. Lamar Jackson was there, friendly and affable, and Renee Valente. This must have been the first time I met her. There was instant antagonism — at least, to be honest, on my part. I longed for Stacy Williams.

Renee pretty much took over, outlining where we were and what we were up to. And then came the shocker. We had gotten into casting.

"And," she said casually, "we're all agreed on Ryan O'Neal."

I screamed like a stuck pig. George looked stunned. The name of Ryan O'Neal had never been mentioned to either of us. I couldn't believe it. I saw Moony as lean and dark, physically the exact opposite of Ryan O'Neal. I said so. George was less vociferous, but he did wonder if Ryan was right for it.

Nobody cared what we thought. Before our very eyes, the powerful Miss Valente picked up the telephone and called O'Neal's agent. We listened to the conversation. Ryan O'Neal wanted what Farrah Fawcett got, which was a million dollars. That came down very quickly to $700,000. But Kate was getting $400,000 and that's what Ryan's agent settled for. It was a done deal as we sat there. I was in a state of shock.

We weren't aware that Ryan O'Neal had a contract with CBS, left over from his sitcom flop. They owed him one. This was their way of paying it off. That he might not be right for the part didn't concern them. He was still something of a name — big enough, at any rate — and

they had Katharine Hepburn for major name value anyway. It was a way
to get O'Neal off their backs.

I went home in utter despair.

On a Saturday morning, Renee and I met with George at his house in
Beverly Hills. She had huddled with the network and had further notes
about the script. They were mostly of the "Moony should be more dangerous" variety, but not unreasonable. She also told me I had to break
the script into seven acts "because the network wants it." I explained
that we didn't work that way. We'd done two very successful movies together, and it was George who took my script and broke it into acts.
George backed me up. So we got over that one.

I now heard again how hard up Burt Reynolds was. He had made
"bad investments." This was to be harped on throughout the entire production. I found it difficult to shed the appropriate tears. I should be so
hard up.

Certainly Renee was called in to deliver this movie as cheaply as possible. I suppose she reaped advantages—a percentage or something—if
she did this, but what do I know? I only know it was my first experience
with this kind of thing.

They were due what we call "a first polish" of the script.

I rudely said, "You'll get the script when I get the check."

"You don't trust Burt?" said Renee.

I remembered Stacy's having to take it to the Directors Guild to
get paid.

"Nope," said I. Do you wonder that I was not Renee's favorite? Can
you blame her?

I had also insisted on two things. I wanted Walter Lassally as director
of photography. Only he could photograph Kate flatteringly at her age.
This was vital. It was a fight, but I finally got him.

Also, I'd written the part of Molly, Kate's cook, for the Irish actress,
Helena Carroll. Aside from being a brilliant actress, she was almost as
short as Kate and certainly rounder than Kate. Next to Helena, Kate
would look taller and slimmer.

Renee didn't know who Helena Carroll was and wanted to hire a
local actress in Vancouver. I dug my heels in. Nevertheless, George
sided with Renee. He said he'd once worked with Helena Carroll and
she was one of the few actresses he'd never work with again. Difficult.

I couldn't believe it. So I threw a cocktail party, inviting George and

John and Helena Carroll. John didn't know Helena, either, but he took one look at her and said to me, "She's perfect! We've got to have her!"

George took one look and called me into the bedroom for a private chat. "I'm sorry," he said, "I was thinking of another actress. She's ideal." Had it not been for that party, we'd've lost Helena and she'd have lost the job. Scary.

I delivered the first polish and finally got a check, although it was postdated.

Renee went off on her own to Vancouver to scout locations. When she got back, we gathered in Burt's office—Burt wasn't there—to look at the videos, a gathering that included George and John and Lamar and our production designer, a delightful man named Trevor Williams.

Renee was smoking. I used to smoke. I once thought I couldn't work at the typewriter without smoking. I was as hooked as anybody. But twenty-five years ago I quit—I just quit, and I've never had a cigarette since. I'm fully aware that it's the toughest habit in the world to kick, but I also figure if I could do it, anybody can do it. Consequently, I'm intolerant of smokers. I'm rabid. This is partly due to the fact that I've lived in Los Angeles long enough to have slight lung problems and have been told by doctors to avoid secondary smoke.

Anyway, Renee was smoking. She alone. I thought it inconsiderate with all those people in so small a space. I can't remember whether I mentioned it. I'm sure if I did Renee doused it immediately. She was good about that.

We watched the videos she had brought back. She had found the perfect house to use as Kate's home.

"That's a Hepburn house," I told her and congratulated her. I wasn't all bad.

For some reason I wasn't free to go with him, but George Schaefer went up to Ryan O'Neal's house to meet him and hear him read Moony. He called me the next morning, very excited. Yes, Ryan was a bit overweight, but he was working on it and his reading was wonderful, just wonderful. He couldn't wait for me to hear him.

I went to the video store and got a cassette of *What's Up, Doc?* At that point, Ryan had one of the great bodies of the world and, furthermore, he was very funny. I suspected George was right. Ryan O'Neal could really act. I also ran *Paper Moon* and was bowled over by him. He was playing a con man, which was just what we needed. Could it be we had lucked out?

It was arranged that Ryan and I would meet the next afternoon at 5:00 at George's house. Luckily, George and I had planned to meet earlier to do a little work on the script, because at 4:30 the front door flew open and in came Ryan O'Neal.

He had changed. It was difficult to find the handsome young man he had once been. But he was pleasant and enthusiastic and laughingly said he'd do anything to make Miss Hepburn like him. He also said he was working out, exercising. Seeing Ryan, and sensing the quality he could bring to the character, I didn't care if Moony was a little pudgy.

I was quite happy about him.

On the early evening of June 29, 1992, John Dayton, George and Millie Schaefer, Adie Luraschi, and I flew to Vancouver to make the movie of *The Man Upstairs*. The weather was beautiful and we flew over Mount St. Helens, serene and majestic, but ominous to me because my friend Reid Blackburn had died there doing photography for the *National Geographic*.

It was dark when we landed in Vancouver and two limousines took us immediately to the Coast Plaza Hotel, which was the new name of the old Denman.

I awoke the following morning at dawn and, leaning over the balcony, drank in the tremendous view. My spirits soared. I had breakfast sent up, and then met John downstairs in the lobby. We were driven to a small studio that first morning, where we filmed several shots of two newscasters, a man and a woman. George was there and Renee, who had flown up to Vancouver earlier to establish an office. Linden Soles and Teryly Rothery were actual local newscasters, not actors. I had written their dialogue, but when George asked for additional lines (ad-libs, as it were, at which I'm terrible), Linden came up with better lines than I ever could. Unfortunately, the lines were eventually cut.

It was very exciting, of course, to get these first scenes in the can. And to see old friends. Among others, there was Jimmy Chow, the wonderful prop man who'd worked on my other films.

I was also determined to be friendly with Renee, who was cool and very much in charge. After all, didn't we have to make a movie? I suspect she felt the same way. Had I merely been the writer, I'm sure I would have been dispensed with very quickly. But I was again coproducer, not to mention the old friend, and link, with Miss Hepburn. I had to be put up with.

Renee stayed on there, but John and I drove to the office Renee had set up. We met the people who would work there. I had always been very friendly, and even formed lasting relationships with the people who ran such offices, but here I detected a little attitude. It was a jolt.

The accounting lady handed me my per diem. It came to fifty dollars a day. I couldn't believe it. I said there must be some mistake. No, she assured me, this was the per diem she was instructed to give me.

I discovered the actors, too, had been cut from their normal one hundred dollars a day to fifty. No actor in my films, who had been flown in and had to live on it, had ever received less than one hundred a day. Vancouver was expensive. I went from a lovely enthusiasm over the film to a fuming rage. I girded my loins for battle. I wasn't so concerned over Brenda Forbes, who had independent means, but Helena Carroll was another matter. She was working at what was, for her, a very cut rate to begin with and she'd have to be in Vancouver for almost the entire four-week shoot. I wasn't sure she could do it on fifty dollars a day, especially with restaurant meals and the like.

I would have to deal with this, but I wasn't quite sure how.

After lunch, John and I went to check out the apartment Renee had leased for Kate. Here no expense had been spared. It was only two doors from her former building (which wasn't available) in the neighborhood she loved and it was in a ten-story, spanking-new steel-and-glass building called the Presidio. The apartment was spectacular. It was the entire ninth floor, as I recall, with enormous windows affording sensational views in every direction: the park, the bay, the sky. I knew she'd carp a bit—the gas fireplace with glass in front of it; the difficulty of coded elevators and doors—but she couldn't carp much. Her own private suite was at one end and, at the other, rooms for Phyllis and Jimmy, each with a private bath. It was perfect for a movie star and legend.

Kate and her entourage were to arrive from New York late in the afternoon. This time, through some kind of pull, it had been arranged that we could drive straight to the plane; Kate wouldn't have to go through customs. John and I would go to meet her, of course. We drove to the airport, but got there an hour early. There was a sentry box and guard at whatever back entrance we were sent to. He said we couldn't drive through until the plane had landed. Therefore, we parked and waited in the heat and dust for the plane to arrive. A full hour. Just as it did, we saw a limousine pulling up.

"Oh, my God!" said John. "Would you believe this?"

It was Renee. She lowered her window and said what with Phyllis and Jimmy, as well as Kate, there wouldn't be room for us in the car so she'd go and meet Kate and we'd see them as they came out. With that her limo roared on, leaving us standing in the dust. If it hadn't been so outrageous, it would have been funny. John was furious. I was amazed.

(Later Kate said she'd asked Renee where her friends were, and Renee told her we preferred to meet her outside.)

When they came out, Kate opened the car door and we both gave her a hug. Phyllis, too. Kate looked in remarkably good shape. Renee was beaming at her little triumph.

"Meet us at the apartment," Kate said and they drove off.

We got there first and waited for them at the entrance to the garage. (They'd stopped for ice-cream cones; Kate could never pass up an ice-cream store.) Only John could explain the code that opened the garage door and the code in the elevator that got them to their floor and the code at their front door. It wasn't easy, and I had no idea how Kate or Phyllis would ever cope.

I think Kate was really overwhelmed by the grandness of the apartment and thrilled with the view. She didn't even seem to mind the glass in front of the fireplace.

Two real-estate ladies from the Presidio were there "to greet Miss Hepburn."

"I think we need a drink," said Kate, even including the two Presidio ladies as we headed for the kitchen and Jimmy got ice. We all stood, leaning on a high table in the center of the room, having a drink. After the first one, I saw Kate begin to fade.

And then came a frightening moment. I shall never forget it.

Kate looked right at me and said, "Where's Jim Prideaux? When does he arrive?"

There was a stunned silence.

"Kate," I said, "I'm Jim Prideaux."

She then tried to make a joke of it, but she'd been gone for a moment. Most disturbing. I went home and John went out to buy more groceries for them. As always, Kate wasn't satisfied with the stocking of the apartment.

"We're in danger of starving to death," were the last words I heard as I headed for the elevator.

Noel Taylor flew in and I gave him and his two assistants drinks in my suite. John and I then went out to dinner, recalling the events of the day and wondering, once again, if Kate was up to this. As always, John was sure she was. I was almost sure she wasn't.

We walked back to the hotel around 11:00 P.M. It was still light out, which threw us a bit. It felt like 7:00 P.M. But this was Vancouver in the summertime and night fell late. We were in the North. I'm not sure I'd care for it in the wintertime.

The next day was her routine "first day" when Kate wanted to check out the locations, especially her house. So we piled into George's car, Kate and Phyllis and John and I, and George attempted to find the house, which was quite a ways out of town. Much trouble, and laughter, finding it. We stopped; George consulted a map; we asked directions of pedestrians; it all seemed hopeless until we found ourselves down a little street, looked up a driveway, and there it was.

Kate was pleased with the look of it. But once we got inside it was another matter. She hit the ceiling over her bedroom and the way it was decorated.

"Cheap," she said. "No taste."

This, I might add, was not the fault of Trevor Williams, the production designer. He hadn't really decorated it. Most of it was stuff already in the house. And it was all sort of thrown together. After Kate finished with her critique, it was all changed the next day. When it came to the rooms she lived in, Miss Hepburn had very firm ideas.

She also attacked me (I think *attacked* is the word) over the attic, where much of the action was to take place because Moony was hiding up there.

"Why does it take place in the attic all the time?" she hooted. "That's idiotic!"

"It's not idiotic!" I told her. (We were old friends.) I said that was the plot. She said she'd die of the heat and wasn't assuaged for a moment when we explained that we'd have air conditioning piped in. She poohpoohed that. And, in the end, she was absolutely right. With actors and crew and lights in that small space, when the time came it was a nightmare up there, even with cool air being pushed in the windows through great tubes from a generator on the lawn. Kate hated small, airless spaces. And the air conditioning had to be turned off the minute they started shooting. It became a serious problem.

On the drive back into town, Kate said she wanted a hot dog. We found a Wendy's, a drive-in. That was a mistake. No hot dogs, only hamburgers, and no ginger ale, which is what Kate wanted to drink. We sat in the car gloomily munching hamburgers.

Our spirits revived, however, when we drove the entire six miles around Stanley Park and Kate declared that she was reoriented at last. Now, she said, she knew where she was.

I went home and napped, and had dinner with an old friend, Alan Poole. We walked down the street to the English Bay Cafe for fish and chips. Not cheap; dinner came to sixty-one dollars. I was even more devastated by the prices in the liquor store. The Canadian government was in the liquor business, and a bottle of vodka that would cost you ten dollars in the States cost thirty in Canada. It was a great little racket.

Trevor Williams called to say that he couldn't possibly do what was needed on the budget he had, and then Noel Taylor called to say the same thing. There was nothing I could do about it.

The next morning, John and I drove Noel Taylor over to Kate's for a fitting. We were astonished to find her sitting in a reception room on the main floor with all the other tenants around her. ("Well, the cover's off," said one of the lady tenants, referring to Miss Hepburn's anonymity.) It seems the fire alarm had gone off and all the tenants were required to walk down the stairs to the lobby. Kate had walked nine flights.

"But where's Phyllis?" John asked. Kate said she'd stayed up in the flat. When we registered dismay at this, Kate said, "Let her burn." There wasn't any fire, of course, and the elevator was soon back in operation. We left Noel there.

Renee called a couple of hours later and said that Kate was feeling unwell and she was sending a doctor over. I worried, but after lunch John called and said Kate had telephoned and said, "You and Jim come over. Let's take a walk."

When we got there, she seemed fine and was waiting for us with Phyllis in the lobby. Stanley Park was right there so we walked into the woods, Kate and John going on ahead, and I followed with Phyllis on my arm. Kate was, naturally, our leader, and Phyllis and I struggled to keep up with her. By this time it was late afternoon and, once out of the woods, we were invited up for a drink. It was like old times with Kate, funny and pleasant. We laughed a lot. John kept firing questions at her about the making of *The Philadelphia Story*.

"Stay for dinner," said Kate, and poor Jimmy had to come up with steaks for four, which he did with John's help, while Kate kept shouting into the kitchen, "How soon?"

Over dinner, she queried us about Renee. (Poor Renee. She was, after all, just trying to get the job done with what she had to work with.) We complained about the per diems, of course. Kate had all sorts of suggestions as to how to deal with that. She said she'd tell Renee that she, Kate, would pay all our per diems.

"Would you really do that?" asked John.

Kate laughed. "Well, I'd tell her I would." And then she went on. "You destroy the creative process if you're penurious. All I'm interested in is perfection."

We went back to the hotel, having had a wonderful time. I don't know what the "unwell" business was about. Kate was absolutely on the ball.

Ryan O'Neal was to arrive the following day, so John and I went once again to the airport. No limousine with Renee this time; Ryan wasn't a big enough star. (But we had a limo.) Nor was Ryan spared the customs people, which was unfortunate.

He met us looking rather scruffy and unshaven. And he was grumpy. At the customs desk, the officer had looked at him and said, "What are you going to do on the film, Mr. O'Neal?" How would you like to hear that if you'd once been one of the biggest stars in Hollywood? Ryan told him he thought he'd act.

He calmed down on the ride into town, and we talked about his son-in-law, John McEnroe, who was playing at Wimbledon. The car phone rang and it was Renee, calling to welcome him. George came on the phone, too. Ryan O'Neal wasn't a big enough star to be met, but something had to be done. When he'd hung up, Ryan made clear his feelings about Renee.

"God, she bit my lip," he said.

He had worked with her before. Renee and I might have our differences, but that was nothin' compared to the enmity between Ryan and her.

And that night George Schaefer and I had the first fight, over the telephone, that we had had in twenty years. He said that I was not to go to "the house" the next morning with Kate to check it out. Nor was John. He said he was tired of this feud with Renee. I had never known

George to be in a rage before and this was a rage. I said I was sorry, but I felt there was some injustice to the actors and to Trevor and Noel and . . . but I didn't get very far. When he hung up, I sat staring into space. Was I in the wrong?

Anyway, I stayed away from the house the next morning and met them all later in the day for our first reading of the script. We were once again in the Ryerson Church, in the very room where we had first read *Mrs. Delafield*. George seemed to have forgotten our fight, which was fine. Onward and upward.

But first Katharine Hepburn and Ryan O'Neal were to meet.

I had just parked on the curb outside the church when Ryan was driven up in a van. As he was getting out, Kate's car pulled up and parked directly behind the van. Ryan got out and walked toward Kate's car as she got out and walked toward the van. By this time, I was standing in the middle.

"Miss Hepburn, this is Mr. O'Neal," I said.

She looked up at him and suddenly turned on a dazzling smile. If there was anything Kate understood in this world, it was a troubled, overweight Irishman. I won't go so far as to say she saw traces of Spencer Tracy in him, but I wouldn't be surprised. At any rate, it was clear to me from that moment that we were all right. This was going to work. The chemistry was there.

As to what Ryan's trouble was, who knows what anyone's trouble is? Whatever it was, it was Moony.

We gathered around a long table for the reading. Unfortunately, Helena Carroll wouldn't arrive for a couple of days (it was cheaper) and Renee read her part, which upset Kate a little. Renee also lit a cigarette immediately and I surprised Kate by snapping, "Renee, would you put that out, please?" She did, and we began the reading.

Kate gave a reading that had every nuance, funny and moving. And Ryan was every bit as good. Very touching, in fact. I swear I actually saw glimpses of a great actor.

I cried during the reading, but everybody did, Ryan most of all.

After the reading, which thrilled everybody, I think, John and I had lunch at our favorite fish restaurant, the Kettle of Fish, and went to Kate's at 5:30. We piled in to her car and drove into Stanley Park. Kate wanted to walk in the deep woods.

"Stop here!" she told Jimmy, and Kate and John and I got out, leaving Phyllis and Jimmy in the car. We started walking into the woods and I thought, how beautiful! The forest primeval! There was only one unusual thing about the forest primeval. There seemed to be a single man standing behind every tree. And, looking down, I noticed that the floor of the forest primeval was littered with used condoms. (At least, they were practicing safe sex.)

Kate was quick to pick up on it.

"This is a strange place, isn't it?" said Kate. We laughed about it. She wondered if John and I were safe. I'm sure I was, at my age.

As we were walking back toward the car, an elderly man, very nice and polite, stopped us and said, "I never thought I'd see a living legend when I came out this afternoon. Thank you, Miss Hepburn, for all the joy you've brought into my life." It was very sweet and Kate smiled and thanked him.

When we got back into the car, I told Phyllis about it and what a lovely moment it had been. "Yes," she said, "and he'll go home and tell his wife about it."

"Roommate, Phyllis," I said, "roommate."

We drove slowly around the park. Slowly was the only way Kate wanted to be driven so that she could comment on how fascinating everything was. We went back to Kate's place for drinks. Jimmy had created gorgeous appetizers of shrimp and mussels, which was followed by a superb dinner of lamb.

I was beginning to think Kate had a little crush on Ryan.

It was a Sunday and John and I took the limo out to the airport again to pick up Helena Carroll. The limousine made her feel like she was going first class, I figured. It was the least we could do.

John had called Kate earlier in the day to see if she didn't want us to bring Helena around for cocktails so they could meet. Yes, yes, she said, but all she could talk about was whether Ryan could come. Go to the telephone now, she had insisted. Find out.

The previous afternoon we had had a private rehearsal at Kate's place. George and Ryan and I all rode over in a tiny open car belonging to the script supervisor, Pattie Robertson. It was time to have the script supervisor on hand. Rewrites might be brewing.

At that rehearsal, I had caught Kate eyeing Ryan as he bared his arms, still golden and good, and I suspected she might even be a little frightened of him, just as I suspected she might have been of Spencer. And she was obviously impressed with his talent.

We sat in her living room and the two of them read brilliantly together. Kate started tearing the first act apart, but George calmed her
and with a couple of very minor changes she seemed satisfied. We re-
arranged a few lines here and there, but nothing major.

After that, Jimmy gave us lunch, actually sitting at the dining room
table—rare for Kate. It was cold cuts and English muffins. Ryan ate
sparingly, I noticed, obviously determined to lose weight.

We went back to reading the play and I was weeping, of course, at
the end of it (as was Ryan). Kate called me a jackass. I said if she were
the emotional mess I was, she'd cry, too.

On the ride home, Ryan said of Kate, "She's very acute." And we
agreed that she was. Ryan was perfectly friendly throughout the afternoon, but when we got out of the car he disappeared into the lobby
without a good-bye, as if we'd suddenly vanished from his life. Odd.

And so, that rainy Sunday afternoon, John and I gathered Helena
and Ryan and off we went again to Kate's. We had a rousing time. Here
we had two Irish actors playing off one another with gales of laughter
and I thought at first Kate might be miffed at not being the entire center of attention, but she seemed to have a good time. Didn't want us to
leave, in fact, until well past her dinner time. Ryan was very much on,
and there were many Irish stories from Helena. She talked about her
father, the great Irish playwright, Paul Vincent Carroll.

Ryan said to Kate, "You've never married, have you?" And Kate swore
she couldn't remember, which was, I trust, a joke. What was fascinating
was to watch her watching him. She was hooked. I did notice that the
vodka bottle emptied rather quickly, with only Ryan and me at it, so he
obviously wasn't off the sauce. And Helena could drink anybody under
the table.

Phyllis and I sat on the sofa and mostly listened.

"Actors," I said and she nodded. I think Kate was hungry for it, the
talk of actors.

Kate walked to the door with Ryan's arm around her.

Helena and Ryan then, very raucously, went to Bud's Restaurant for
fish and chips, but I'd had enough of the raucousness and went home
to a quiet dinner. Well, at least the actors were getting along.

A meeting was planned the next morning at my suite to hear Helena
read. I knew that George and Adie and Pattie would be there, but then
Renee called and asked what time she should be there.

I said, "What for?"

Now, that wasn't meant in a rude or hostile way. In all my experience, the producer—Merrill Karpf, for instance—had never sat in on such a meeting.

"This is for the creative team," I went on. I actually assumed that she had plenty of business matters to attend to, much more important than sitting in on Helena's little reading.

"I'm not creative?" Renee shouted and she hung up on me.

She was there in a flash, sat and listened to the reading, and had some very good suggestions to make. At the end, as the others were leaving, she said to me, "I have to have four minutes with you alone, Jim."

We went into my bedroom.

We had it out. Talked quietly. Aside from the damn per diems (it turned out that Renee—and everyone else—was getting the same fifty dollars per day), it was nothing more than a personality clash, really. She said she hadn't acted as a line producer in years—a comedown, I assumed—and she was thoroughly unhappy and wished she had never gotten into this. I said, sometimes I wished I hadn't gotten into it, too.

"But Renee," I said, "I think we can make magic here." I honestly believed that at this point, if Kate could remember her lines. I went on to say that I wanted to prevent a blowup with Kate (which I feared) if Renee hovered around the set.

She said she'd take care of Miss Hepburn. I thought, oh yeah? She'd told us the other day we should have said "no" to Kate when she first wanted to inspect the house. Try saying no to Kate!

And suddenly she started crying and, for the first time, I glimpsed a human being in there. She ran out the door, crying.

And straight to Burt Reynolds, of course.

I didn't have time to think about it. I had to get to Kate's, where Helena was going to read with her and Ryan. Helena came off as far too mean. Worried, I told her that Molly really liked Miss Browne, possibly even loved her employer. I was concerned because Helena was the one member of the cast I'd really fought for, and if she didn't work out there was nobody to blame but myself. (She did work out. That suggestion was all she needed. She was wonderful in the part.) Kate worried about her, too, but she needn't have. When the time came, they worked together like a dream.

Ryan had sent Helena a bottle of Scotch as a gift. That cemented their friendship, although I don't think the relationship accelerated as Helena might have liked.

After that, there was a production meeting, but George said there was no reason for me to be there. And possibly a very good reason for me not to be there. I stayed away.

It was the next night, when the call sheet was slipped under my door, that I discovered a little something with it. It was a letter from Burt Reynolds addressed to John Dayton, James Prideaux, and George Schaefer.

Here it is in full:

Gentlemen,

It has been brought to my attention that Renee Valente was to be excluded from a rehearsal of *The Man Upstairs* by Mr. Prideaux. Let me take this opportunity to clear up what I think might be a few misconceptions. Firstly, considering that this is a Burt Reynolds Production and according to my agent I am indeed Burt Reynolds I would like it made perfectly clear that in my absence Ms. Valente is running the show.

Creating camps and a divisive atmosphere is a destructive and uncalled for action and as professionals frankly I'm a bit taken aback. It is through Ms. Valente's efforts that this film is being made and thereby hopefully furthering all our reputations. I have complete faith and confidence in her abilities and as my producer she is to be afforded the same respect that you surely would have given me. If this pettiness continues a very tired, very grouchy Burt Reynolds will make a trek to Vancouver to deal with this in person, which believe me will not be pleasant.

Let us all cut to the chase and get this movie made and save all the unpleasantness for the wrap party.

If you have any questions, please feel free to call me but know that I stand behind Ms. Valente like the 800 pound gorilla that I am. I don't want to hear of any other instances where she is treated poorly or with the lack of respect so far demonstrated. I trust this message is very clear and that things will begin to get on track.

Sincerely, Burt

I began to pack.

It seemed to me, at the time, to be a threatening letter. But so what? Who needed me? John had taken over the role with Kate that I had played heretofore: dining with her, riding with her, cueing her lines. Which I thought was great. Kate wouldn't miss me as she would have on prior films. With John on hand, she wouldn't feel deserted. The writer could go home.

The thought of escaping was bliss.

I slept fitfully, though. It did seem like defeat. We hadn't really even started to film, and simply because of this personality clash with Renee I was ready to walk out? The sleep was fitful, indeed.

In the morning, there was another letter under my door. It was from John Dayton. It had been written at 5:00 A.M., after he'd received Burt's letter. He must have sensed I was packing. It said, in part:

> Let's get on with the show and put ill feelings aside for the good of all of us . . . Jim, the script is too good, the company spirit is up, Kate is ready, Ryan is wonderful . . . Don't desert the project . . . I have asked you to talk to Renee, and I mean to Renee not down to Renee . . . No, she's not perfect, yes, she can be irritable, etc., but at least I have talked to her and I understand much of what she's got to cope with—the least being making this picture on a budget whose deficit is coming out of Burt's own personal pocket . . . If you would bury the hatchet and move on in trust, this could be your best TV movie yet . . . Jim, for the sake of a beautiful project, which we all care about, let's move on—it's a new day . . . In your own mind, give Renee a chance.

And then George Schaefer telephoned.

He was clearly upset by Burt's letter and he was certainly tired of "that feud," but he was loving and supportive.

But it was Noel Taylor who really got my suitcase back in the closet. I don't know how he knew about all this, but he called and, in his quiet way, said something like, "If you leave, she's won. If you stay, you've won. Don't be foolish."

I dressed and drove to David Street to a screening room to view a makeup test that Kate had made the day before. It seemed as if years had passed since Burt's letter was slipped under my door. I felt drained. But the decision was made.

I smiled at Renee.

This makeup test was important. Even Kate, who claimed never to look at herself on the screen, was there. If she didn't like what she saw, it could frighten her into abandoning the entire project. And she was in a foul mood that morning. John, who had driven over with her, said she had yelled at Phyllis and Jimmy.

Thanks to the genius of Michal Bigger, who did Kate's makeup, Miss

Hepburn looked fabulous in the test. We all cheered with genuine enthusiasm. Kate couldn't possibly wriggle out now. But it didn't help her mood.

I said to Renee, "That was quite a letter Burt wrote."

She said to me, "I loved it."

I'm sure.

We went on then to the Ryerson Church, where we had a good rehearsal—Kate and Ryan and Helena—with Kate warming up and really beginning to enjoy it. It was not as long as expected. We started at 10:30 and were finished by 12:30. Generous Kate then said Ryan and John and I should come home with her for lunch, but when she telephoned her apartment there was no answer. Obviously, Jimmy and Phyllis weren't expecting her so early and had gone to do the shopping. Perfectly reasonable.

Kate exploded, however. She wanted what she wanted *when* she wanted it—always.

"They're dumb!" she cried. "They're just so *dumb!*"

I thought that was pretty bad behavior, considering that Phyllis and Jimmy devoted every waking moment to her. I wished she'd stop it. Anyway, we got to her place and she yelled at Jimmy and Phyllis, who hopped to and—with the help of Michal Bigger, who is a lady, by the way—provided us with soup and egg sandwiches and ice cream.

George appeared and Ryan and Kate went through all of their scenes again, just to run lines. Kate's energy—maybe the yelling did it— was really up. And Ryan was simply wonderful. I cried, as usual, when he read the poem. The guy really got to me.

We started filming on the morning of Wednesday, July 8, out at the house, which I had a hell of a time finding. It would be days before I could go back and forth without getting lost. (I had to cajole a car out of Renee. Not easy. She would put every obstacle in the way—the budget couldn't stand it, you know—but when forced would call and say, triumphantly, "I've managed to get you a car." Ryan never got one, which was a serious and insulting matter. I swear he never forgave her.)

That first day was remarkably pleasant. I met some old friends on the crew, Cyrus Block and Duncan MacGregor, and made some new ones, like our production manager, Fran Rosati (who appeared to be terrified of Renee) and assistant director, David Rose. We first did two small scenes of Ryan, as Moony, sneaking into the house, and then Kate worked through the entire day. She was rising to the occasion and seemed to be having a wonderful time. She looked so good I thought she looked almost too glamorous for an eighty-year-old woman. And she was so amusing in her scenes, I wondered how her character could have been the town recluse. She'd have been the most popular gal in town. I still wasn't sure Kate could memorize lines, but she certainly had the old Hepburn magic.

The second day was equally pleasant. (We weren't into the attic yet.) Kate was early on the set and rarin' to go. I showed Ryan the dailies of the day before, which were very good. But George was annoyed with me for letting him see them; he said the actors should never see the dailies. Poor Ryan was justly cranky at the end of the day, having waited through most of it in full costume and makeup to shoot a couple of scenes that were then postponed.

But the third day was horrendous. It was a difficult day, starting with Kate and Ryan doing their very physical first scene together in the kitchen where they fought and fell to the floor. Tough on a lady of Kate's age.

After that, she couldn't remember lines and began to panic.

"I'm having a stroke," she said. "I'm having a stroke!" We began to panic. A doctor was summoned immediately. We stumbled through a few more scenes, but Kate was saying, "You'll have to replace me." (It was a fairly safe statement. If there was one thing Katharine Hepburn knew, it was that Katharine Hepburn was irreplaceable.)

Finally, she and John set out to take her to a clinic. At the clinic, it was suggested that she go to the hospital for further tests, so off they went. Because of the press, John checked her in under his mother's name, Mary Jane Dayton. He then called his mother in Arizona to inform her of the deception, lest she faint when hearing it. (Nobody was fooled. The next day everybody in Vancouver was saying that Katharine Hepburn was in the hospital. Actually, by that time, she'd visited Granville Island, walked the seawall, and been to the lighthouse.)

She had various tests at the hospital, none of which showed she was having a stroke or anything else. Indeed she was, they said, in perfect health. So she went home and told John to call and ask me by for cocktails. It was quite a day.

It was quite a weekend, too. The days were beautiful and on Saturday, while John and Kate were doing Granville Island, the seawall and the lighthouse, I mosied through the Hudson Bay Company. Then the bookstore, where I bought a copy of *Me* to give as a wedding present, appropriate—I felt, if Kate signed it, which she readily agreed to do.

Going to dinner in the evening, though, and down in the hotel elevator, Noel and I stepped in to find Ryan, and for the first time we observed the O'Neal nastiness. He was in a vile mood and that famous temper was very near the surface. It was his turn to turn on the star stuff. He said nobody knew what a terrible day he'd had on Friday, what he'd gone through, that he was tempted to fly home to L.A. for the weekend just to get away. Very unpleasant. We assured him how much Kate adored him, which was true. I think he felt he'd lost his grip on her on Friday when she went off to the hospital, that she should have turned to him whereas she was, of course, totally concerned with herself. At any rate, we did what we could with Ryan, who stalked off without so much as a good-bye.

Sunday was another beautiful day and at 11:30 A.M. John and I appeared at Kate's door. Jimmy had prepared a picnic basket for us. He and Phyllis were staying home. "Phyllis isn't interested in anything anymore," said Kate. I was never quite sure how serious Kate was when she talked like that, but, at ninety, I felt Phyllis had earned the right to avoid a rigorous drive if she wanted to.

We took the winding road to Squamish, a stunning drive with mountains to the right of us and islands rising out of the sea to the left. Everywhere there were warning signs about falling rocks. "Fascinating," said Kate.

We started on Monday morning in fear and trembling. Could Kate or could Kate not do it? But we had a fine day of shooting. Only once did Kate falter when she couldn't remember her lines.

"I think I'm having a stroke!" she said, but George paid not the slightest attention. (Some of us thought she might at least have come up with a new word. Why not *seizure*?) They went right ahead setting up the lights and she never mentioned it again. She sailed through the day beautifully and wasn't ready to leave at 4:30, her appointed hour to depart. Ryan was also back in good form and looked really great in the dailies.

It rained for most of the day, but we were inside the house so it didn't affect us. After work, John and I went to the drugstore to pick up a prescription for Kate and then strolled over in the rain to her place for drinks. She appeared in her nightie and robe, face scrubbed and hair up. Over drinks, she said that Ryan was "a sweet man and a wonderful actor."

I told them my friend, Winfield Ogden, was coming to visit. Phyllis said good, she was looking for a husband. How old was he? She was disappointed to hear that he was only thirty-five. "Far too young," she sighed.

John said his parents were coming up on Thursday, and Kate said she'd keep herself free to entertain them on Saturday. When she was in a good mood, Kate could be such a good soul.

But I didn't think so the following day.

The day started out badly and I behaved stupidly.

Kate and I were sitting in the house on the stairs, watching them set up for a scene in the hallway. Her stand-in was under the lights.

"She's a dwarf," said Kate. "Am I as short as that?"

"You want the truth?"

"Yes, of course."

"Yes," I said. How could I have been so dumb? Would I never learn that honesty is never the best policy when dealing with stars? Why didn't I say, "Of course not. Somebody has obviously goofed." That would have pleased her and saved me what was about to happen.

Later in the day, I got involved in something and missed two of Kate's scenes. When I came in, she turned on me in an absolute rage. Right in front of the cast and crew and everybody.

"I do a brilliant scene and you never say anything! You disgust me! You're loathsome! Get out of my sight!" And with that she whirled around and went upstairs to her dressing room.

It was really appalling. I was sick to my stomach. I stumbled to the car and drove back to the hotel, fuming. I knew her ankle was possibly hurting her and she was in pain, but I didn't think anyone had the right to speak to another human being like that, especially in front of his coworkers.

It was the second time I almost left Vancouver.

Instead, I had friends in for cocktails. Why not get drunk? Gary Simpson and Wayne Steele came by, as well as Noel and John. Then we walked down the street to an unhealthy dinner of fried chicken with mounds of fattening French fries. Who cared what one looked like? I was loathsome, anyway. Katharine Hepburn had said so.

After that, I walked alone along the bay.

It was late and the sun was setting and the stars were coming out. I tried to get control of myself. I wrestled, half-amused, with the meaning of life. What did I believe? What was important—if anything?

Well, I believed in any number of things.

I believed, with Tennessee Williams, that cruelty was the only sin.

I believed that man and animals were as one in their capacity to suffer. No difference.

I believed that the hot blood of religion was the devil's greatest joke on humanity.

I believed that men and women were equal, but of different species.

I believed that we were ants on a fiery ball whirling through space and knowing nothing.

I believed that the NRA wouldn't be satisfied until every citizen in America carried a gun.

I believed that all love—with whomever or whatever—was good and demanded respect.

I believed that sex between consenting adults was nobody else's business.

I believed that every human heart was important—except on those days when I thought *blow the whole damn thing up.*

I believed that the arts were more important to a civilization than business.

I believed that leaf-blowers should be illegal.

I believed that there was no longer such a thing as an honest politician.

I believed that one could not live without music.

I believed that all stars should be drowned at birth.

I didn't really believe that all stars should be drowned at birth, but I did think, if detected early, they should wear signs saying STAR TENDENCIES—APPROACH WITH CAUTION.

I decided not to go to the set the next day, but I did because Pattie Robertson called and talked me into it. Good girl.

I made a point of avoiding Kate, but there was one encounter.

"Good morning," I said and she sailed past me without a word. I stuck around through lunch and consulted with George Schaefer. Kate had started cutting lines. If there was too much of that, I was afraid we'd lose the wit and humor.

After my soul searching of the night before, I had gone home and written a note to Renee. I was mending my fences. In this note, I said to Renee everything I could honestly say. I said, in effect, that on the set you are the most efficient, diligent, and caring producer I have ever worked with. It was true. I slipped it into her chair when she wasn't looking. What I didn't know, until lunch, was that it was her birthday. There was a bit of a celebration. Her husband had arrived, an elegant, handsome gentleman. He was noticeably cool to me until the note.

George told me Renee said later that my note was the best present she'd gotten for her birthday.

But what about Kate?

I awoke the next morning thinking about her and what to do—if anything. John reported that she had started on him yesterday, too, the single person who had been beside her every moment and, indeed, made this production possible. He was trying to help her with her lines when she said, in her dressing room, "Get out of here before you make me angry."

I tried to be understanding. She was eighty-five years old, she was often in pain, she had practically no memory left, which terrified her, and she was carrying the weight of this entire production on her shoulders. So why not a little testy?

And what patient George got on the screen, take after take, was magical. One could forgive her almost anything when one viewed the dailies. She might not know her lines, where she lived, what town she was in, or the name of the movie, but the clarity of her thinking when she acted was astonishing. Every little nuance, every little thought was crystal clear. And the woman who was totally selfish in real life came across on the screen as utterly endearing.

My note to Renee was so happily received, I decided to write one to Kate as well. Laid it on, but it was true:

> Dear Kate: In the event that you really are not aware of it, let me put this on paper. Having seen all the dailies, I can honestly say that the work you are doing is among the finest you have ever done. There is not the slightest reduction in the Hepburn magic; indeed, I think it's more magical than ever. You may say I'm being "emotional," but I'm also no fool. This is Hepburn at her best. I'm proud and excited. We all are.

I strolled down the street and slipped it under the door of her apartment. Then I went home and watched a bit of the Democratic

National Convention on the television set. Gore was powerful; Clinton a bore.

Winfield Ogden arrived from New York that night. We sat up talking. It was fun, but I started the next day tired.

That was unfortunate because it was a bad day on *The Man Upstairs* set. Ryan didn't get his call sheet the night before. The chap who should have stuck them under all our hotel doors was lax. He left them, instead, downstairs with one of the bellmen, who overlooked Ryan. And so Ryan arrived on the set to discover for the first time that he was playing three of his biggest scenes that day. Some stars would have left the production then and there.

Instead, he made life difficult for everybody, I was told, although he did it up in the attic and I couldn't get in there—and didn't want to. The place was packed with people and Ryan didn't want anyone at "eye contact" level, which wasn't possible in the small space. Renee talked to him—"chewed him out," some say—which didn't help. Rumor had it he harbored a grudge against her for some earlier misdemeanor when he was a young actor and was going to "get her."

It all sounded pretty awful and Win Ogden and I, with several others, stayed outside the house drinking coffee and praying.

But when I ran into Ryan as he was leaving the house, he was all huggy and kissy and thanked me for a photo I'd given him of the two of us together. He even posed for some tourists who wanted to photograph him. They said, "Aren't you Ryan O'Neal?"

"I used to be."

I asked Renee later why he was suddenly so cheerful and she said, "I gave him a bottle of brandy."

I only saw the back of Kate's head as she was being made up in her dressing room. Just as well; avoiding confrontation.

Renee talked with CBS on her cellular phone, and they were complaining that there was not enough "threat" in the dailies, meaning violence. They couldn't see beyond the cops-and-robbers cliché and realize that they had something better here.

There was also a good deal of grumbling about the tightness and heat in the attic, and Noel reported to me that evening at the hotel that they were talking of moving scenes down into the kitchen. I thought it would be a disaster if they did, and duly despaired. (When we finally did move down, it was not into the kitchen but into the dining room. And the move only enhanced the scenes.)

I had left the set early and thereby missed the arrival of Farrah Faw-cett, who had come to stay with Ryan for a couple of days. When I did meet her, she couldn't have been nicer. I showed her the dailies so she could see (and tell Ryan) how wonderful he was.

That evening, Noel Taylor and I grabbed the limo and met our dar-ling Brenda Forbes at the airport. She was the last member of the cast to arrive, but far from the least. Her brilliant contribution to the film was immeasurable.

It was a lovely weekend, but the following Monday brought another difficult day with Kate. I sometimes thought it was like working with the matron of a prison.

I'd been avoiding her, but suddenly she came out of the house and there I was. I'd stuck a spring of holly in my hat. She walked right up to me.

"Take that off," she commanded, pointing at the holly.

"Why?" said I.

"Because it looks idiotic."

Had we not been making a movie, had she not been the star, I would have told her it was none of her business what I wore in my hat. And that it was rude to talk to me like that. But we were making a movie and she was the star, so I took the sprig of holly out as if I were a naughty lit-tle boy in school and tossed it away. But, oh, how I wanted to simply say, "I like it. It amuses me." However, I didn't dare face the consequences. But wasn't it sad? She hadn't always been like that. The crew might have respected her for the great star she was, but I don't think she was gener-ally liked now.

Well, we had less than two more weeks with Kate and she would be gone.

I continued to pray.

We struggled on.

We had our good days and our bad.

Ryan was still thrilled to be working with Kate. He didn't even mind it when she slapped him, playfully, when he started to complain about something and said to him, "Hey, I'm the only bully around here." He said he'd never worked with anyone like her, that it was a great "life experience."

Kate actually said, "How do you do?" to me one morning, an indica-tion that our little altercation was resolved. John went driving with Kate, who said that Prideaux hadn't been around and why? John hemmed and hawed and said she'd hurt my feelings apparently through something she'd said. Kate said it was probably something like, "What a ridiculous script!" and laughed. (I would have laughed, too. That wouldn't have hurt me.) I assumed she'd totally forgotten the "you disgust me" incident. Anyway, he told me she wanted me to call, so we were over that.

The next evening, John and I were to have dinner with Ryan, but he called John in a rage, furious that Renee had flown to Los Angeles for the day without telling him because she could have brought his young son back. When Ryan got mad, Ryan got mad.

But there was another side to him. On the day he did his big scene where Moony told of his mother's abusing him as a kid, I waited outside the house until they had finished shooting. Ryan came out crying; everybody had been very moved. He went past me and walked across the lawn to his trailer. Suddenly, without turning, he called out, "Prideaux!"

"What?" I yelled.

He still didn't turn, but he raised his arms to the heavens and he shouted, "Thanks for the gift!"

It was the nicest thing any actor had ever said to me.

We were all getting tired and edgy.

George even turned on Renee when she questioned why he hadn't gone on, late at night, after work, to check out a prison location needed for a scene. Patient, good George said, and I quote, "Fuck the scene!" She'd pushed him too far. He was there from dawn until dusk, coping with Kate and Ryan with the patience of a saint, and she wanted more.

Fay Kanin came to visit the set, a pleasant interlude in days that weren't always pleasant. I liked and admired her.

Ryan flew into a temper one afternoon, lashed out at Renee, and said the one thing she could not possibly accept, "No producers on the set!" He stormed off across the lawn, and it was Kate who went after him, calling out in a voice that rang over the countryside, "Hey, Ryan!" It stopped him, of course, and she went right after him and brought him back by the hand.

Our big reconciliation came when, to engage me in conversation, Kate came up to me and said in the friendliest way that I was fat and had lost the contours of my face. I thanked her for the information.

Renee went to the network to complain about Ryan. Why had they foisted him on us, the way he behaved? I thanked God that they had.

Standing next to Ryan on the set one afternoon, he looked at Kate and Brenda and whispered to me, "They're so old!"

"So will you be," I said.

"Yeah, this afternoon," he said.

Brenda got a little upset because Kate insisted on staying late to feed her lines for her telephone scene when Brenda would have preferred the script girl. Because, even reading them off camera, Kate kept screwing them up and making changes. Brenda said she couldn't change the lines because "James isn't here," but somebody else helpfully said, "We've done it before."

My masseur went with John to Kate's to give her a massage. John waited while he "did" Kate and, when he'd finished, Kate said, "Go and do Phyllis." Kate and John had drinks, but it was ominously quiet in Phyllis's room so Kate got up and listened at the door. When she came back, she said blithely, "I think he's killed Phyllis. Let's have another drink."

I was surprised, one morning, to see an elderly woman bent over picking wildflowers in the field as I drove down the dirt road toward the house. I could only see her rear and, as she raised a little, her hair, but it looked just like Kate. I slowed down, thought it was Kate—that she had come out early and was picking wildflowers, just like her—thought, no, it wasn't, then looked again and decided it certainly was. I stopped the car and shouted, thinking that it would give her a laugh, "Hey, you wanna be in show business?" And a perfectly strange woman—one of the neighbors—straightened up, turned, looked at me, and said politely, "No, thank you."

I told Kate the story and she howled. We were friends again, despite the contours of my face.

Most gratifying to open the newspaper and find Liz Smith in her column calling me "the talented James Prideaux" and following up with three paragraphs about me and the movie. Some days you need that.

By July 30 it had really gotten hot and, even downstairs in the house, the air conditioning didn't seem sufficient. It was easy for the actors to get grumpy.

At John's urging, Kate tried cue cards, but brushed them aside after about two seconds. Despite our explaining to her that Lucille Ball used them and Angela Lansbury never learned a word, she said she could either read or act, but she couldn't do both at once.

I'll never forget one scene when she and Ryan had only one line each. Easy, you'd think. He stood over her and said, "Do you really care about me?" She, sitting, was to look up and say, "Is that so hard to understand?"

Well, she studied that line and studied that line. Finally, George said, "Lights! Camera! Action!"

Ryan looked down at her. "Do you really care about me?"

Kate looked around at the crew. "I don't know," she said. "Do I really care about him?"

George said, "Never mind."

"Well, I need the script!" said Kate. So she studied it some more. And once again, George said, "Lights! Camera! Action!"

"Do you really care about me?" Ryan said, looking down at her.

She looked right up into his eyes and said, "No, no, no!"

But when she got there, when she finally said, "Is that so hard to understand?," it was so touching and so real you wanted to burst into tears. This awful process of aging and what it does to the memory is especially heartbreaking in actors.

Just before one scene, Kate, playing a lady curmudgeon, said to George, "Why do I have to hate Christmas?"

George looked at me. I took him aside.

"Because if she doesn't," I told him, "there's no movie."

Well, I wished this movie would be over.

Ryan threw a major tantrum and came yelling onto the set that nobody gave a shit about him. To give Ryan his due, with Kate you were always second fiddle, unless you were Spencer Tracy. She got a car; he didn't. She had her own makeup and hair people; he didn't. She lived in a fantastic pad; he was tucked into the hotel. You could hardly blame him for feeling a bit slighted. I think if Renee had just sprung for a car for him, we'd have seen a different Ryan.

And Kate was buckling somewhat.

I asked her one afternoon how she felt and she said, "Sick."

"Tummy?"

"Head."

"But it looks good," I told her. And it did.

John Matoian, vice-president in charge of television movies for CBS, came to visit. He spent most of an entire day on the set and was fun. He actually seemed to be mad about the film. We went off into a trailer and looked at the dailies together.

"There's no way this one can miss, is there?" he said.

"No," said I, "no way." Would we be proven wrong? They'd slated it for Sunday, December 6 at 9:00 P.M. following *60 Minutes* and *Murder, She Wrote*. How could we do better than that?

John said he laughed out loud as he watched the dailies and saw Brenda in her tea scene. Laughing at the dailies was something he'd never done before, and people were stopping in amazement at his door. He also asked what I'd do next for them. Did I do adaptations? I assured him that I adored doing adaptations.

We talked, too, about stars that I might work with and he mentioned Jessica Tandy and Hume Cronyn. My heart sank a little, despite my love and admiration for them. Would I never work with a young star? Say, somebody seventy?

We were in the home stretch—only a few more days of shooting—but before that we had a three-day weekend, Monday being a Canadian holiday.

I drove with Kate and John on a sentimental tour of Vancouver, looking at all the places where we'd filmed *Delafield*, the Kievel house and the Casa Mia. Kate had no recollection of it.

"Did you write that?" she asked me.

There were three nights of spectacular fireworks displays from ships in the bay, a competition between Canada, the U.K., and Australia, each having a night.

Ryan and Farrah were invited for a drink at Kate's. Not for dinner, but at least Farrah, who somehow hadn't met her yet, got to spend a little time with Kate, which was the point. Kate was never very good about wives (although she claimed to care more for women than for men), but this wife was also a star.

Their son, seven-year-old Redmond, was also staying in Vancouver. He was a great, tousle-headed kid with a fabulous pitching arm. He and Ryan would throw balls back and forth between shots. Redmond also played a small part in the movie: one of the Boy Scouts in a scene in the woods. Ryan was nervous as a cat about it, the doting father. Redmond came through, although I don't think it made him want to be an actor.

We went back to work—the final week—and Kate did what I considered to be the most important scene in the movie: that last moment when the camera moved through the night and the snow closer, closer on that extraordinary face and she spoke her last words, "Merry Christmas, dear." I had described this scene carefully in the script—after all, it might be Kate's last appearance on a screen—but I had no hope that it could be done as I visualized it. I stayed home while they shot it. John came rushing into the hotel later, very excited, having watched. But John was always positive, always excited.

But when I saw the dailies, I was dazzled. The scene was more wondrous and Kate more beautiful than anything I could have envisioned. George and the astonishing Walter Lassally had outdone themselves. And Kate, whose "shakes" made her the butt of many jokes, was absolutely still as that camera moved slowly in on her. I felt if I had done nothing else, I had provided Kate with a final shot that was worthy of her distinguished career.

I sent Ryan a note in which I told him how valuable he had been to the project and that, frankly, as far as I was concerned, we couldn't have done it without him. True. I could imagine no one who would have brought to Moony the sensitivity that Ryan had.

Ryan said Farrah read the note and burst into tears.

We did the scene with the Boy Scouts in the woods at Capilano and moved on to St. Paul's Cathedral, the parish church on the reservation of the Squamish Indians, who were probably better off with their own religion. Here we shot the scene where Helena, as Molly, confides in the priest that she thinks "there's a man upstairs," and he suggests she call the cops.

As close as we were to the end, though, there was a bit of rebellion among the troops. John was alarmed because some of the crew were, he said, threatening to walk out due to Renee's treatment of them. He calmed them saying, like Burt, "Let's finish the movie first and then rebel." They went back to work.

Kate's spirits began to climb. She could see, now, that she was going to get through it.

She had only one more scene to do, the one in which she drives up to the jewelry store and buys Moony a watch for Christmas.

Kate insisted on driving the car herself, although she hadn't driven in years. She also stunned everybody by running up the stairs two at a time in one scene. She did just fine.

We used a beauty parlor, two doors down from the jewelry store, for her dressing room. She grumbled at her 2:45 P.M. call, wanting it earlier in the day, of course. (Poor George and Ryan and the crew had to go on from there and film all night at the prison.) But once in makeup and knowing it was her last scene, she was in rare good humor; she even held my hand, which was most unusual.

Kate finished her scene in the jewelry store and then got in the car to drive it around the corner, as if she were arriving. This was to be the last for her. I began to choke up. Phyllis was there, of course, for this historical moment, as were several reporters and newsmen and Carina Sayles, our PR lady from CBS. Not to mention half of Vancouver.

She had to do the little scene twice, but finally our assistant director, David Rose, said those remarkable words that both Kate and I had wondered if we'd ever live to hear.

"That's a wrap for Miss Hepburn!" he shouted.

We exploded! We yelled! We shrieked! We applauded! I rushed up and kissed her and then George, more emotional than I have ever seen him, hugged her and kissed her and she kissed him back.

We all piled into the beauty parlor, where Renee had champagne ready and an ice cream cake that read THANK YOU, MISS HEPBURN— WE LOVE YOU on the top.

Kate was simply glowing. I've never seen her happier.

I kept saying, "You did it! You did it! You did it!" Couldn't stop. John, who had more right than anybody to be proud of what she'd accomplished, was beside himself. He, and he alone (including Kate), had been the only one who believed from the very first that she could do it. And she hadn't let him down.

Everybody came up and congratulated her, every member of the cast and every member of the crew.

I whispered that I'd see her for a drink at her place if she wanted, and she whispered back, "Yes, of course."

I arrived at Kate's just as she did with Phyllis, John, Michal Bigger and her husband, James Sarzotti, who did Kate's hair. There were bouquets of flowers all over the place. And there was the most tremendous, almost overpowering, sense of relief and satisfaction. We were all exhausted, but the job had been done and well.

Our Miss Hepburn would always be a legend, no question of that, but she had proved that she was still a star as well.

She could still deliver.

I went home, fell into bed, and slept as I hadn't slept in weeks.

The next day was an easy one for us. Nobody was scheduled to work until evening, when they'd do Ryan's final scenes at the prison. It could take most of the night. After that, it was really a wrap. For everybody. *The Man Upstairs* would be in the can.

John and I had planned to drive out to the prison for that last night of shooting, leaving around 8:00 P.M., but at 7:30 the telephone rang in my room, where we were having drinks, and John answered it.

It was Ryan and he was fuming. He was calling from the lobby. Seems he was to have been picked up at 7:00 and he wasn't. He was furious.

I was chicken, but John rushed down to the lobby, which was the last I saw of him that night. All thought of going to the prison was abandoned, as far as I was concerned. *The Man Upstairs* would have to wrap without me.

I got a full report from John the next day.

There was simply some mix-up and the teamster hadn't picked Ryan up when he should have. Ryan was, I think, humiliated enough to have to sit there in the lobby (a star, remember) and be forgotten. It triggered every hostility he'd harbored—or not—throughout the production. (And I only suggest that if Renee had provided him with a car none of this would have happened. She did ask me to lend him mine for a day once, but I refused, saying I'd never see it again.)

John had the great pleasure of driving a raging Ryan O'Neal to the prison. At one point, John said, he threw a full can of Coke out of the car window. Once he got to the set and started working, however, he was fine. The work got done and at 3:00 A.M. Renee had champagne and cake for Ryan, just as she had for Kate.

But Ryan disappeared. He was never seen again. He somehow got to the airport and somehow got a plane to Los Angeles. He said good-bye to nobody, just skipped.

I've never seen him again, although through his agent I requested an autographed picture (he'd given Kate one) and it was sent to me, affectionately signed. It hangs prominently on my wall.

And anytime Ryan O'Neal wants to work with me, I'm ready.

Our official wrap party was slated for two days later, so Kate chartered a seaplane and spent a day with her nephew on Bainbridge Island, off the coast of the state of Washington, and the next day with an artist friend of hers near Victoria. John accompanied her on both excursions, along with Phyllis and Michal Bigger. John's a pilot, but he didn't get near the controls because the plane turned out to be the same model that

Howard Hughes had first taught Kate to fly in. So she took over, John said, understood all the instruments, read the map, and told the pilot what to do and where to go. Typical Hepburn stuff. She must have been in heaven.

They flew back just in time for the party. Kate staggered in saying she was "exhausted" and badly needed a drink. It was like no other wrap party I'd ever known. We were told it was "Cocktails — 5 to 8," which is exactly what it was, atop the hotel in Windows on the Bay, a beautiful setting with a panoramic view of the city. But subdued. It hadn't been an especially happy shoot, obviously, and I think people were just kind of damn glad it was over. I'd always known wrap parties where you had plenty of booze, a full dinner, and then danced the night away. Not this time. A rather limited bar, some finger food, and at exactly 8:00 P.M. the bar was locked tight and we were told we could have no more drinks. Renee was frugal to the end.

Nevertheless, Miss Hepburn managed to down her drinks before closing time, seated at a large circular table. She asked about Ryan, wanted to see him, and I told her he'd flown the coop. I think she was sorry. I think she wanted a proper leave-taking with her costar.

Kate and her entourage flew back to New York the next morning. I don't know why I didn't see them off at the airport — neither John nor I can remember — but John escorted them and said it was quite impressive. Kate was led into a room at the airport restricted exclusively to the use of the British royal family, a room in soft royal blues with gleaming Victorian furniture and a large oil painting of Queen Elizabeth and Prince Philip. Kate, who acted like royalty, oftentimes got treated like royalty.

And it was here, John said, that Kate began to cry as they parted. I'd never heard of Katharine Hepburn crying and couldn't imagine it, but he said she did and so he did. They hugged and cried.

It was over.

We flew back to Los Angeles the following day. I was greatly relieved, as I walked into my apartment, to see that the plants were still alive.

It wasn't until early September that I saw a "cut" of *The Man Upstairs*, not a "rough" cut, but a "first" cut. It was the only time I hadn't been invited into the cutting sessions. They were restricted to George, Renee, Adie, and the editor, Dann Cahn. Nor was John Dayton, who was an executive producer, permitted in. I believe we were considered recalcitrants.

When I saw it I despaired, of course. I thought the fun had all been removed from the first part of the picture and it was clunky. Also, George had moved an early scene, introducing Brenda, into the middle of the film. He claims to this day that's where it belongs; I claim to this day it belonged where it was. I also felt that some of Ryan's best moments had been left on the cutting room floor, and even some of Kate's.

George, justifiably annoyed, told me Burt Reynolds had said that the whole thing should be rewritten. Lovely.

On a gray October morning, we gathered in a sound studio at Capitol Records in Hollywood to see the picture scored. Billy Goldenberg had composed the music and it sounded great. Only the credits weren't right. I don't think he said anything, but John was supposed to have a separate card credit, whereas he was sharing one with Lamar Jackson. And I was aware that I was, according to the Writers Guild, to have two cards: one as writer, one as coproducer. They were combined in one. Cheaper. I couldn't have cared less. What did it matter?

(The Writers Guild cared, however, and Burt Reynolds Productions was fined $500 in punitive charges—which was sent to me—and informed, after the initial airing, that the film couldn't be aired again until this was corrected. I was astonished that the Guild was so alert.)

Invitations were sent out, over Burt's signature, to eight hundred of Hollywood's elite for a gussy preview screening of *The Man Upstairs* at the Directors Guild on the evening of Monday, November 9.

Kate would not come out, of course, but I knew she'd be eager for a report. Brenda Forbes did come out, which added to the festivities. Brenda deserved her little moment in the limelight. Helena Carroll was there, too, and even Henry Beckman, our wonderful "sheriff," had flown in.

The lobby was filling up as I arrived and I hurried, nervously, into the auditorium. The first person I ran into, standing in the aisle, face to face, was Burt Reynolds.

We hugged. This was, after all, Hollywood.

"Your letter did it," I said. Irony? Tongue in cheek? It was all I could think of to say.

I can't remember what he said, if anything, and luckily he was quickly distracted and turned away.

Old friends, and new, began piling in. And suddenly there was loyal Patrick Duffy, come to offer me moral support. We sat in the back row and watched the auditorium fill up. The moment of truth would soon be upon us. But first, Burt, unfortunately, made a speech. It was rambling, but his "charm" was intact and some of it was funny. It was the content that was disturbing.

He related that first telephone call to Kate, selling her on the fact that he had "a James Prideaux script and George Schaefer to direct." So we got mentioned. Then he digressed and somehow got onto his and Loni's attractiveness. He said people must look at them and wonder, "Who do those two people fantasize over?" There was an uneasy titter. I stared at this fifty-six-year-old man, heavily made up and wearing a fairly phony-looking toupee. Why in the world was he bringing this up? Didn't he know?

He then got back to business and began to thank those responsible for the movie we were about to see. He thanked Lamar Jackson for his wonderful contribution. (Lamar, likable as he was, had spent exactly two days on the set.) He thanked several others. Mostly, however, he thanked Renee Valente, who had brought this production in under budget, and he shocked some of us by going on and giving the exact figure under budget she had brought it in on. I can't remember the figure, but I thought, well, there's our per diems and the niggardly wages for the actors.

He then, very theatrically, said there was one more person he wanted to thank. He brought a small blue card out of his pocket and looked at it.

"Oh," he said, "I need my glasses. Doesn't matter." And he put the card back in his pocket and told us to enjoy the film.

I knew what had happened. He had not thanked his executive producer, John Dayton.

John was sitting with his parents. His mother burst into tears. His father said, "We're leaving right now." But, of course, they didn't. John wouldn't let them, despite the fact that he'd gone cold all over.

It was among the meaner acts I'd ever observed in Hollywood.

The publicity on the movie was terrific. I think we made the cover of every television supplement of every Sunday newspaper in the country. I did endless interviews, the best of which was front page in the calendar section of the *Los Angeles Times* by Robert Epstein entitled "A Leading Light." Meaning me. Momentarily.

The reviews weren't especially good in the Hollywood trades, but most of the rest were and practically all America watched. At the end of the season, *The Man Upstairs* was no. 7 in the ten top-rated telefilms of the year. (And we'd have been higher than that if it hadn't been for the ever-popular Amy Fisher and her two movies.)

Very gratifying.

Kate got the most mail and the greatest response she'd ever had from a television movie. It so lifted her spirits, she stopped talking about it being "the last" and began to talk about doing another one. Which she did.

I made myself scarce. I felt it was time to protect the Hepburn legend. In short, time for her to stop. Only Garbo, however, knew when to stop.

Attention, after all, must be paid. Right to the end.

EPILOGUE

It was a wintry Sunday afternoon in the early 1940s.

My father and mother adored one another and a quarrel was out of the question. But they were arguing a bit. My mother was still religious enough, having been brought up in a strict Victorian household, to feel that going to the movies on a Sunday had a taint of sin about it. But my father remained firm, kissed her on the cheek, and told his young son to get in the car. This was important.

We drove the seven miles into Indianapolis. But instead of going to one of the smaller movie houses on the south side, with which I was fairly familiar, we drove to a larger theatre in the very center of the city. As we got out of the car, my father explained that we were about to see his favorite movie star. He could hardly contain his excitement and, ever dramatic, I got caught up in it.

The name of the movie was *The Philadelphia Story* and it was, to me, dazzlingly sophisticated. I wonder, even now, why I was chosen to accompany him on this pilgrimage when my two brothers—one older, one younger—were not. But I was the one he wanted to share this experience with.

We walked out of the theatre on a cloud. The nation was at war and a certain fear seemed always to hang in the air. We were Americans and, consequently, confident of ultimate victory. We would win, of course. And yet there was that nagging fear. What if we didn't?

On that Sunday afternoon in Indiana the fear was forgotten. Indeed, the war itself was forgotten. Nor were we quite as provincial or penurious as we thought ourselves to be. That was all wiped out, at least for the moment.

Because a magical creature had come into our lives. She was beautiful and aristocratic and loving and funny. She was Katharine Hepburn.

How my father would have laughed had I looked up at him and said, "Daddy, one day I'll know her. One day I'll write movies for her."

Instead, we got into the car and drove out into the countryside. It was bleak and flat and the sky was graying as a light snow began to fall. That didn't matter to us. We hardly noticed.

"Isn't she the greatest?" my father said, turning to smile at me.

I smiled back.

She was.